Carrie Mae Weems

Reflections for Now

HATJE CANTZ

barbican

kunstmuseum basel

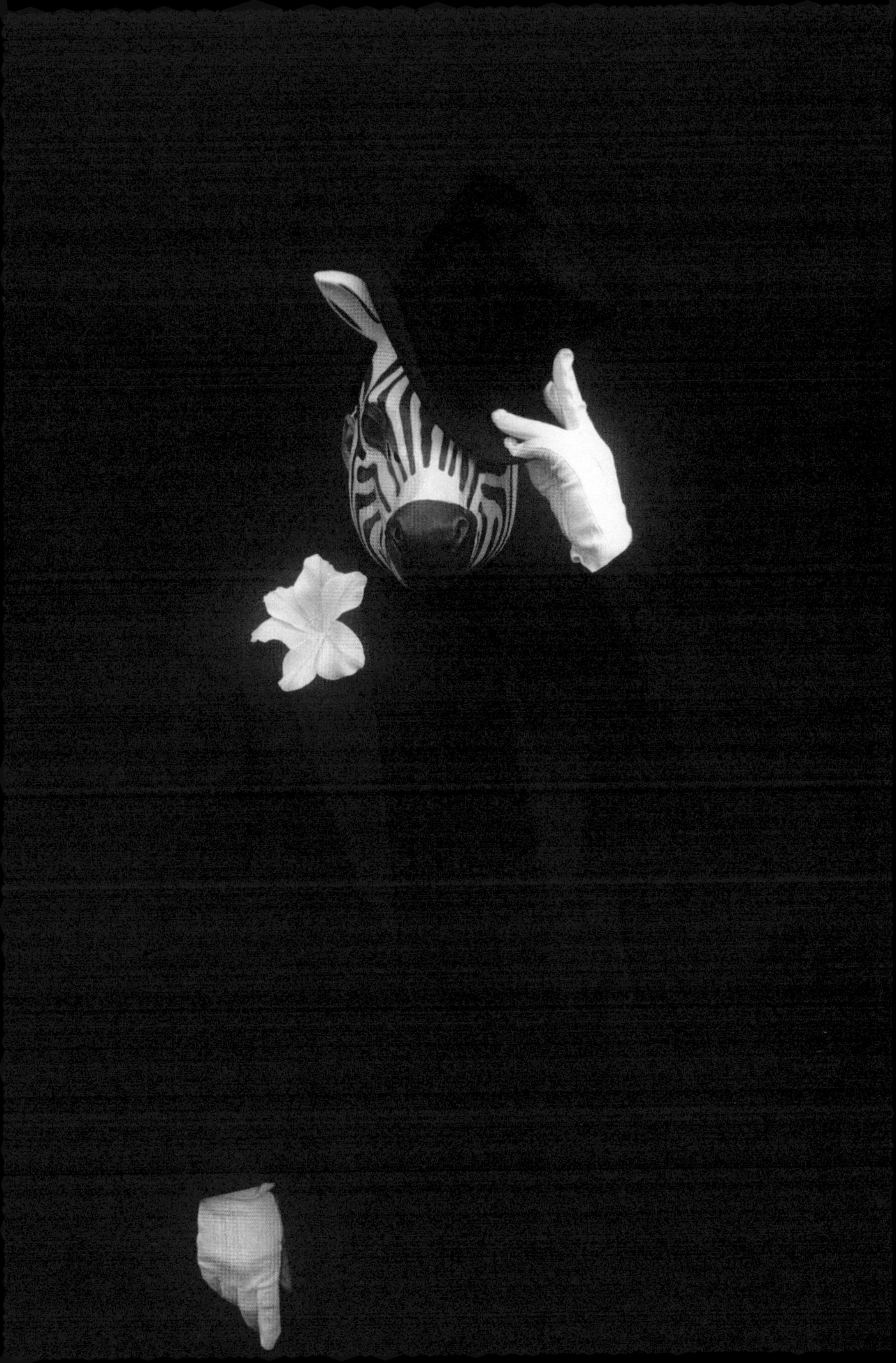

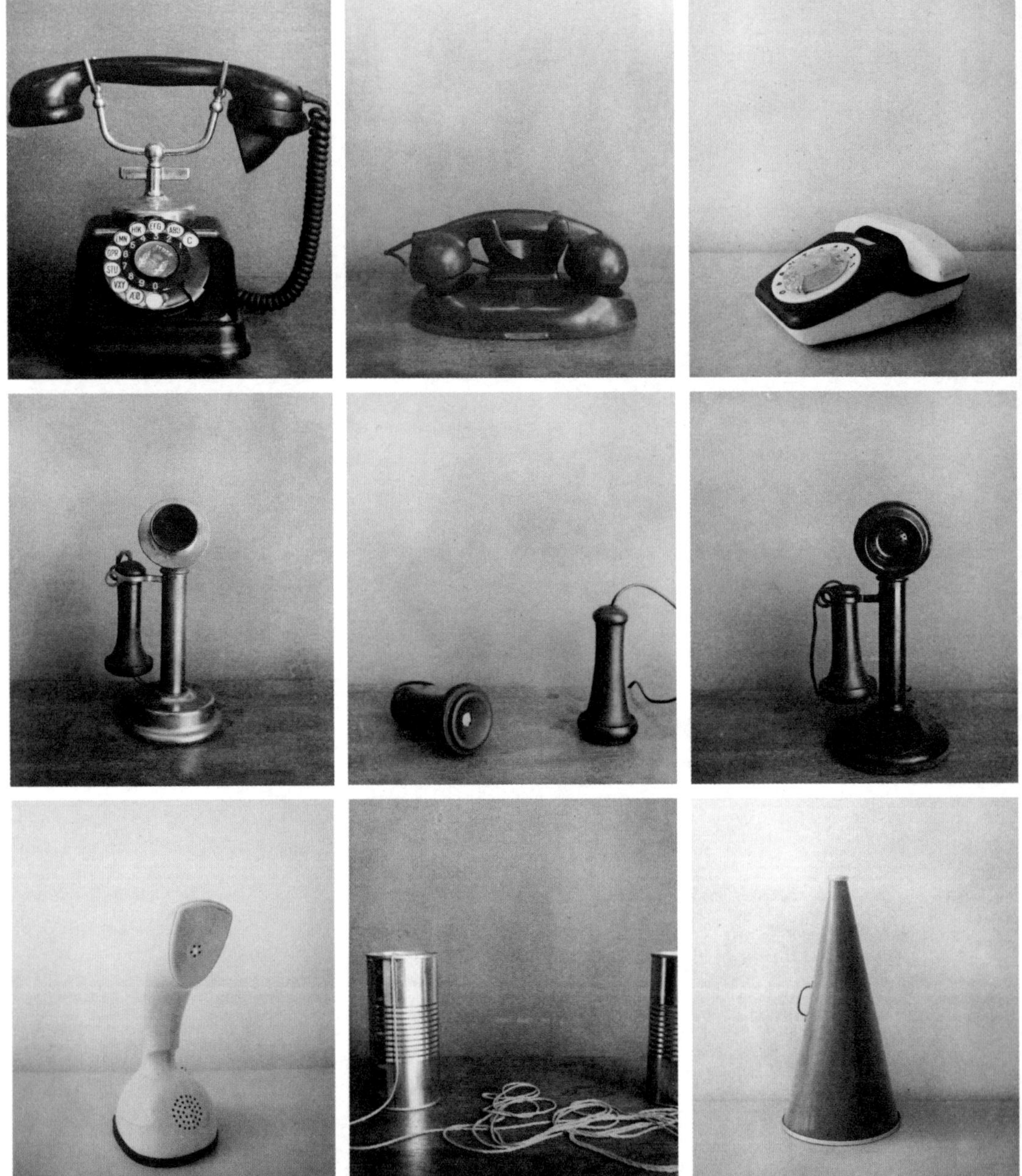

14 How Do You Measure a Life

18 A Woman in Winter

26 Mutual Beliefs
Carrie Mae Weems + Dawoud Bey

32 Ritual and Revolution

42 Constructing History

54 Histories of Violence

64 The Man Was Rejected, The Woman Was Denied

74 Architecture and Power

86 Becoming an Artist
Carrie Mae Weems + Terence Nance

94 Art for Social Change

106 Appropriation and Influence

114 On Music, Machinery, and Meeting
Carrie Mae Weems + DJ Spooky
Carrie Mae Weems + Nona Hendryx + Hans Ulrich Obrist
Carrie Mae Weems + Hans Ulrich Obrist

128 Home

136 Family Stories

150 Black Love
Carrie Mae Weems + Theaster Gates

154 While We Can

158 On Grace

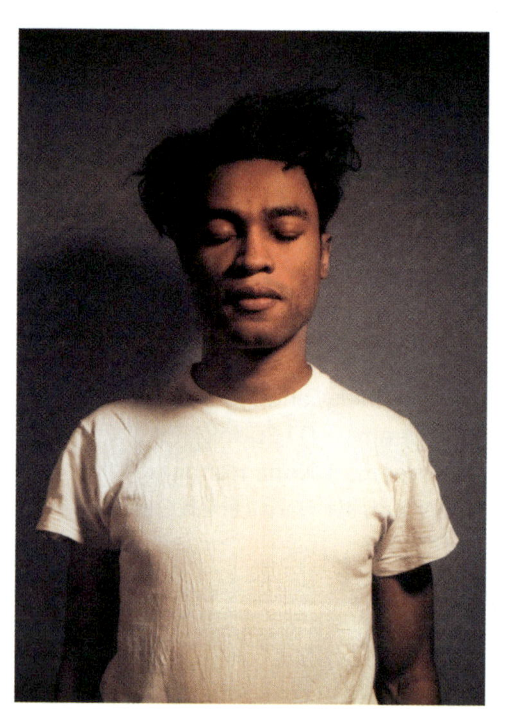

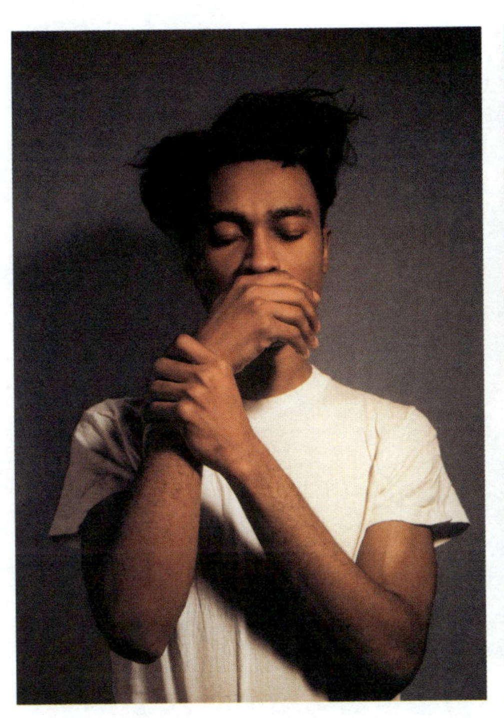

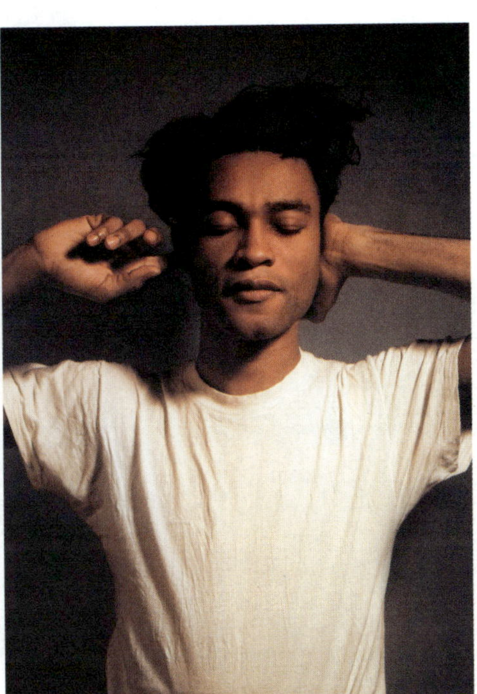

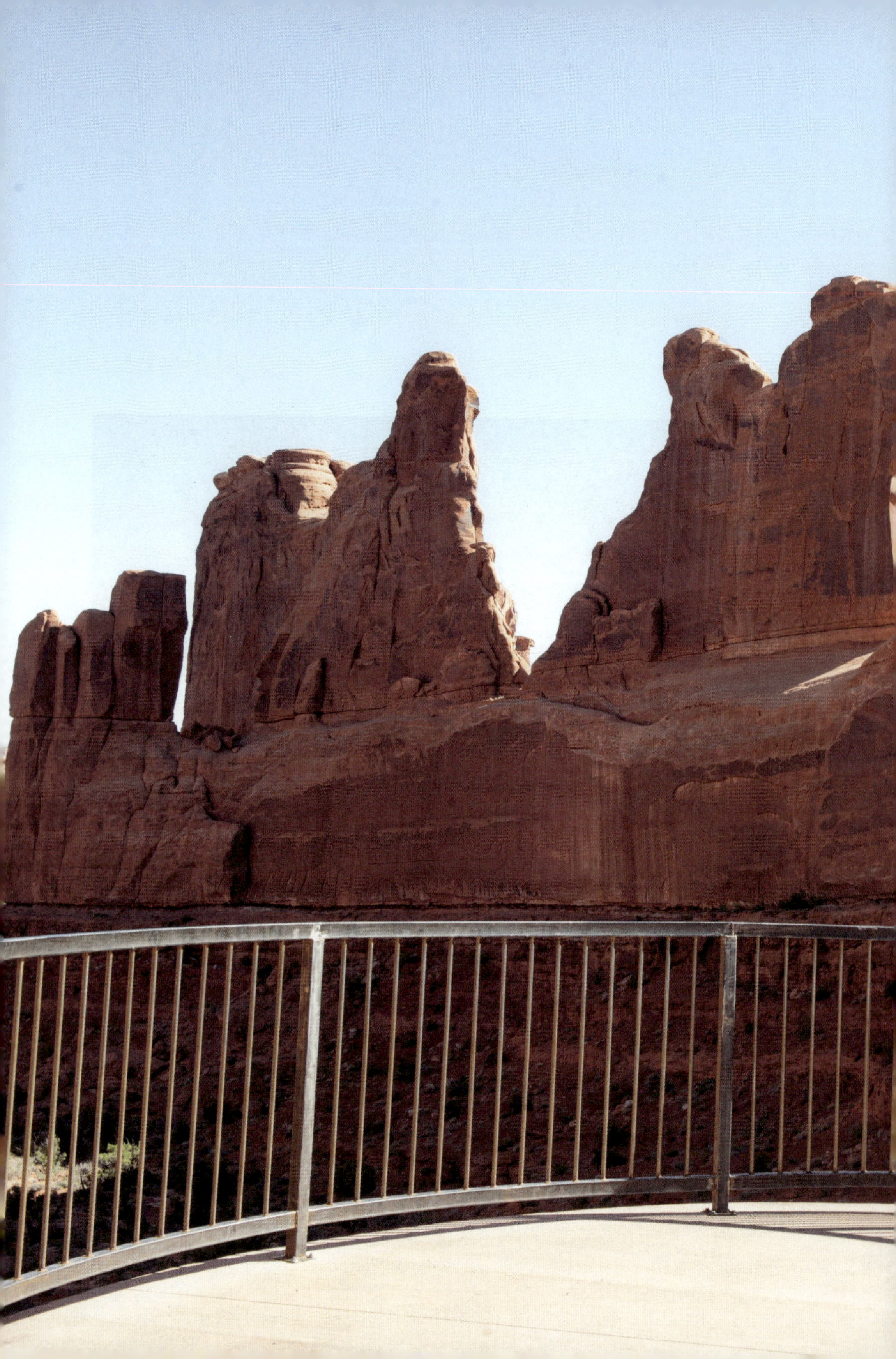

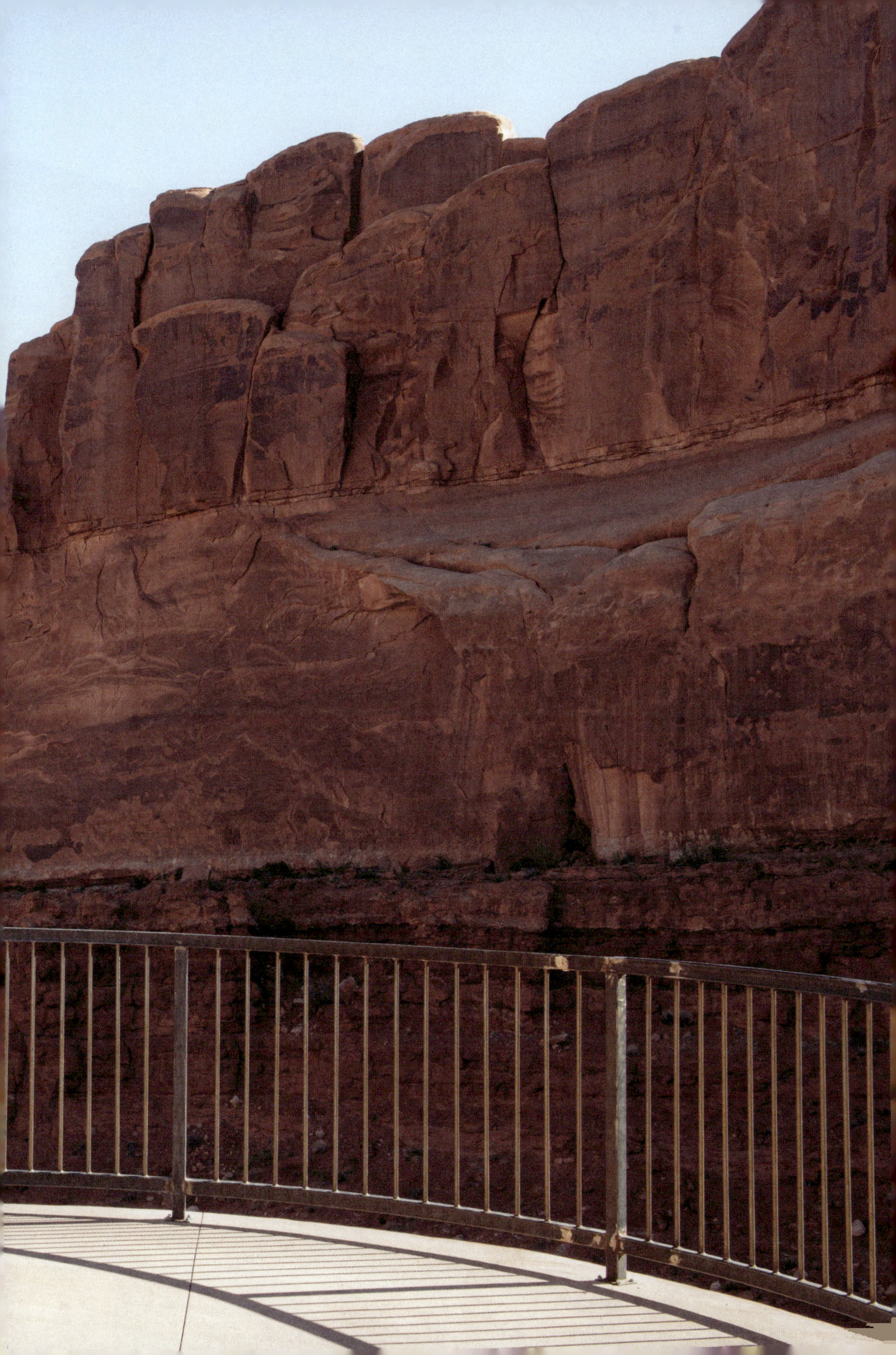

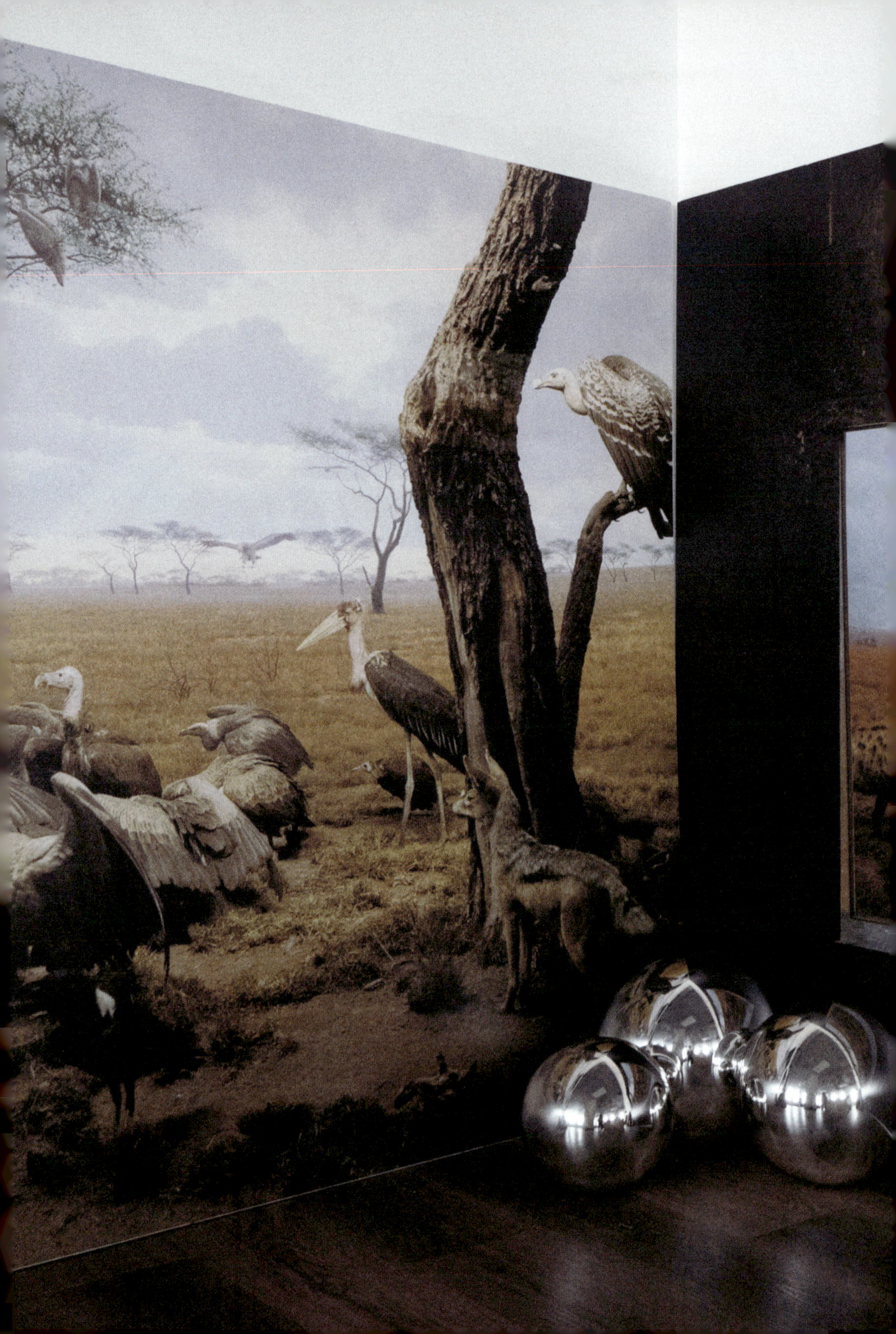

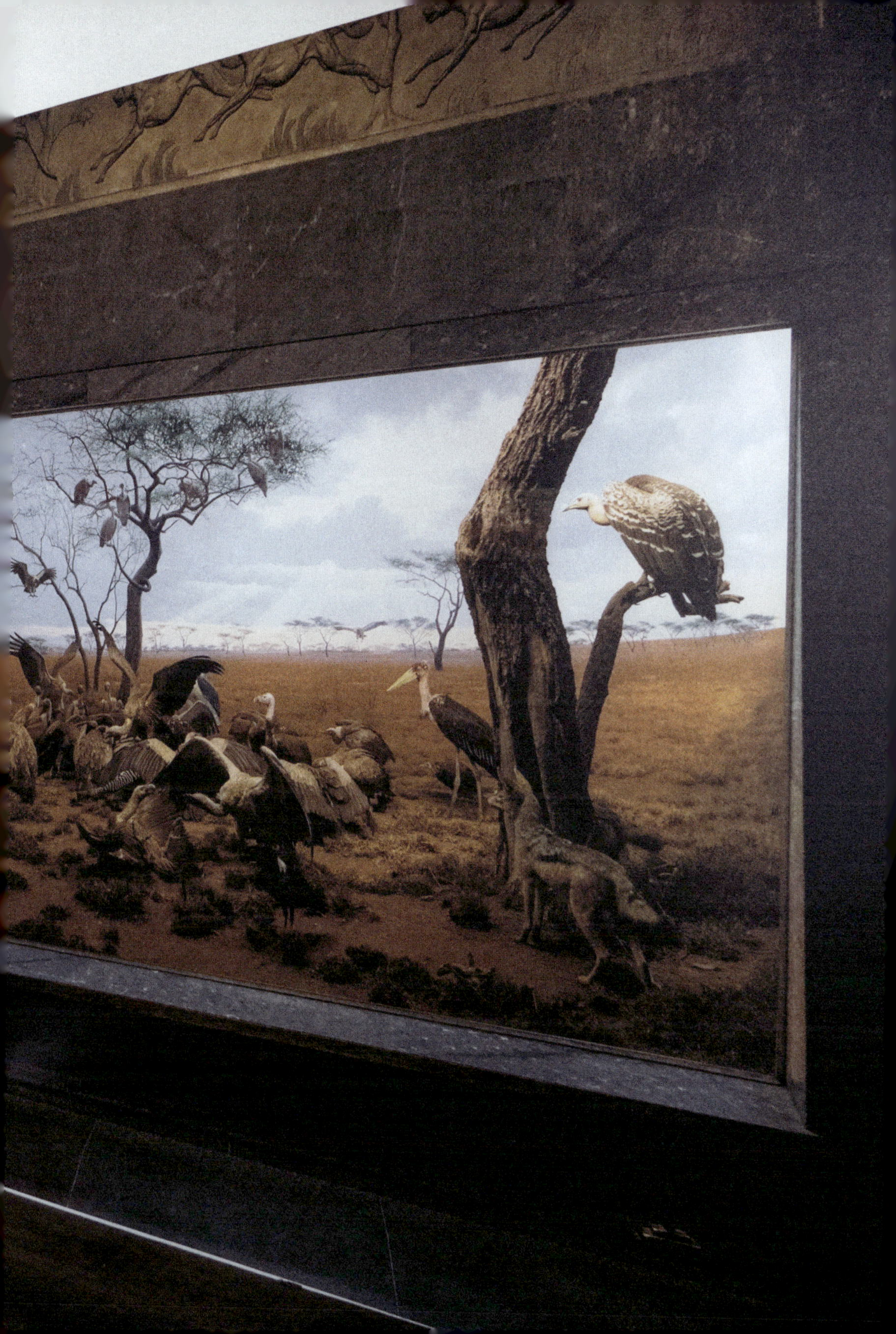

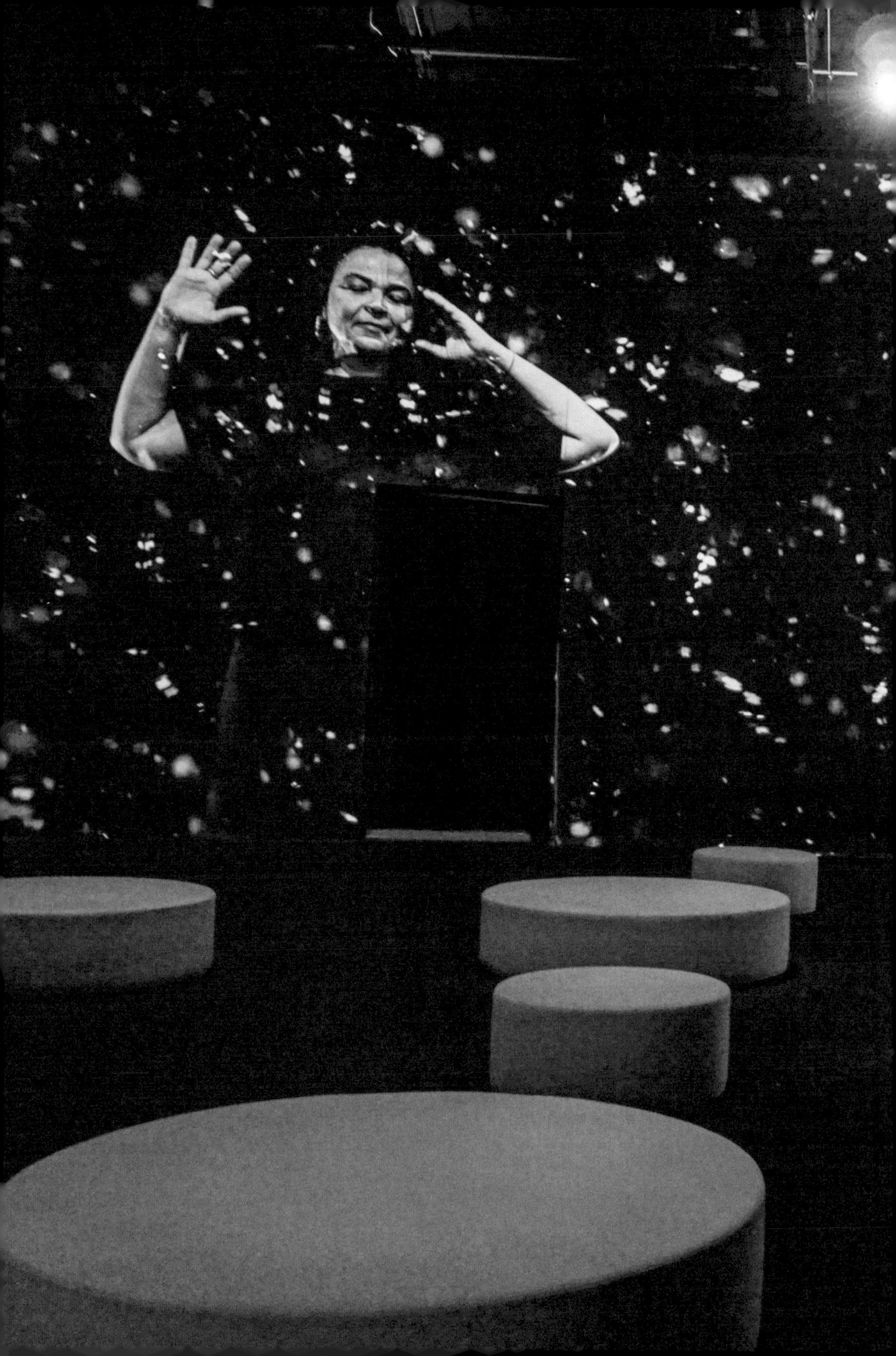

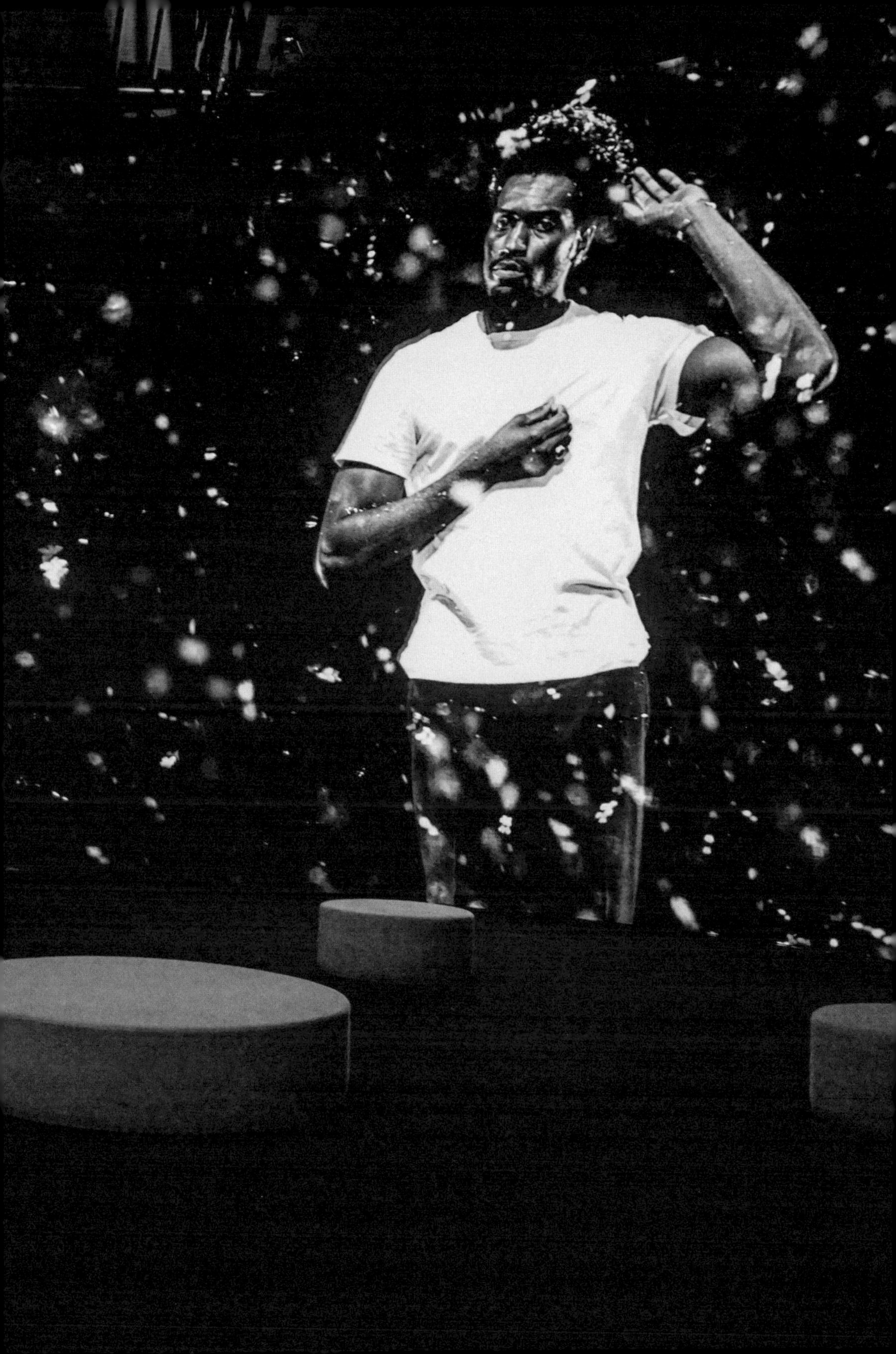

How Do You Measure a Life

In this mystery of all mysteries,
In the alpha and in the omega
On a day coming in a world without end,

I humbly ask:
By what means
By what measure
Do you measure a life?

Do you measure it
inch by inch,
foot by foot,
yard by yard,
or step by step?

Do you measure it by the moments lost,
or by the moments gained?
Do you measure it by yesterday, today, or tomorrow?

Or by the miles walked,
the mountains climbed and the valleys explored?

Or do you measure it by the dreams imagined,
or by the hopes dashed?

Do you measure it by the wisdom of wise
words spoken,
or by the sorrow suffered in silence?

Do we measure it by the wealth accumulated or by
the amount spent,
by success or by failure,
by the monuments built or by the walls scaled,
by victories and defeats, large or small?

Do we measure it by the forgotten or over
    the remembered?
By all of the near misses, by the exhaustion
or do we measure it by the will,
the determination to endure?

Or do we measure it by race, by class, by gender,
    by beauty,
by your lover's love or your hater's hate?

Do we measure it by pushing against the wind,
against the tide,
against family and against tradition?
Or do we measure it by the suffering of our friends
    and enemies alike?

Do we measure it by the beginning, or by the end?
Do we measure it by the way we confront life
or by the way we confront death?
Or by the number of friends and family that are
    gathered during a lifetime?
Or do we measure it by the remaining few
who go as far as they can with you,
shedding copious tears when they lay your
    body down?

How do we measure this life?
Do we measure it by the road travelled—
the journey taken?
Or by the effort, the will, the drive to endure?

Do we measure it by the kindness displayed in the
    act of living,
or do we measure it by the grace offered
or the grace received?

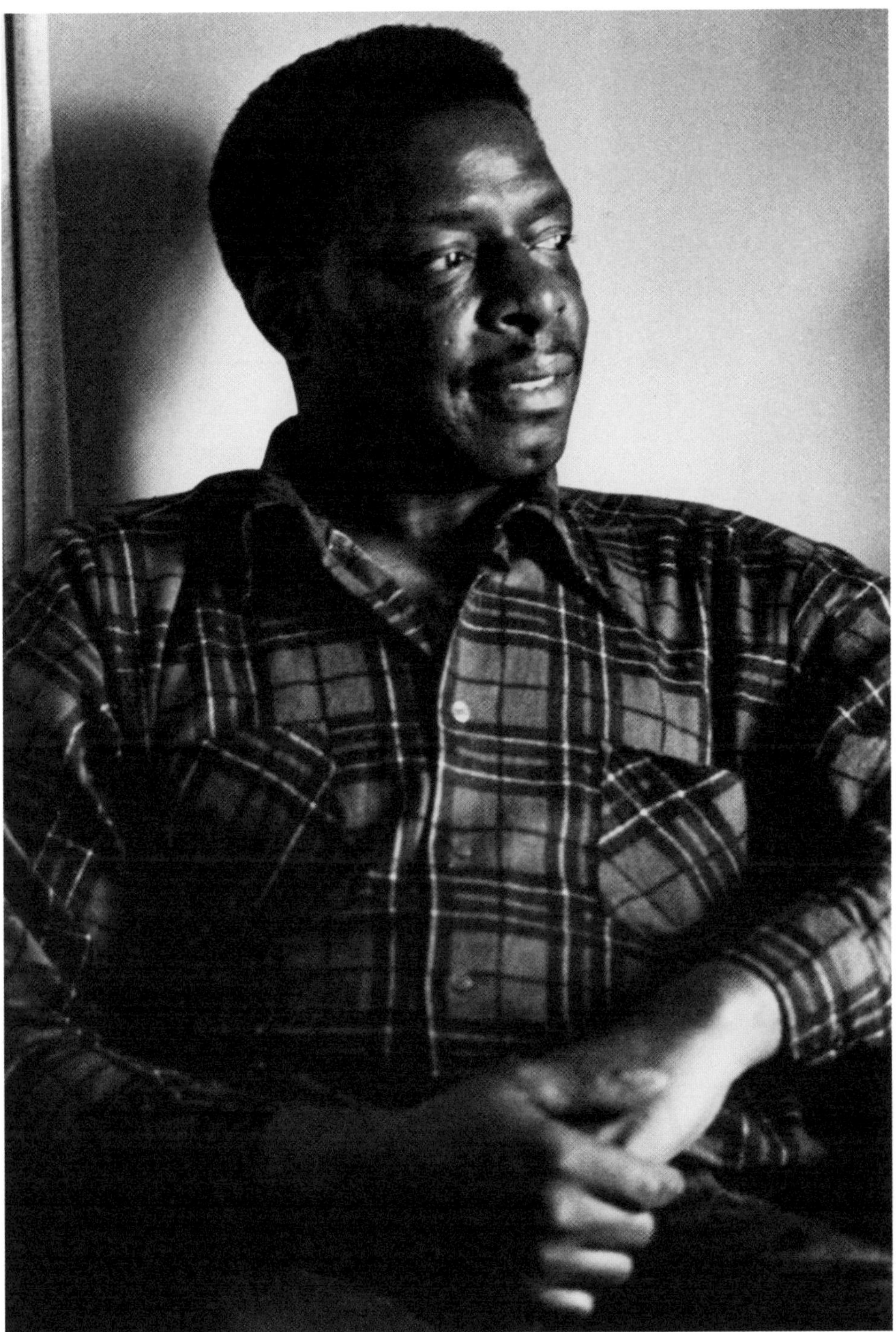

A Woman in Winter

A woman stands in the thaw of winter, the beginning of spring; reflecting, considering, imagining; contemplating the past, imagining the future. With one step she could be in the future in an instant or in the past or in the moment, the now. But to get to now, to this moment, she needs to look back over the landscape of memory.

Lost in memory, the woman faces a history, a history with a story that has been told a thousand times before. If you look on the horizon, here and there, first seen now hidden are little sightings of hope, of dreams, of memories. If you look closely, through the corridors of time, even within the horror, one could see the fluttering wings of doves, wings like time, batting out beats of hope. Hope was the thing missed, the thing hoped for, you could almost taste it. But it was just out of reach, just above your head.

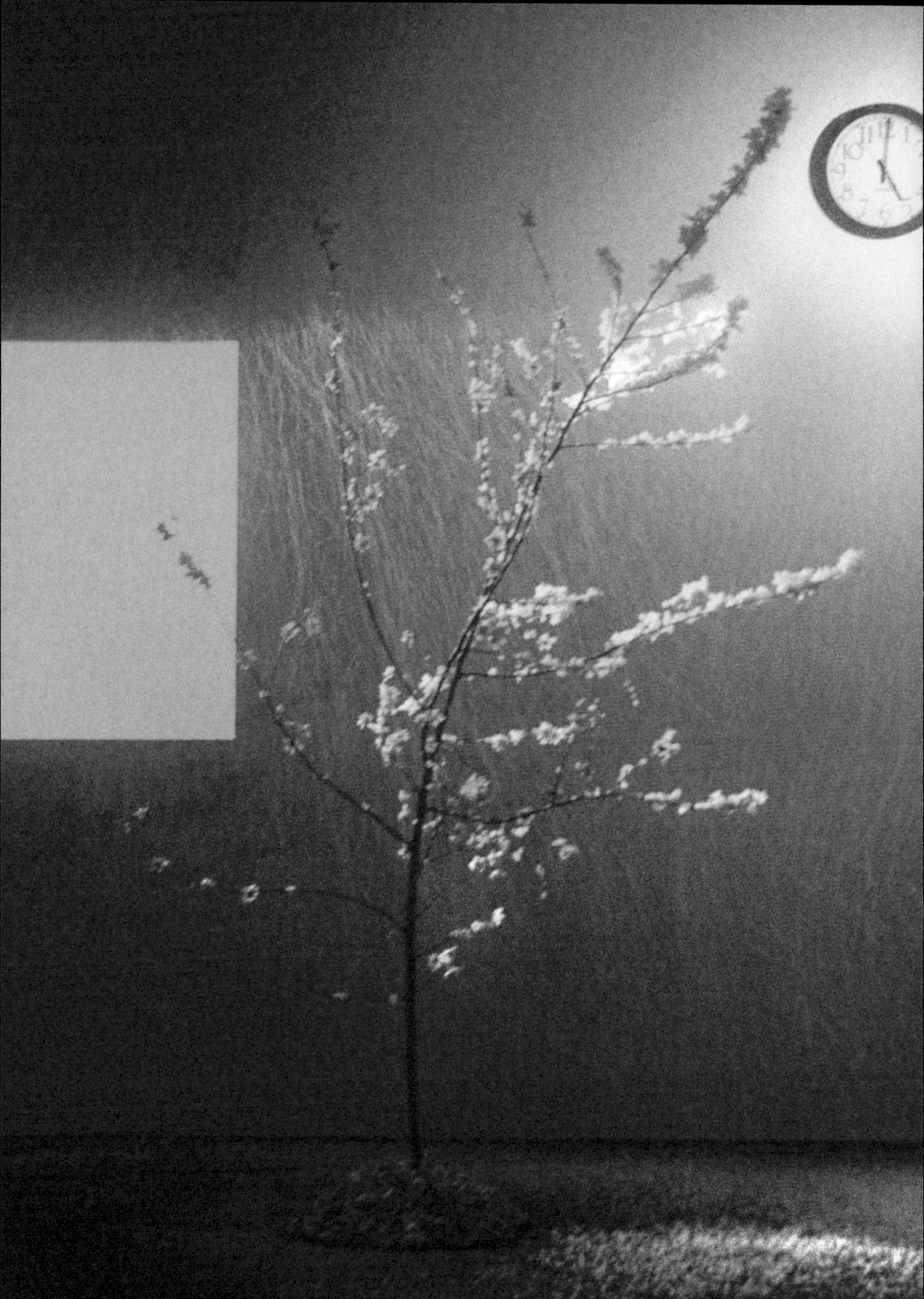

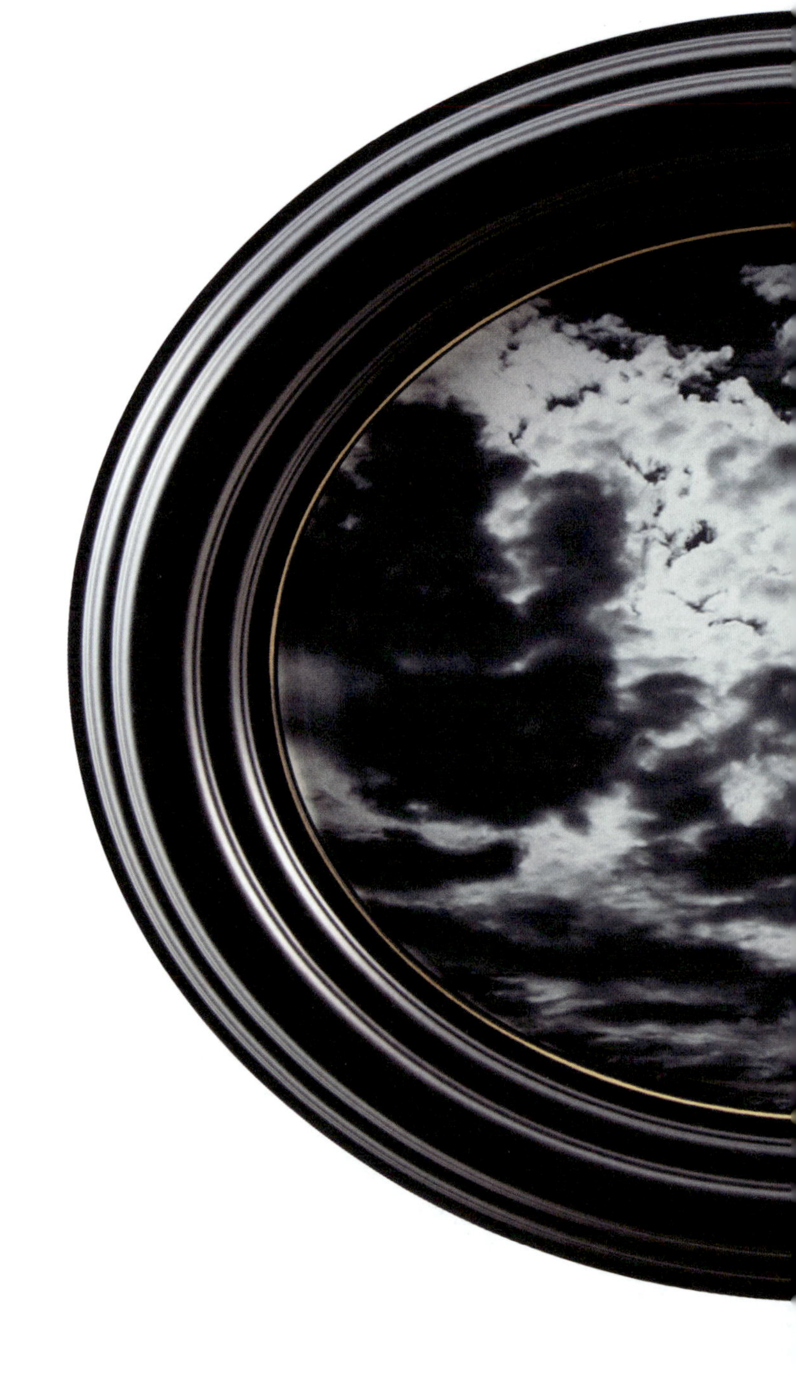

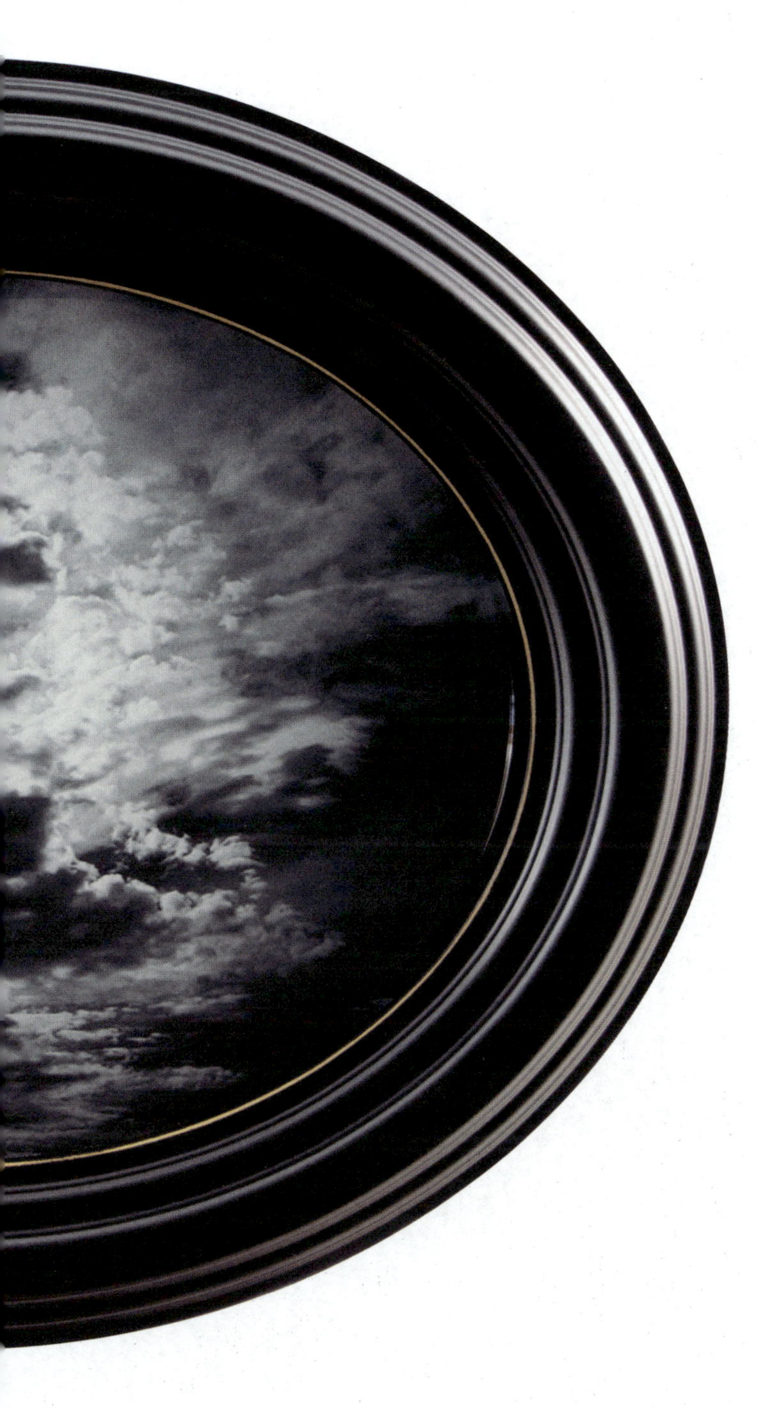

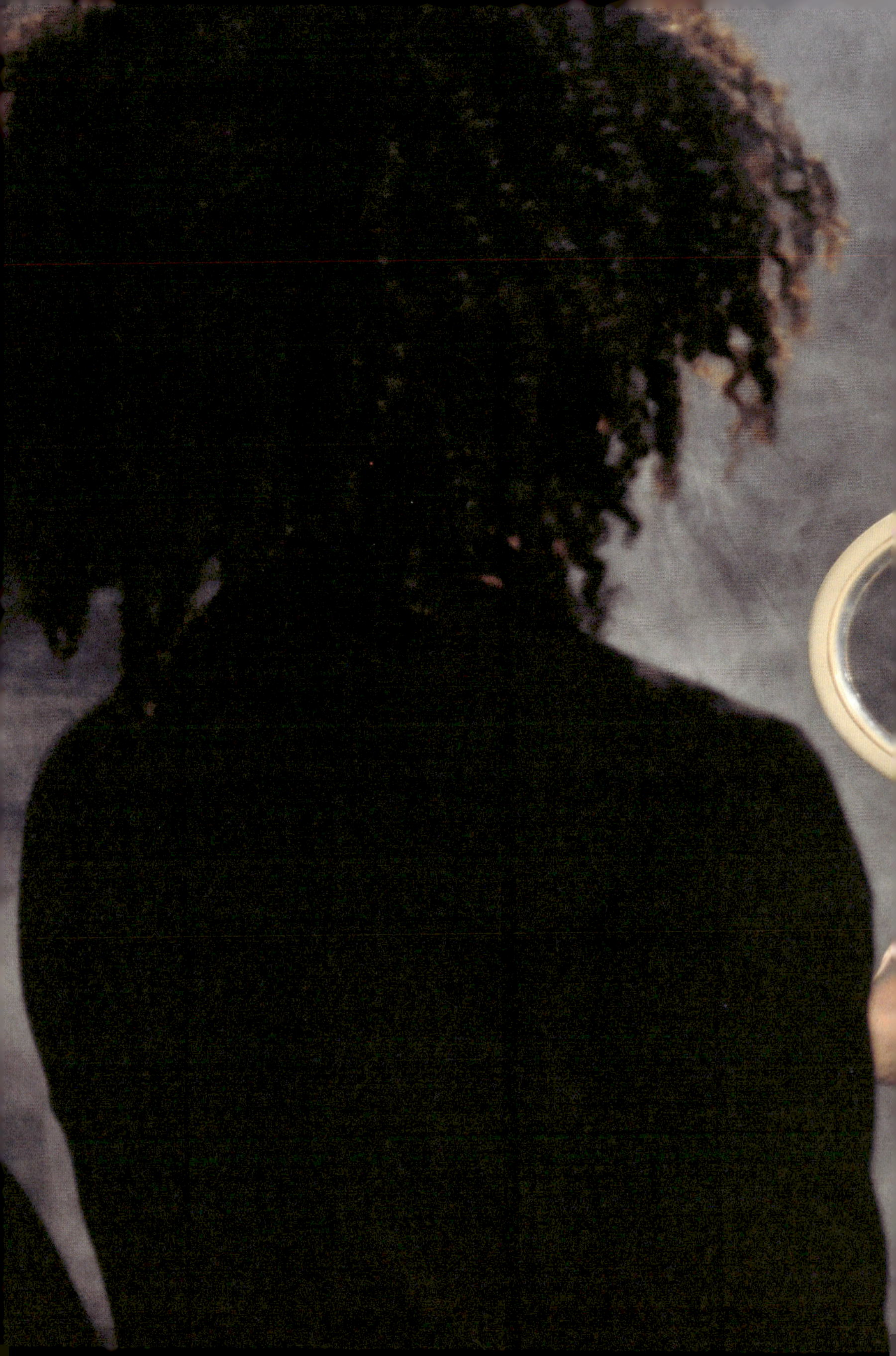

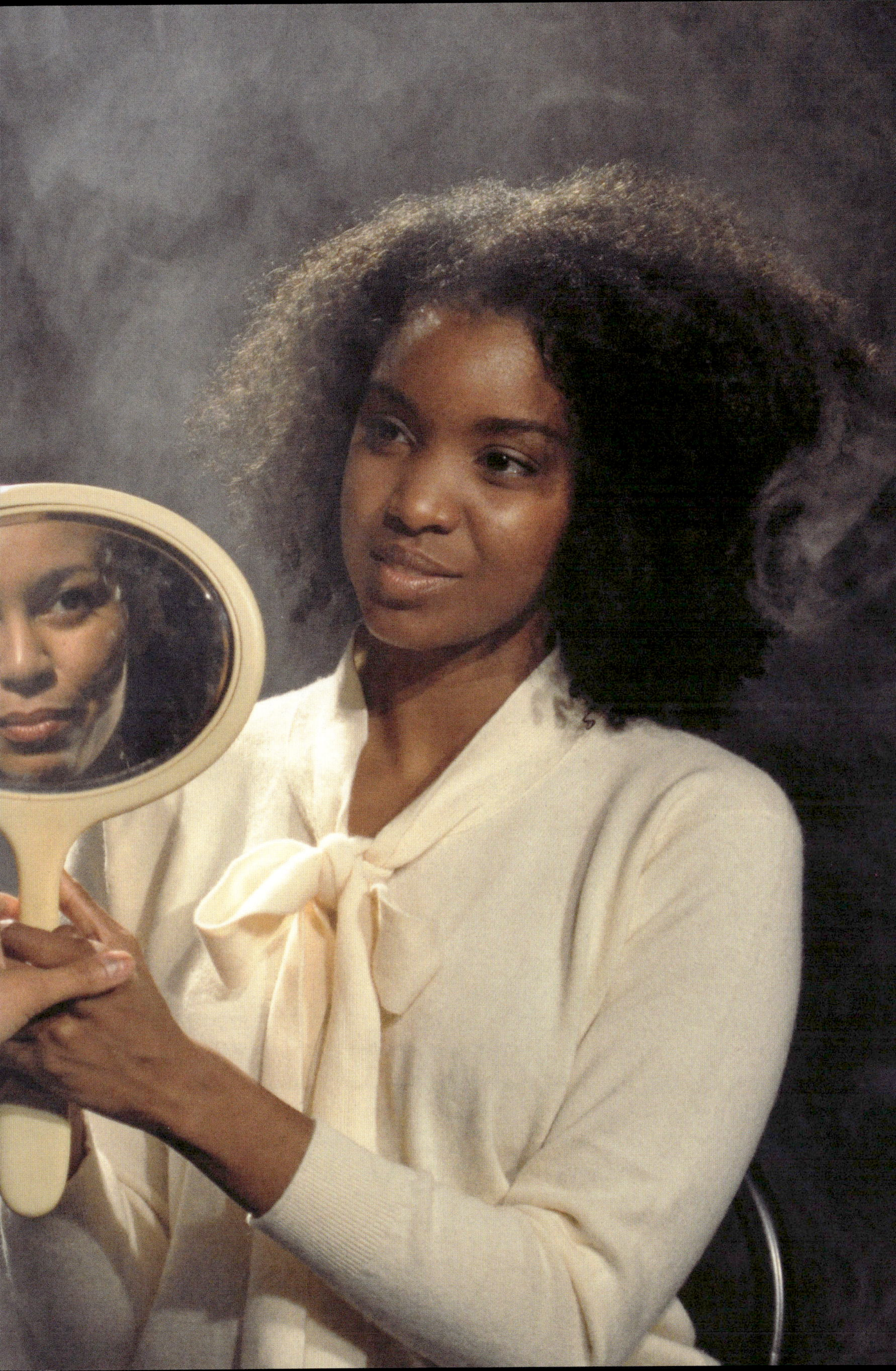

Carrie Mae Weems

Mutual Beliefs
2009

Dawoud Bey

From the very beginning, Carrie Mae Weems has had a sharp intelligence that was looking for a way into the world. From her early documentary photographs to the more expansive and materially varied recent works, she has consistently set out to visually define the world on her own terms and to redefine for all of us the nature of the world that we are in. After all these years I still anticipate her work with a fresh sense of wonderment, knowing that her restless search for the deeper meaning of things will yield a continuing rich trove of objects and images. On a Sunday morning in May I called from my home in Chicago to reconnect with my dear friend while she was travelling in Seville, Spain.

—Dawoud Bey

DAWOUD BEY: We're doing this interview while you're in Europe, and of course I'm wondering what you're working on there; I know you were in Rome previously, and now you're in Seville. What's going on over there?

CARRIE MAE WEEMS: When I first decided to return to Rome, I wanted to relax a little bit because I was working very hard and I knew that I needed a mental break before I had a mental breakdown. I decided to leave the country and come to a place that I knew and felt comfortable in. I also wanted to finish some aspects of the work that began in Rome in 2006. So I've been standing in front of all these monuments and palazzos, thinking about questions of power. I've stayed because I'm working on an exhibition here that opens in October, and I wanted to see the space and start preparing the work for the exhibition and the catalogue.

DB: Your work has had a very grand sweep since we first met in 1976. I'm wondering if you could go back for a minute and just talk briefly about where you were when you decided that the camera was going to be your voice. What influenced you, and who were your models at that point?

CMW: The thing that surprises me most about the early work is that it's not particularly different from the work I'm making now. Of course, I was trying to find a unique voice. But beyond that, from the very beginning, I've been interested in the idea of power and the consequences of power; that relationships are made and articulated through power. Another interesting thing is that even though I've been engaged in the idea of autobiography, other ideas have been more important: the role of narrative, the social levels of humour, the deconstruction of documentary, the construction of history, the use of text, storytelling, performance, and the role of memory have all become more central to my thinking than autobiography. It's assumed that autobiography is key, because I so often use myself, but it's never about me; it's always about something larger.

In *Family Pictures and Stories*, I was thinking not only about my family, but about the movement of Black families out of the South and into the North. My family becomes the representational vehicle that allows me to enter the larger discussion of race, class, and historical migration. So, the *Family* series operates in this way, as does the *Kitchen Table* series. I use my own constructed image as a vehicle for questioning ideas about the role of tradition, the nature of family, monogamy, polygamy, relationships between men and women, between women and their children, and between women and other women—underscoring the critical problems and the possible resolves. In one way or another, my work endlessly explodes the limits of tradition. I'm determined to find new models to live by. Aren't you?

DB: Can you talk about some of the earlier relationships that shaped you? I know how important those early relationships were to my formation, and I think yours too—to realise that there were indeed Black people who were out there making this work. There had been Black artists making work for a very long time, but of course they were largely invisible—we didn't know but maybe one or two. So, to discover a whole community of them to whom we had access was just amazing. It was like, We're not invisible; there are others like us. We were in fact part of a long and rich tradition, and it's not merely located in the past.

CMW: Black folks operate under a cloud of invisibility—this too is part of the work, is indeed central to the work. Even in the midst of the great social changes we've experienced just in the last year with the election of Barack Obama, for the most part, our lives remain invisible.

This erasure out of the complex history of our life and time is the greatest source of my longing. As you know, I'm a woman who yearns, who longs for. This is the key to me and to the work, and something which is rarely discussed in reviews or essays, which I also find remarkably disappointing. That so few images of African American women circulate in popular culture or in fine art is disturbing; the pathology behind it is dangerous. I mean, we got a sistah in the White House, and yet mediated culture excludes us, denies us, erases us.

My first encounter with Black photographers was as an eighteen-year-old, when I saw the *Black Photographers Annual*. I remember standing in the middle of the floor flipping the pages, seeing images that just blew me away, like a bolt of lightning. I truly saw the possibility for myself—as both subject and artist.

I knew that I would emulate what they had begun. Shawn Walker, Beuford Smith, Anthony Barboza, Ming Smith, Adger Cowans, and, certainly, the phenomenal Roy DeCarava. Of course, this comes back to you, because you were one of my first teachers. You too showed me the possibilities, showed me a path—I love you for it. But I also learned to find my own nuanced voice on that road toward self-definition. Sometime in the early 1980s, traditional documentary was called into question, it was no longer the form. For my photographs to be credible, I needed to make a direct intervention, extend the form by playing with it, manipulating it, creating representations that appeared to be documents but were in fact staged. In the same breath I began incorporating text, using multiple images, diptychs and triptychs, and constructing narratives.

DB: There are some things that I want to ask you that are more specific to your work. One has to do with an aspect of your work in which you are, conceptually, both in front of and behind the camera. You're the subject and you're the photographer. Certainly the earlier *Kitchen Table Series* introduced that idea quite forcefully. More recently there's a recurring figure that has been appearing in your work; what I would call a silent witness to history. She seems like a witness who, through witnessing, almost carries the weight of each place. This woman—this avatar—who is she? What's her function in relation to places and the narratives you're constructing?

CMW: I call her my muse—but it's safe to say that she's more than one thing. She's an alter ego. My alter ego. The muse made her first appearance in *Kitchen Table*; this woman can stand in for me and for you; she can stand in for the audience; she leads you into history. She's a witness and a guide. She changes slightly, depending on location.

For instance, she operates differently in Cuba and Louisiana than in Rome. She's shown me a great deal about the world and about myself, and I'm grateful to her. Carrying a tremendous burden, she is a Black woman leading me through the trauma of history. I think it's very important that as a Black woman she's engaged with the world around her; she's engaged with history, she's engaged with looking, with being. She's a guide into circumstances seldom seen.

My girl, my muse, dares to show up as a guide, an engaged persona pointing toward the history of power. She's the unintended consequence of the Western imagination. It's essential that I do this work and it's essential that I do it with my body.

DB: How do you think about what the next piece of this conversation is, as you construct this narrative?

CMW: I'm a woman who engages the world. I feel as at home in Seville as in Spanish Harlem [*laughter*]. So, I have these curious interests. I'm walking down curious paths trying to connect the dots. For instance, if I want to know something about the African influence on dance, then I need to know Mississippi and go to Cuba, Brazil, and Spain, because that's how you connect the dots. I can't connect them in my living room. If I can see things and understand them with my mind and body, I might be able to use them. It keeps me out in the world, even when I would prefer to be home, in bed and near my husband.

DB: What about form? There's the how, but there's also the what.

CMW: I think the how is the most difficult and rewarding. Sometimes my work needs to be photographic, sometimes it needs words, sometimes it needs to have a relationship to music, sometimes it needs to have all three and become a video projection. I feel more comfortable now without my muse. I've figured out a way of making pictures that suggests that something is being witnessed.

The work tells you what form it needs to take. What's important is knowing when to put your ego aside so you can see what the work wants to be. Being sensitive to the world around you and paying attention to your aesthetic tools... Once you know that you can make it, you get out of the way.

DB: Talking with you over the years, I've been acutely aware of a particular cultural wellspring of references that runs through your work and indeed through you, informing both the production of your work and the way you choose to be in the world. One of those strong references is music. A while back I was listening to the poet Quincy Troupe read his work, and just as clear as day I was hearing John Coltrane, who Quincy later confirmed as a strong influence. I often hear music when I look at some of your work, too, and even when I hear you speak. So I'm wondering what role music plays in your personal life, your creative and intellectual life; how you have drawn from it?

CMW: Music has saved my life, more than once. Abbey Lincoln is my favourite, I listen to her music often. She sets the tone—she's a woman of yearning and of longing. Miles's forlorn trumpet sets the pace and Jason Moran carries the melodic line. Like Monk, I'm spinning, but hum along.

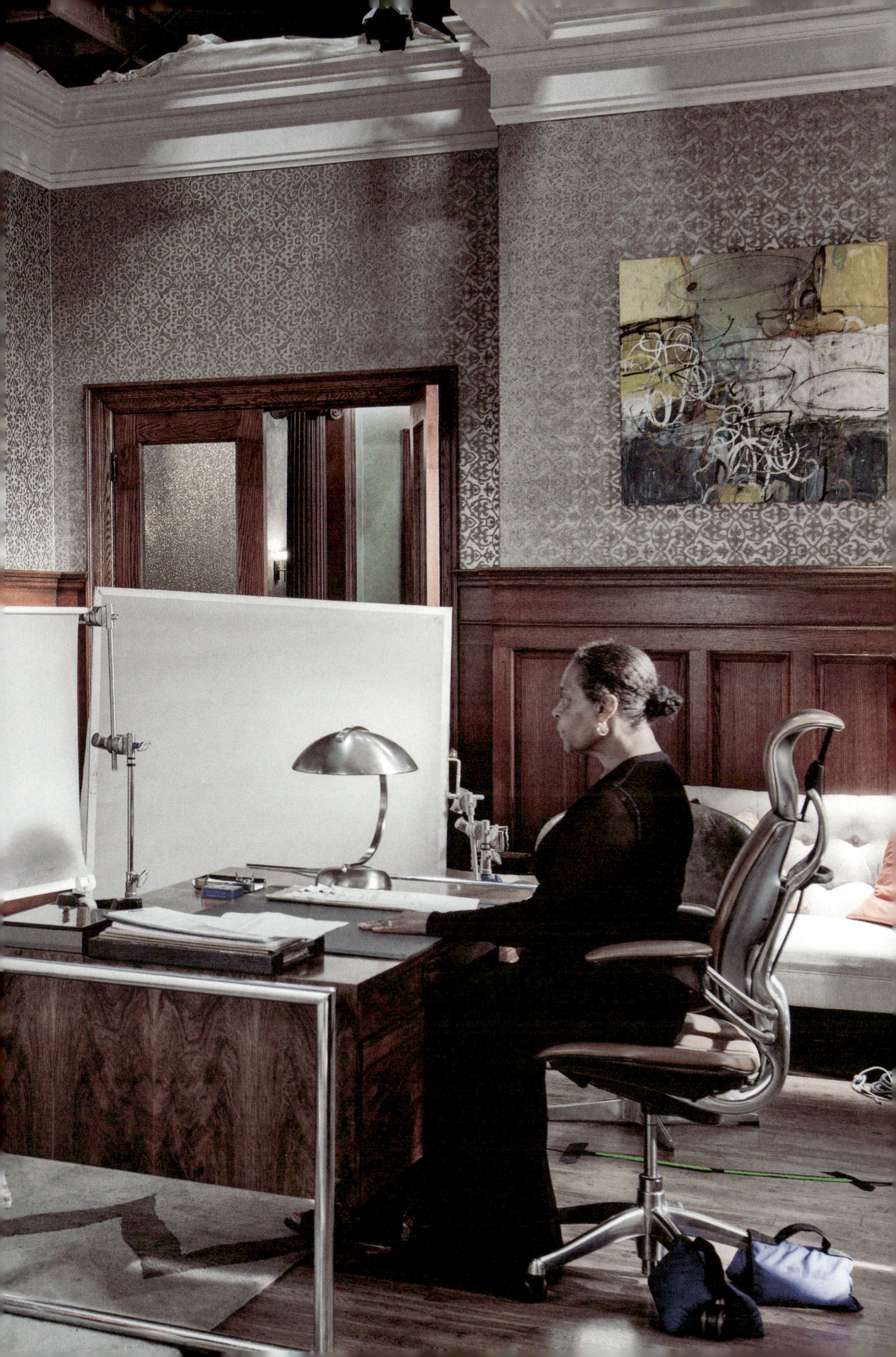

Ritual and Revolution

Between the two worlds
I was with you
but as the wind on the Caspian Sea.

I was with you
in the ancient ruins of time
you rode me a hobby-horse
into the age of revolution.
I was with you
When you stormed the Bastille &
The Winter Palace.

I was with you
in the hideous mise-en-scène
of the Middle Passage
One potato, two potato, three potato, four
& in Ireland, too.

I was with you
in the death camp
shaved head and all
beating the drummer's drum
shaking in my boots and crying.

I was with you
on the longest march
in Cuba & Timbuktu.

I was with you
in Santiago
attempting to block
an assassin's bullet
and again in Harlem
cradling Malcolm to my bosom, crying.

Out of the shadows
from the edge of the new world
I saw your slow persistent emergence, &
saw you spinning jenny's cotton into gold.

Throughout the course of my existence
& I have been here always
I saw everlasting death
& the endless
weeping of women

I saw you and your father
your mother &
all your sisters
frozen static
in the autumn
of the patriarch.

I saw your fear of pleasure
I saw you mistaking sexuality for sensuality
& saw your body fragment into a zillion pieces.

I saw men and women
locked in a futile struggle for power
& saw the declining significance of race.

I saw your hands replaced
by inventions that left you idle
no laurel surrounding your name
no marker to mark
your existence.

I saw nor heard any mention of
working, class, you
& you said little
and did even less.

In the halls of justice, I
spied some of you robbing
the coffers of church & state
smashing the piggy bank
using the shards
to pick your teeth.

I too felt the allure of
temptations' temptress
and in no-time flat
saw my own greed
my own corrupt hand
in the pot.

Lost for a time
I saw you moving through
the shadowy corridors of
an ageless labyrinth
wondering when and where
it would all end.

From the four corners of the world
I saw you bewildered, startled & stumbling
toward the next century
looking over your shoulder
with fingers crossed.

From the ruins of what was and what will be
I saw your longing
felt your pain
and tried to comfort you.

Afraid for you
I swooped down from my hiding place
kissed your brow
& left a bag of square-shouldered courage
at your side.

In the midst of the storm
trumpets blared
& from the top of Tatlin's monument
Stanley waved the white flag of surrender
Lorna turned her head
not once but twice
bell hooked us all
intoning the constant refrain
GO ON
& dear Felix,
beautiful and exhausted
blew us a long red beaded kiss
of farewell.

In the twilight
coming on a day without end
Ana traced the tracks of your tears

& I could see again
the coming of Spring's hope
in the May flowers
of May days
long, long forgotten.

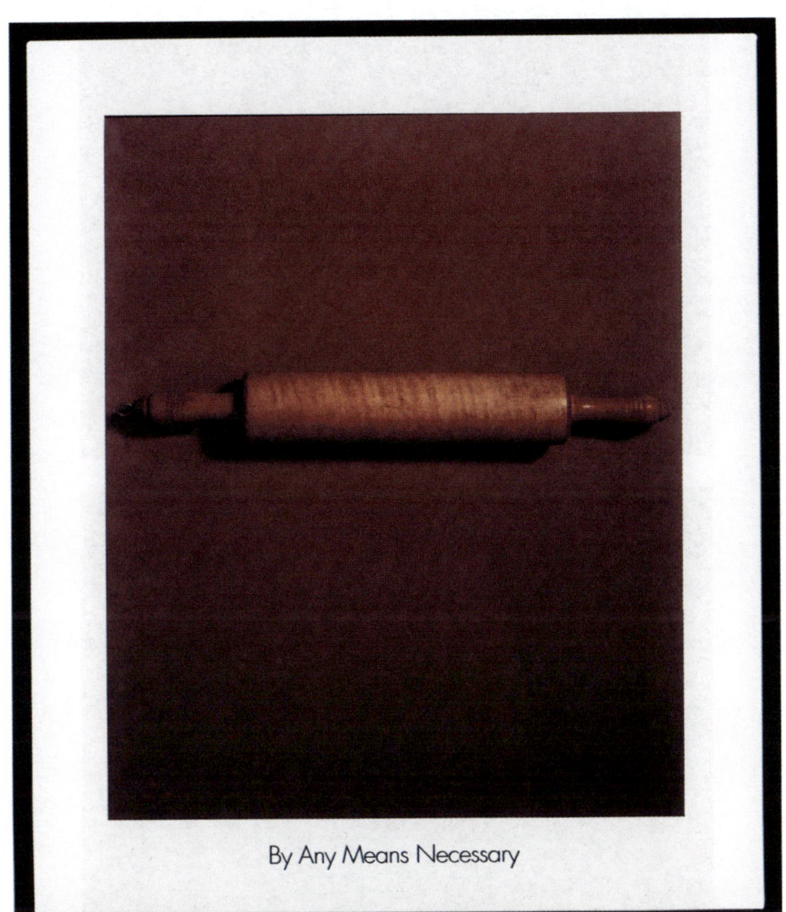

By Any Means Necessary

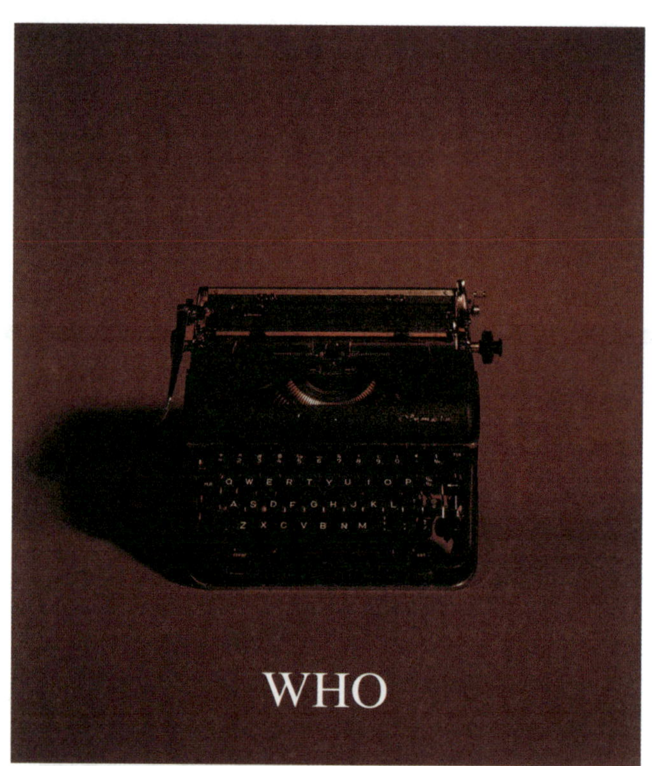
WHO

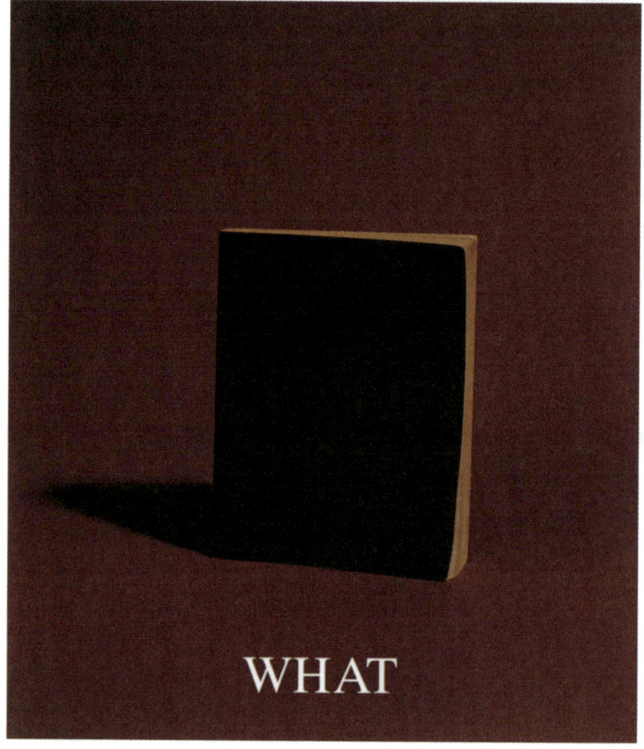
WHAT

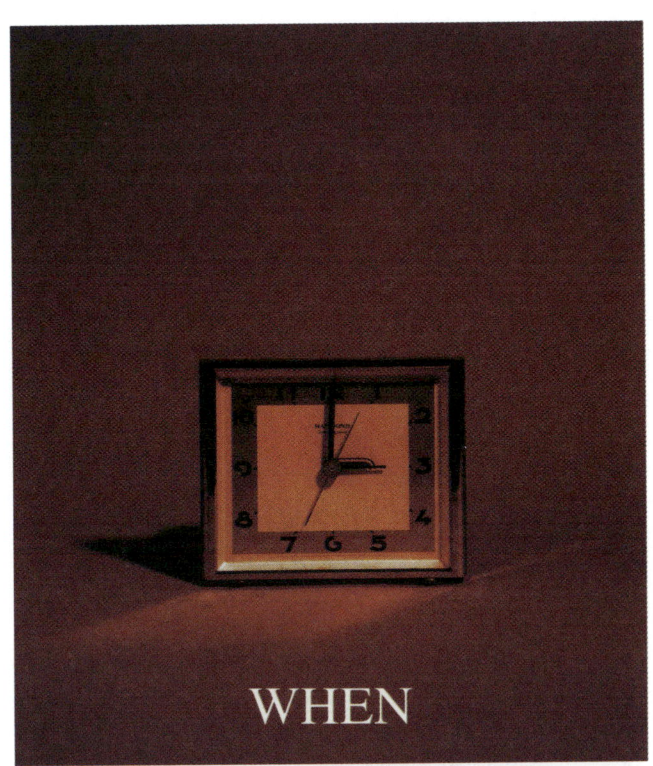
WHEN

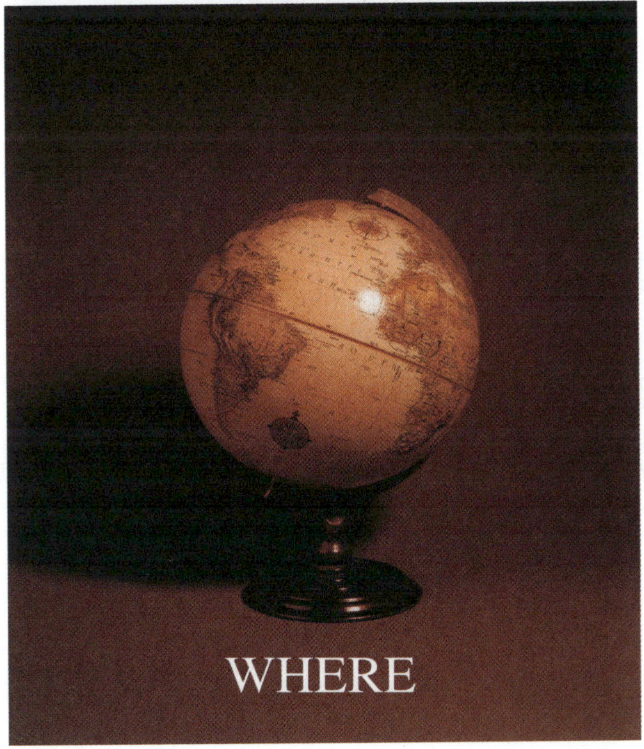
WHERE

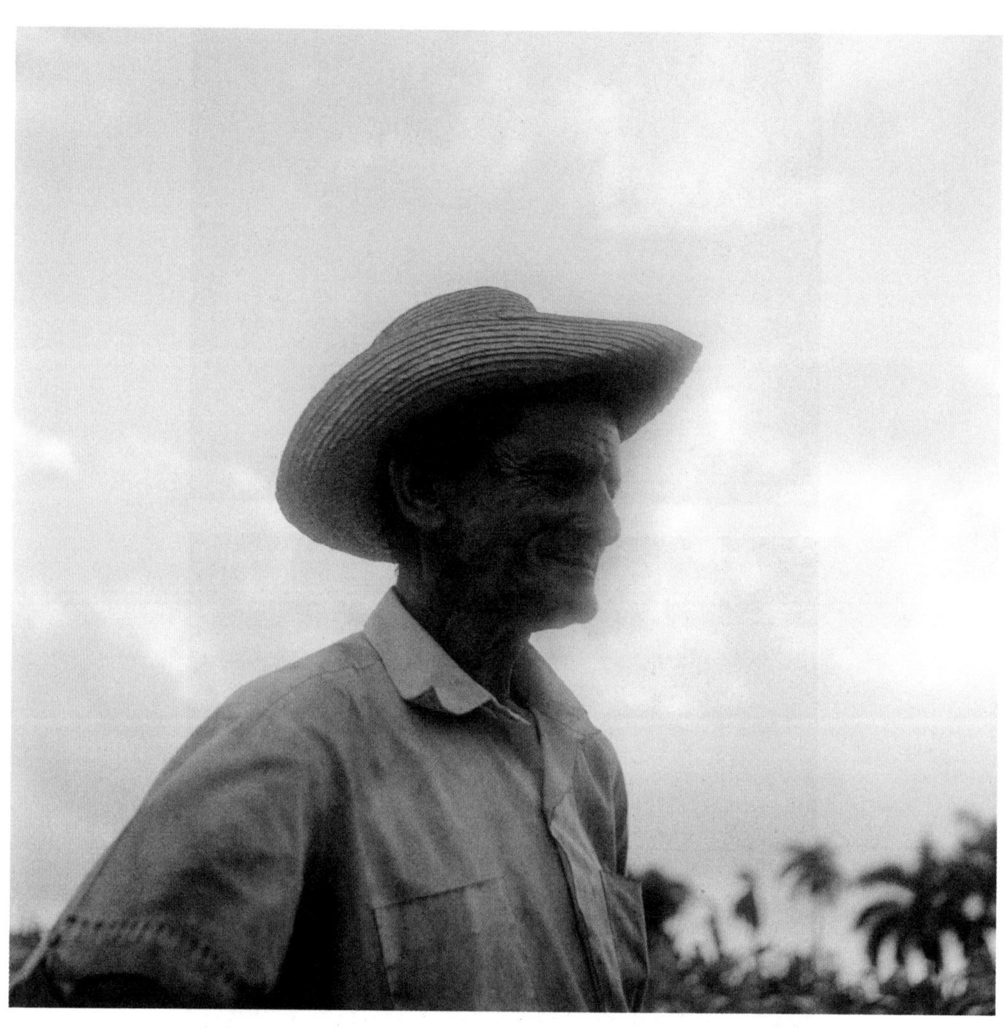

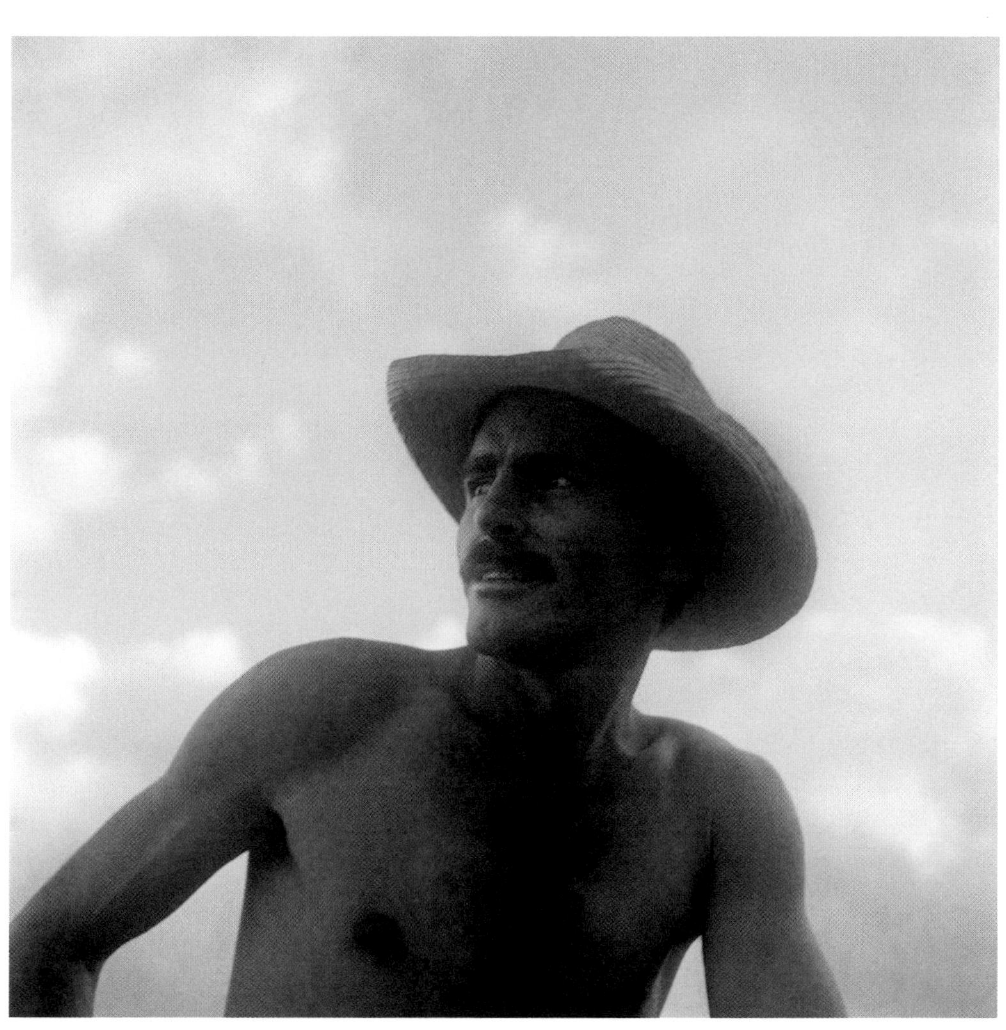

Constructing History

This is a story within a story. How to enter this history? What to show, what to say, what to feel? It's a creation myth of how things came to be as they are. In this constructed place, our classroom, we revisit the past. The students examine the facts and will participate in the construction of history, a history that has been told to them by others. But now, with their own bodies, they engage their own dark truth, their own winter.

Some of the students are young, learning about civil rights, human rights, for the first time. A teacher will guide them through lessons. For many of them, the day will be long and hard; for others, painful. Some things will be difficult for them to see.

Snow is falling. The students are attentive, curious, anxious. They know that the day will not be a normal day—will not be child's play. They will see things meant for older eyes, but they need to know. There are now schools for suicide bombers. Lawlessness is everywhere, corruption rampant.

She tells the students that the bright lights of history are now shining down on them, on her, on you, on us, and now all things are unavoidable. Perhaps in shame, some will turn away, but the crime remains. The age of innocence is past, and you are now responsible for your own future.

How we got to this point is still one of the great questions of the twentieth century, and yet, no viable answer seems to be forthcoming. We simply know that something unimaginable happened, and what happened—how it happened—changed everything.

—

Earlier, in the 1940s, a startling thing happened. A bomb, more powerful than life itself, was dropped on Japan. Hiroshima—Nagasaki. And we knew that the world was now completely ours to destroy and, if left in the wrong hands, would be destroyed! Life gone in a moment, in a flash, in the blink of an eye.

This is a story within a story. A key, a peephole.

The teacher tells the students that when she was young—maybe thirteen, when it all started—her world, like theirs, had been a world for the most part that was filled with play, with fun. Like them, she had been protected from the horror—from the horrors of the world; had been shrouded in comfort, in innocence. Then came the war. The war, the war, the war to end all wars and the assassinations and the murders, and things changed.

There were protests, marches, demonstrations, riots, here and there, everywhere. There were murders of the famous and the not-so-famous. Hundreds, thousands, millions of unknowns gone. Like thousands of others, she joined the demonstrations and felt the crush of the police baton on her back too, and ran for cover, regrouped, and demonstrated again.

Once upon a time you could not vote, you could not enter a store, you could not speak unless spoken to. You could not be unless recognised. You could not, could not, could not...

If you were Black—if you were Black, maybe that was a good place to start, to begin, though it might be hard for students to understand, to believe. But perhaps that was a good place to start the tale, if you were Black.

I went to a diner for coffee. Nothing more. The waitress is beautiful. White. She pours me a cup of coffee, and I talked to her. Jim Crow is almost out of our system. I talked to her about things that mattered. She knew some of these things, but not everything—not everything on my mind, not everything that had happened.

I ask her for coffee. She pours and readies herself to hear a story—to hear the tale. The story makes her uncomfortable. The hard layer of reality rattles her. I can see it in her eyes.

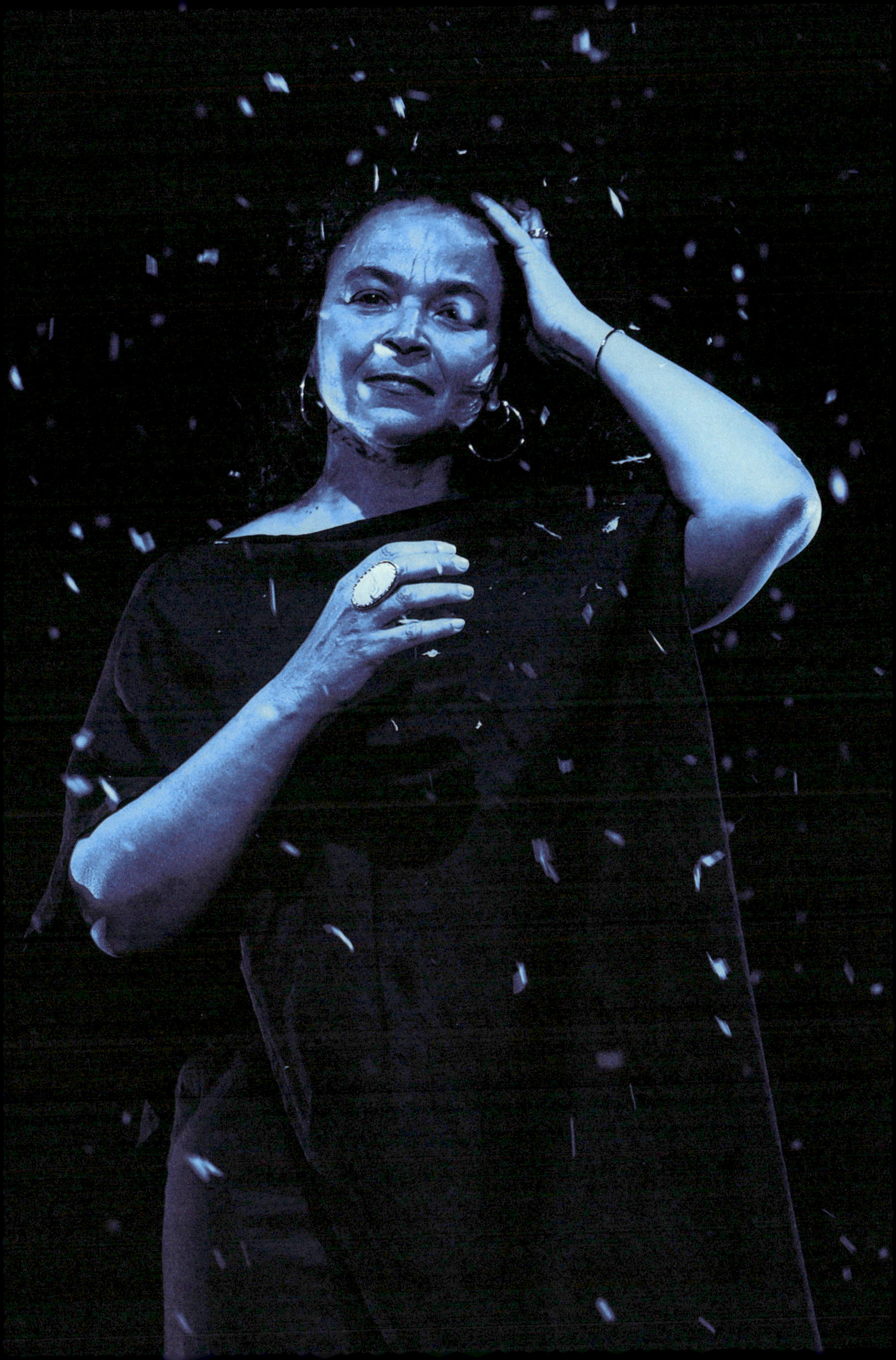

"Negro Progress! Nigger Please..."

Negro you have me laying here in bed on a Sunday morning, which should be my day off—the lord's day—mulling over your request for a 'letter' on my Negro Progress but given my thoughts on the matter it's an impossible task—a truly considered response would require an essay at the very least or perhaps a short novella—but within the limitations you've set out, I'll do the best I can.

Part 1 – America:

Our country is cracking, breaking, shifting—moving from white to Black & varying shades of brown. By the year 2020 manifest destiny will be boxed up and put away. Our progress is linked to this shift.

In relative terms:

The landscape, the contours and dimensions of this country, is rooted in violence—from the assassination of Lincoln, Medgar, Martin, and Malcolm, to John & Robert Kennedy and the recent police killings of young Black men.

We now have senators, congressmen and women, governors, mayors, CEOs of major corporations, and, while he's been called everything but a man, a Black man—Obama—in the White House. This is progress by any measure.

The backlash to Obama's presidency is evident in the rise of Donald Trump and the escalating violence directed against Black boys and men, the slaughter of the Emanuel Nine, and the mass killing of gays that happened only yesterday—violence perpetrated by both vigilantes and the state has often accompanied this 'progress'.

Part 2 – Negro Progress and the Value of the Work:

The first question is: How is progress to be defined and measured, by what means and against what?

In relative terms:

It has never been enough for me to measure myself against myself. My sense of achievement is based on the overall forward movement of my people.

By progress I mean a decided shift in one's relationship to the means of production coupled with the way one is perceived and treated by the larger society.

Trapped by historical circumstance—our work, like our people, is systematically undervalued. This is made evident in the marketplace where the work of Blacks & women artists sells for substantially less than the work of white men.

The highest price paid for a work by a non-living man artist is \$179.4 million — Picasso
The highest price paid for a work by a living man artist is \$58.4 million — Koons
The highest price paid for a work by a non-living woman artist is \$44.4 million — O'Keeffe
The highest price paid for a work by a living woman artist is \$7 million — Kusama

Over \$100 million difference!!!!!

Compared with the above, here are the prices paid for works by Black artists:

Henry Tanner — \$541,000
Hughie Lee-Smith — \$312,000
Elizabeth Catlett — \$288,000
Norman Lewis — \$180,000
Romare Bearden — \$100,000

Part 3 – The Conundrum:

Relative to the field:

Everywhere I look, I see artists of colour playing in the field. Their practice is creating new pathways and fields of exploration; we are inventors redefining contemporary art. While listening to Michael Jackson it occurred to me that a part of our contribution is that we've expanded and extended the field of contemporary art practice. Inventing new ways of making—developing an art practice that would not exist but for us.

In relative terms:

Off the top, without much thought, I could name about 10–12 highly successful Black artists, including you; their work exhibited in galleries and museums nationally and internationally.

However, I can name fewer Black curators, art historians, gallery owners, or museum directors. In the area of critical inquiry we are sorely lacking.

It's important to remember:

That there is a significant interplay between artists and curators and art historians. Each assists the other in defining or shaping how works of art are to be understood and valued.

In relative terms:

It's difficult for Black people to imagine the future, even as we make it. It's hard to create new narratives when you're trapped by what has been. It's a paradox—a conundrum.

Being defined by race has left us holding the bag—while white artists go merrily along being all they can be, dreaming big and tap dancing to the bank. See *The New York Times* Art Section on any given Sunday and you'll understand my meaning.

A number of museums have presented exhibitions by artists of colour representing approximately 2% of exhibitions or holdings.

This is important to remember.

We exist within segregated communities, or what Jeff Chang calls the resegregation of American culture. Our work is expected to deal with social issues related to the Black experience, and when the work ventures into other terrain it is not well received.

Part 4 – The Fact of the Matter:

In 2004, 0% of exhibitions at the Guggenheim went to Black or women artists.
In 2014, I became the first—the one and only—African American/woman to be given a retrospective at the Guggenheim.

In conjunction with the exhibition I organised a four-day convening, inviting over 150 artists, musicians, poets, and public intellectuals to present their work within that hallowed space.

While I can't prove it, the Guggenheim, which has not been heretofore interested in the field, recently received a large grant for their 'new' initiative in Art and Social Practice, inviting several women and Black artists to join them—*on this bridge called my back.*

As you know, artists are often the source of tremendous ideas and cheap labour, and the same stereotypes that kept us rooted to work in the nineteenth century are the same stereotypes that keep us out of work today.

I receive awards regularly, including the MacArthur Award.

I'm currently the 2016 National Artist of the Year. Flying to Aspen soon to retrieve the prize.

I'm invited to participate in any number of exhibitions, rarely with white artists.

I'm invited to any number of events, fancy galas, and fabulous parties with the who's who of the art world.

I live in New York City, the most diverse city in America, but often I'm the sole Black person in the room.

I'm often confused with Lorna Simpson or Kara Walker. Often the confused person insists that I'm not myself.

Within the last twelve months my sales have declined. Fame doesn't translate into fortune.
So this is Negro Progress now, as I see it.

Have a great show, Theaster, and I hope it's well received.

Carrie Mae Weems – June 2016

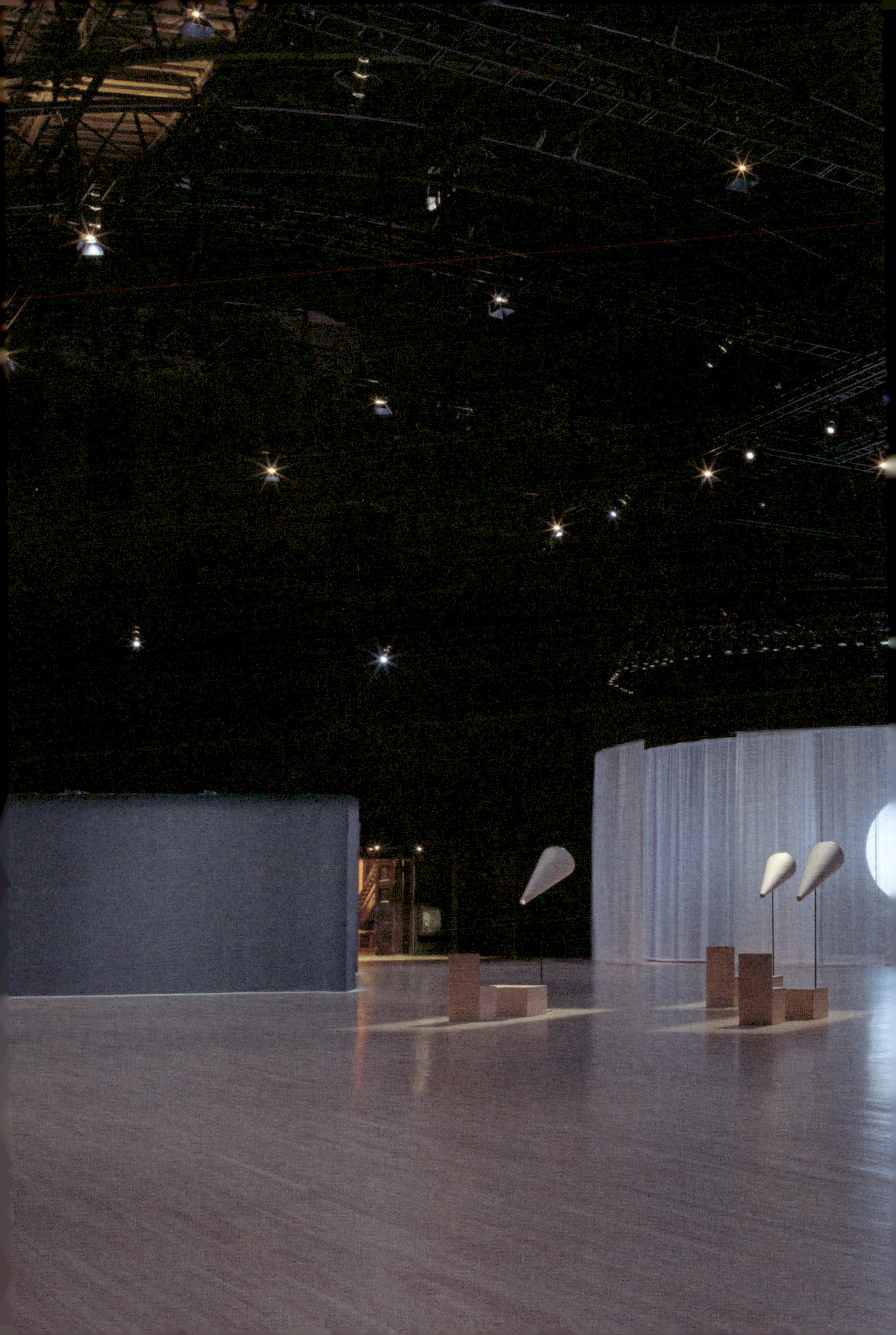

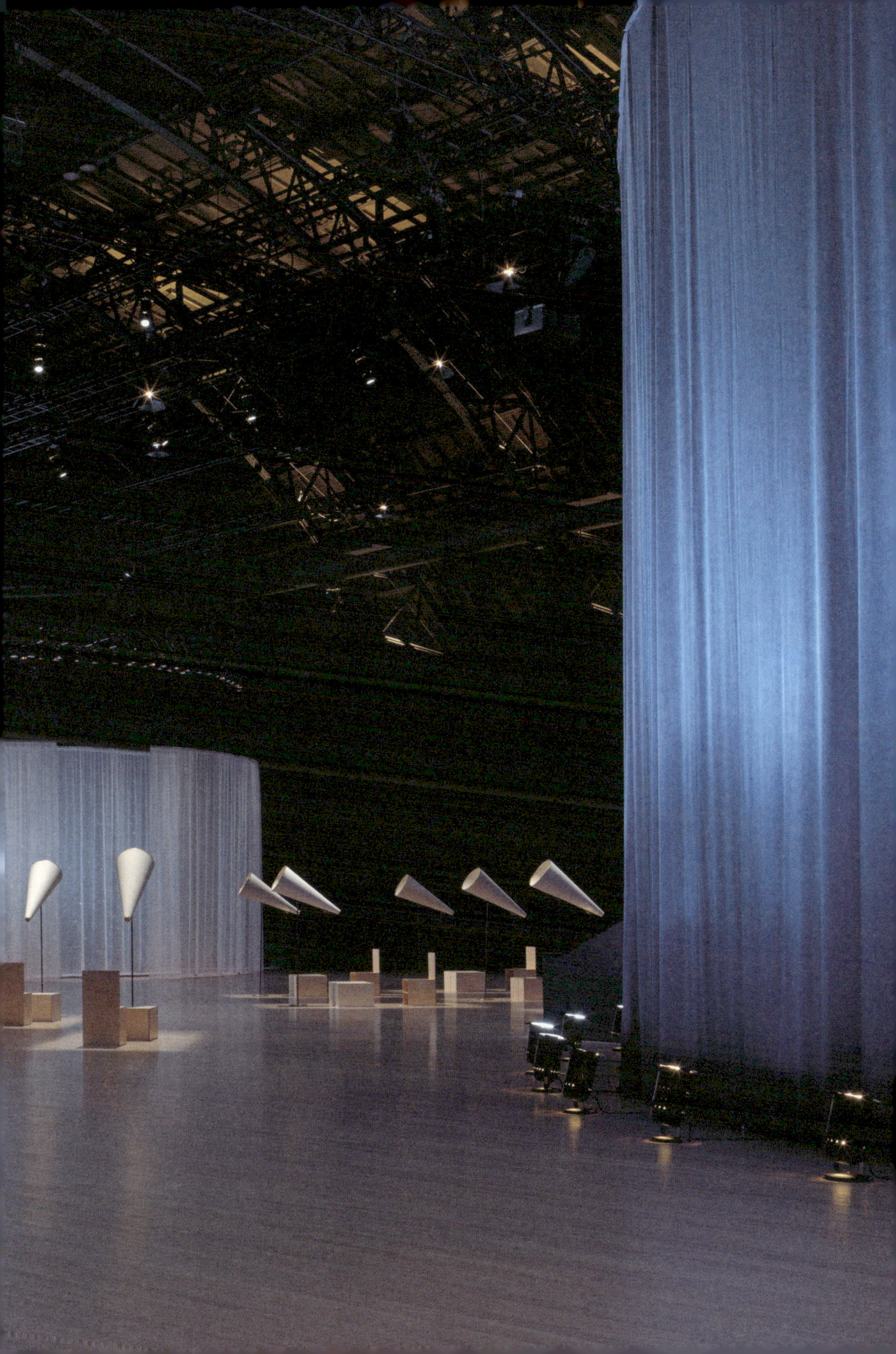

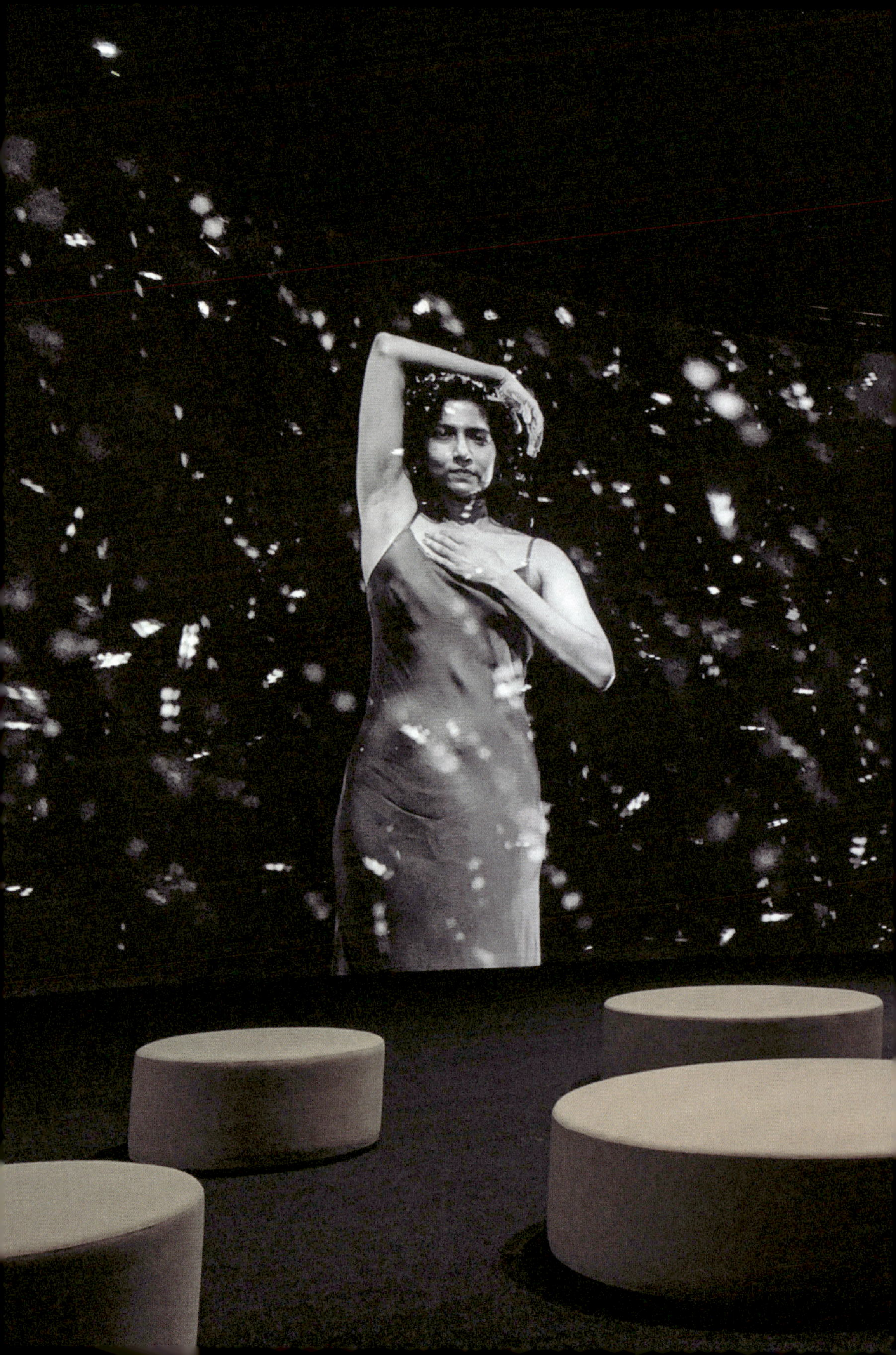

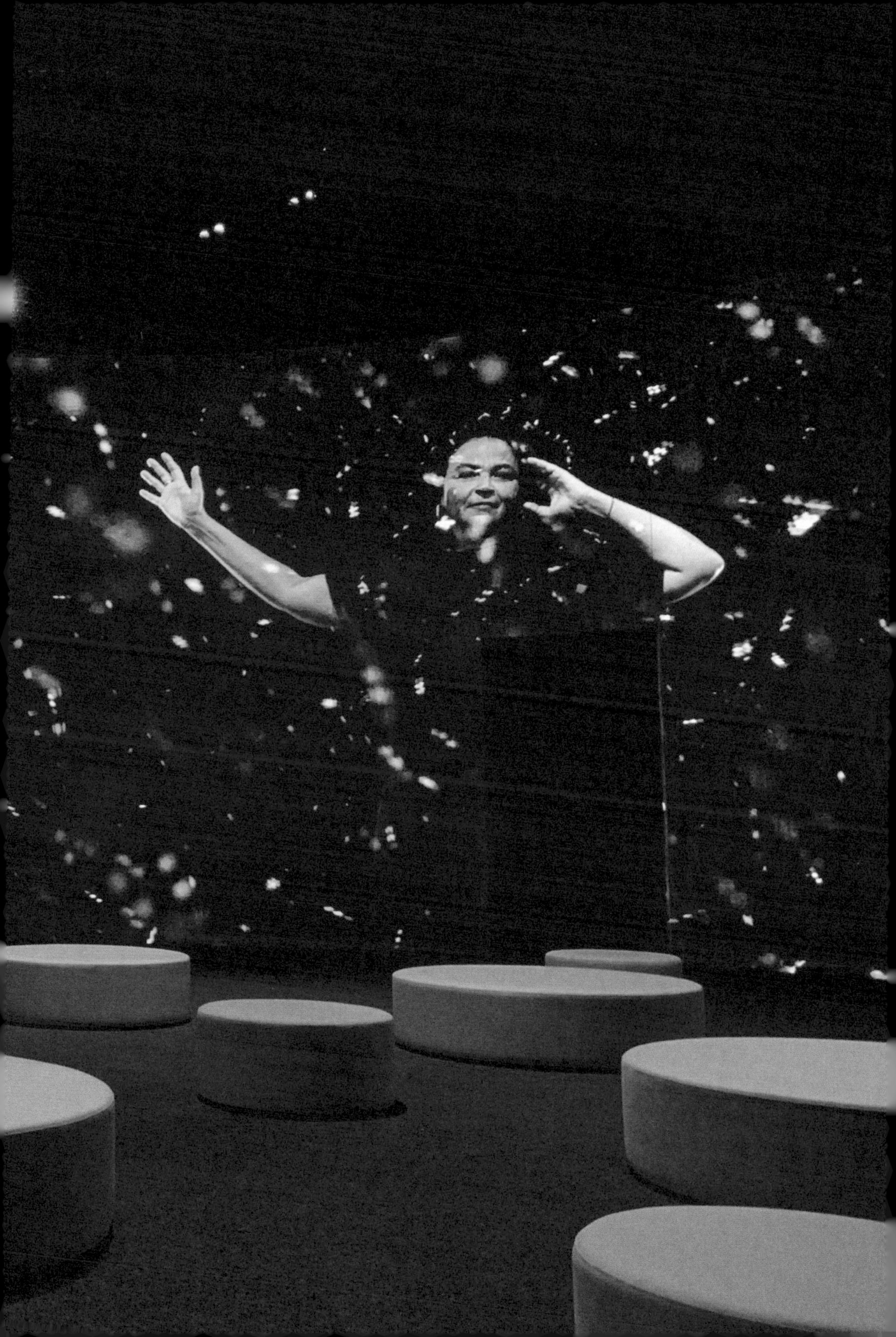

Histories of Violence

Portland Art Museum
'Carrie Mae Weems: An Artist Reflects'
3 February 2013

At a certain moment in my own history, it dawned on me that seminal moments in our common history, our country's history, have shaped who we are and what we are—as Americans, as US citizens.

What was so phenomenal about that, so crazy about that, is that the thing that truly made *us* possible was a series of assassinations that took place in this country; that something meant to destroy us and tear us down is what brought me to this room today—this awful series of awful events that began with the assassination of JFK, and then Malcolm, and then Martin Luther.

These moments in the history of our country profoundly shaped who we were to become, and they continue to shape us today. I thought it would be interesting to construct an imaginary classroom in which a group of students could enact some of these pivotal moments, introducing them to history by using our own bodies to participate in the construction of histories that have profoundly impacted our lives.

•

Grace Notes: Scene 5—A History of Violence

Woman in Black *comes to the stage and stands in the spotlight stage right. She reads the text. One of the* Graces *sings 'Remember Me'.*

IN THIS HISTORY OF VIOLENCE, WE ARE NOT THE ONLY ONES WHO HAVE SUFFERED.

WIB: Imagine that you are out for an evening stroll by yourself or with your friend or your child or with your girlfriend/boyfriend, your wife/husband or partner.

From the corner of your eye, you see a police car speeding by, red strobes flashing. For reasons unknown, imagine that the police car comes to a full stop right in front of you, and the officer, for reasons unknown, gets out and, for no apparent reason, demands your ID. You've heard the news, you know the story, and because recent circumstances have taught you a thing or two about the limits of these fatal encounters, your fingers are crossed.

Fearing the possibility of becoming yet another statistic, you wholeheartedly comply. But as you reach into your pocket for the requested ID, the officer, for reasons unknown, but assumed, imagines that you are reaching not for your ID, but for an imagined gun that is imagined to be in your pocket. And for no apparent reason, but assumed, a shot is fired, and boom! You go down.

Imagine that you are out for an evening stroll, chatting on your cell, kickin' it with your friend, passing the time while making your way home. For reasons unknown, but assumed, you're stopped by a self-appointed dispenser of justice—a neighbourhood vigilante—who imagines that you look out of place and questions your very presence. For reasons unknown and contested, a struggle ensues. A shot is fired, and boom! You go down.

Imagine that you are always stopped, always charged, always convicted.

Imagine you or your child living in a state of constant fear, under constant pressure, constant suspicion, troubled by this unrelenting history of violence, where time and time again, an encounter with those who are meant to serve ends with your death.

Imagine this. See this. Imagine the impossible. Imagine the worst of the worst—and know that it's happening. Imagine Trayvon Martin or Michael Brown, only boys, dying alone on a cold street. Imagine Eric Garner dying alone on a city sidewalk or Sandra Bland dying alone in a county jail, and for no apparent reason. Imagine the grief of their mothers, the suffering of their fathers, and the vengeful hearts of their sisters. Imagine that for these crimes no one is charged, no one is convicted. Then think about it.

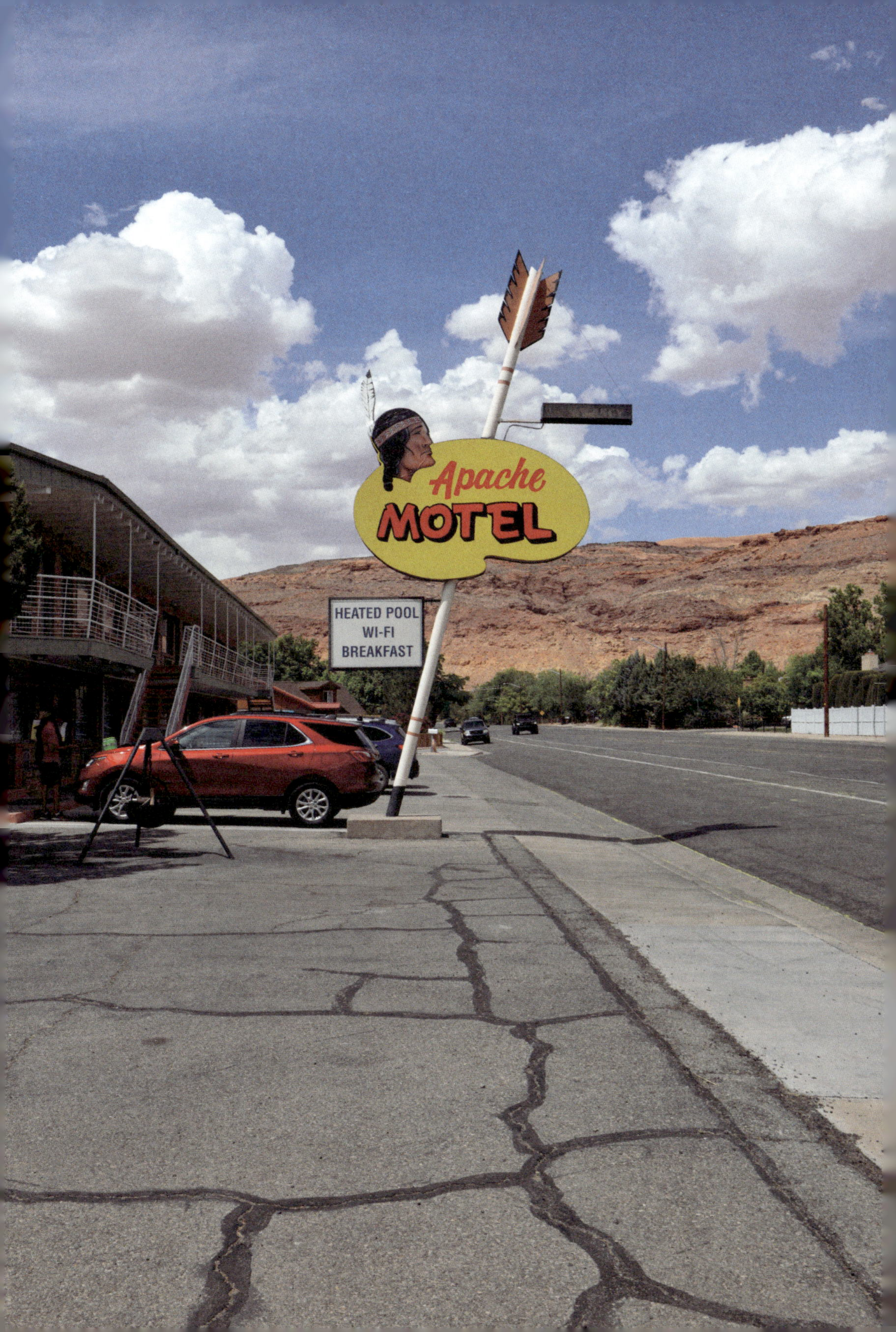
Apache
MOTEL
HEATED POOL
WI-FI
BREAKFAST

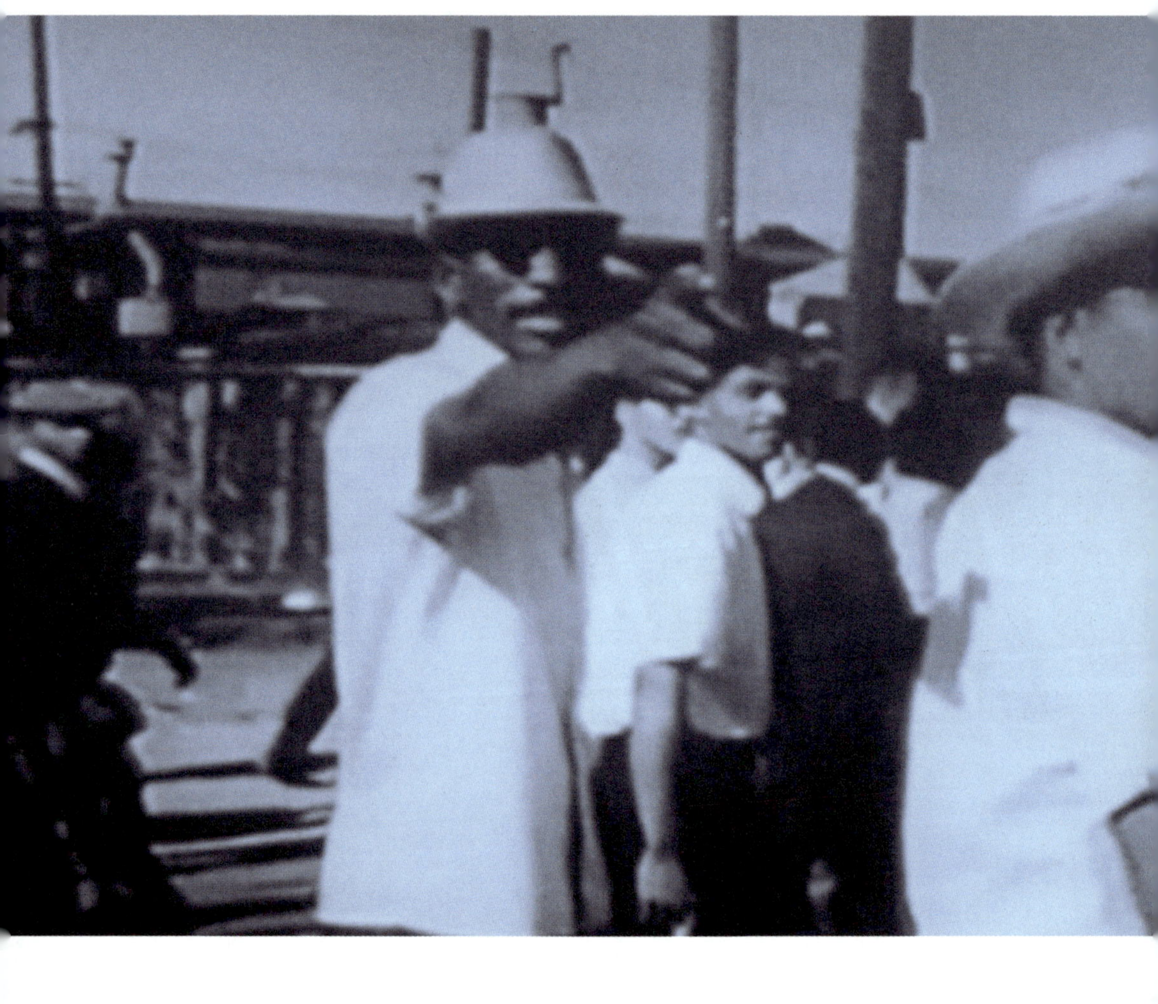

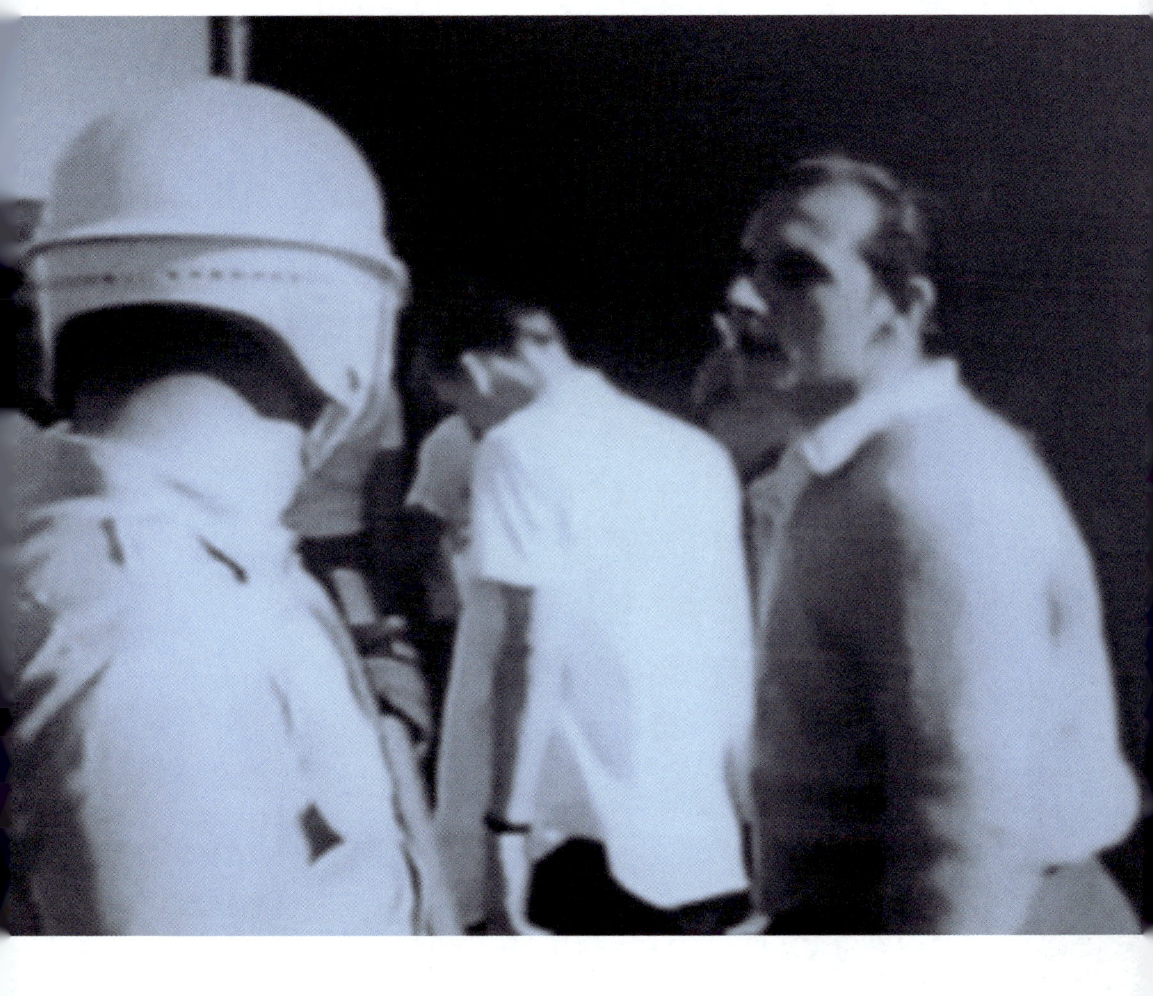

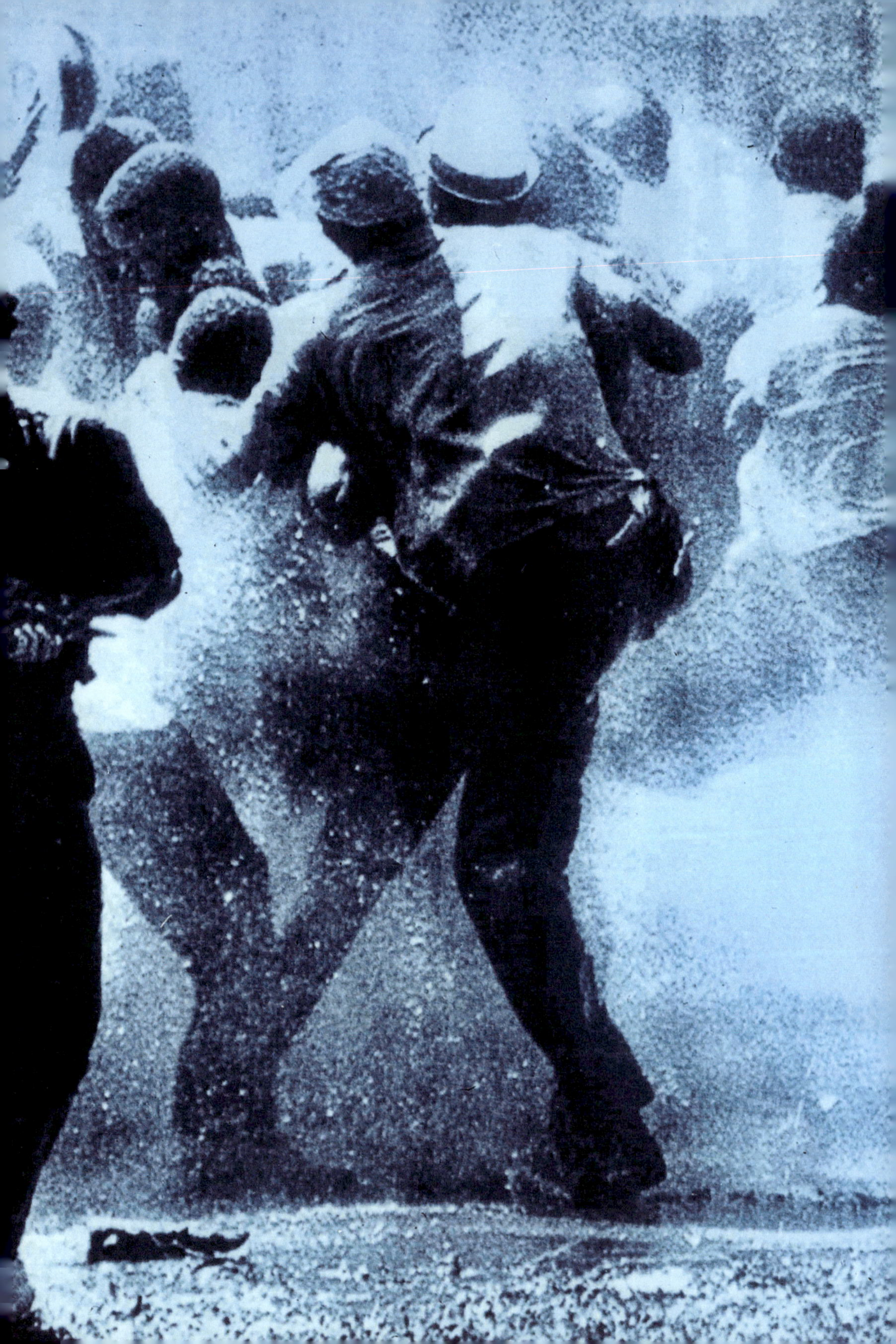

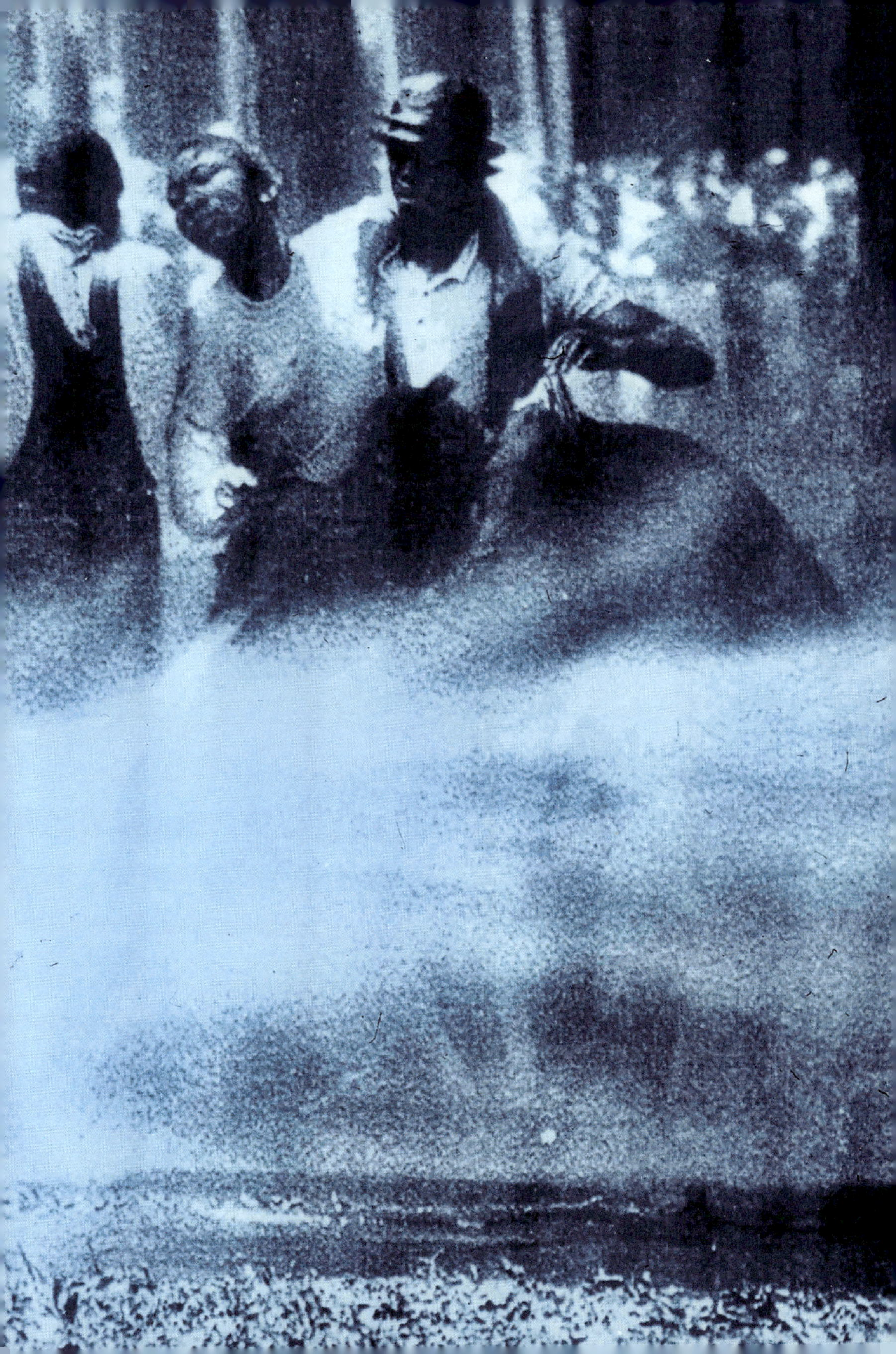

History of Violence Winter in America IV

History of Violence In the Summer in the City V

History of Violence The Killing of George Floyd VI

History of Violence The Forgotten VII

History of Violence COVID-19 VIII

History of Violence The Slow, Steady Rise of QAnon IX

History of Violence The Working Class X

History of Violence Perpetual Whiteness XI

History of Violence The End of Empire XII

History of Violence The Sky is Falling XIII

The Man Was Rejected, The Woman Was Denied

They were no strangers to sorrow.
Time and time again, the man was rejected, the woman was denied.
A man was killed.
The body lay in the open, uncovered and exposed.
Women wailed, and men moaned.
For reasons unknown,
I saw him running
I saw him stop
I saw him turn with raised hands
I heard a shot
I saw him fall.
But for reasons unknown,
I rejected my own knowledge, and I deceived myself
by refusing to believe that this was possible.

The man was rejected, the woman was denied.
Time and time again, they were always stopped, always charged,
always convicted.
The numbers tell the story.
She was twenty-five
he was twenty-two
she was thirty-one
he was twenty-five
she was thirty-four
he was thirty-seven
he was twenty-seven
he was twelve
he was eighteen
she was nine, she was forty-one
he was thirty-nine
he was twelve
he was thirty-seven
he was twenty-four...

She was a mother
a brother
a sister
a daughter
a wife
a mother
a girl
a child
a father
a brother
an uncle
a cousin
a son
a child.

He was thirty-seven
he was twenty-one
he was thirty-one
he was eighteen
he was twelve
he was fourteen
he was seventeen
he was eighteen...

He was a father
a husband
a brother
an uncle
a cousin
a son
a child
a friend.

He was twenty-one
he was twenty-two
he was thirty-seven
She was eighteen...

She was a wife
a mother
a sister
a child.

Time and time again, the man was rejected, the woman was denied.
A man was killed.
The body lay in the open, uncovered and exposed.
Women wailed, and men moaned.
For reasons unknown,
I saw him running
I saw him stop
I saw him turn with raised hands
I heard a shot
I saw him fall.
But for reasons unknown,
I rejected my own knowledge, and I deceived myself
by refusing to believe that this was possible.

Commemorating all of the fallen
and all those who have endured
Commemorating every Black man who lives to see age twenty-one
Commemorating Trayvon Martin, Michael Brown, Eric Garner
Commemorating Tamir E. Rice, Freddie Gray, Sandra Bland
Commemorating Christian Taylor, Samuel DuBose, Walter Scott
Commemorating Tony Robinson, Phillip White, Jerame Reid
Commemorating Tanisha Anderson, John Crawford, Dante Parker
Commemorating Damien Howard, Thomas Allen, and Ezell Ford
Commemorating Jeremy Lett, Lavall Hall, Bobby Gross
Commemorating Brendon Glenn, Frank Shephard, William Chapman
Commemorating David Felix, Spencer McCain, Darrius Stewart
Commemorating Alton Sterling, Philando Castile, &
all of the Emanuel Nine who gave their lives
Commemorating each and every one of them
Commemorating you, commemorating us
Commemorating all those who have the ability to endure
Commemorating every Black man who lives to see age twenty-one

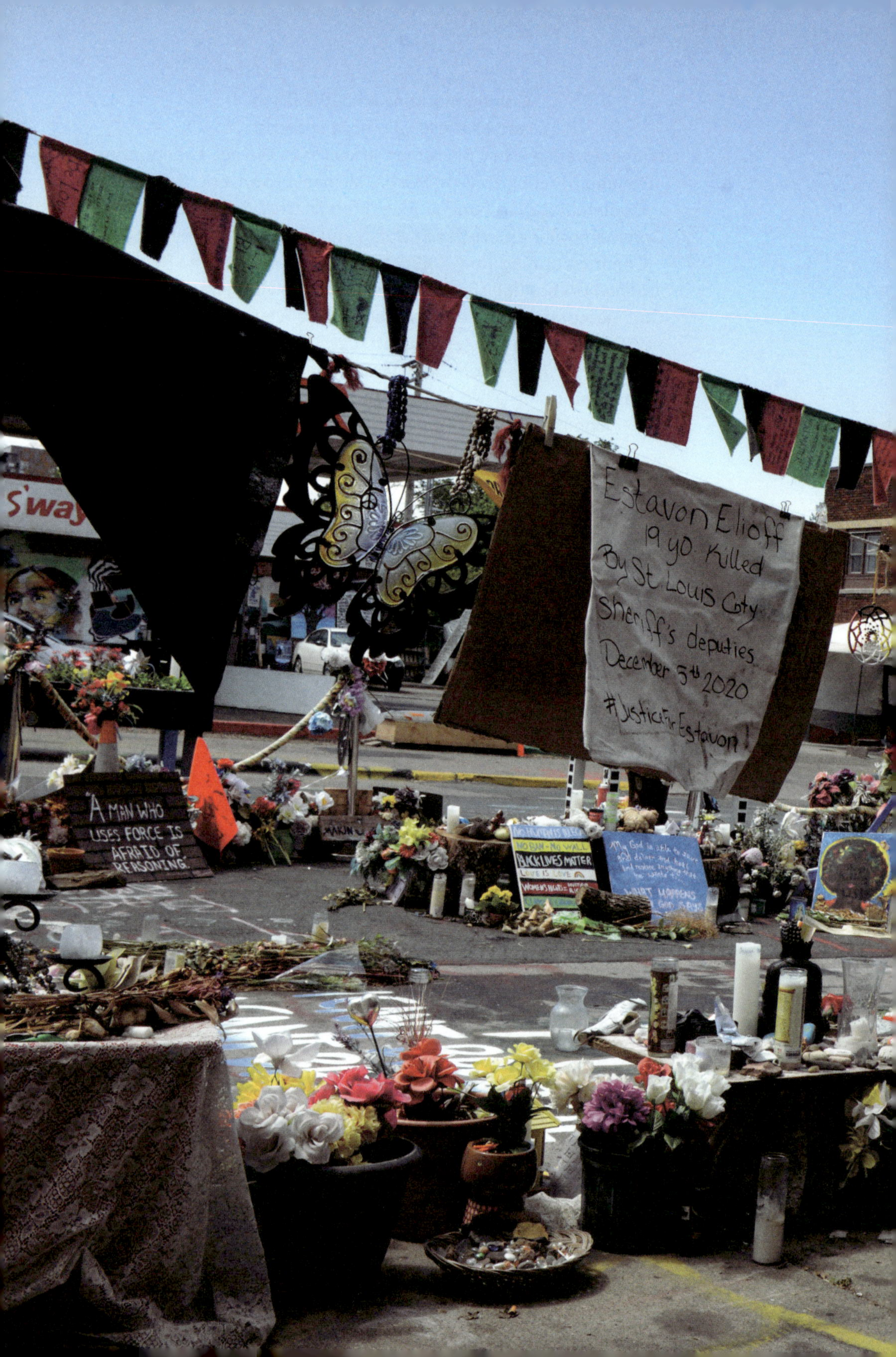

Estavon Elioff
19 yo Killed
By St Louis City
Sheriff's deputies
December 5th 2020
#JusticeForEstavon!
A MAN WHO
USES FORCE IS
AFRAID OF
REASONING.
NO BAN - NO WALL
BLACK LIVES MATTER
LOVE IS LOVE

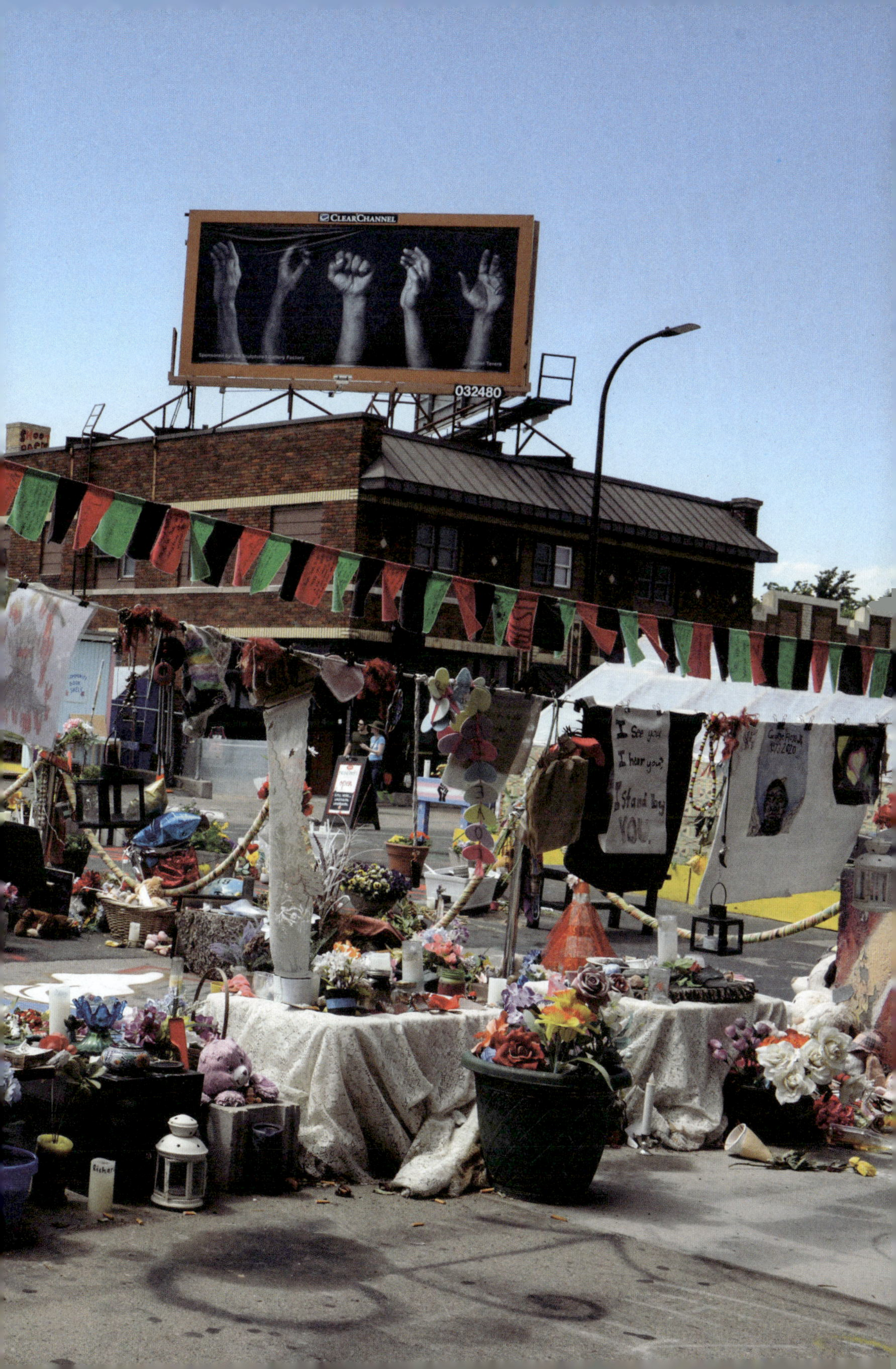
CLEARCHANNEL
032480
I See you
I hear you?
I Stand by
YOU.

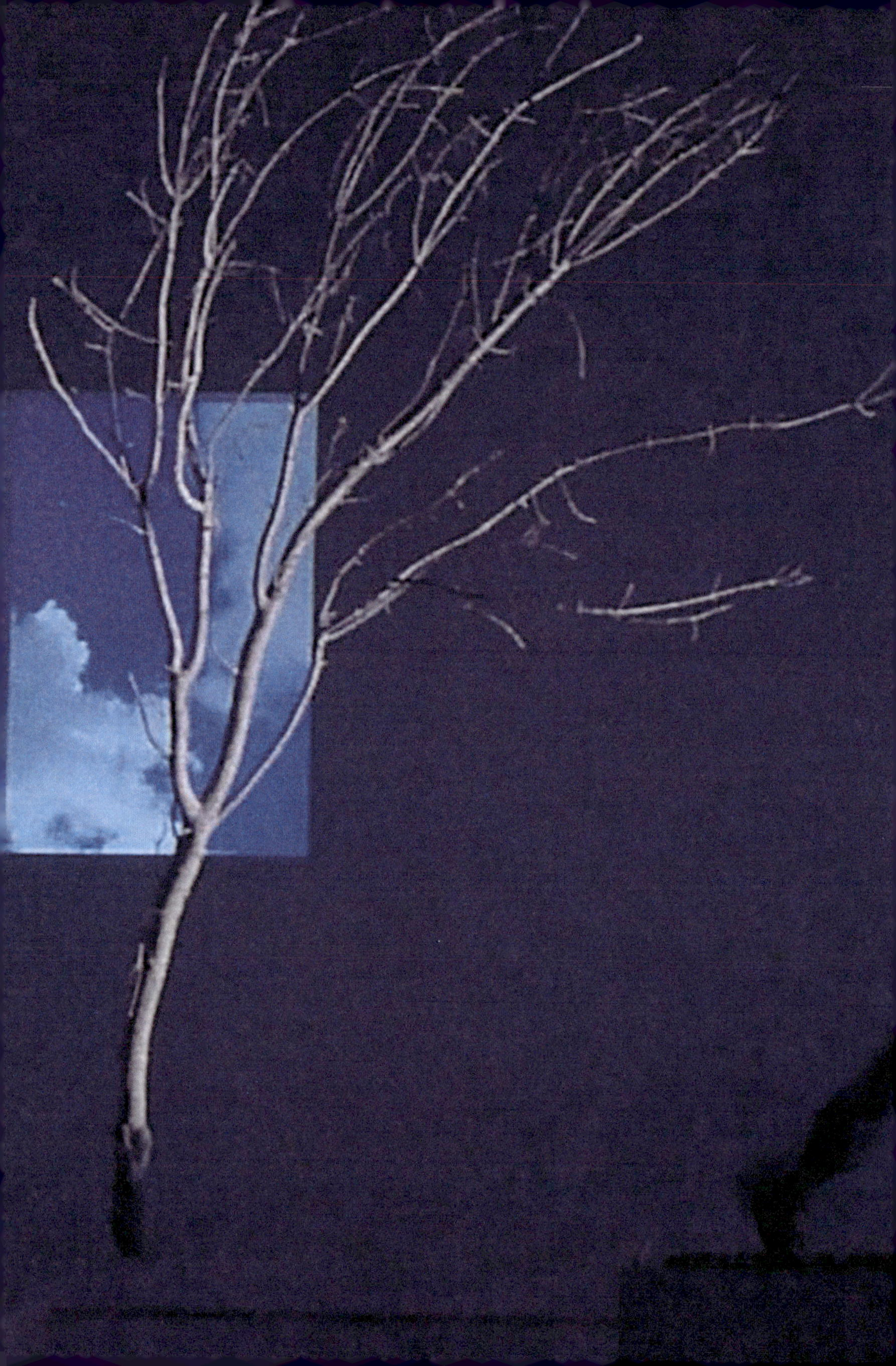

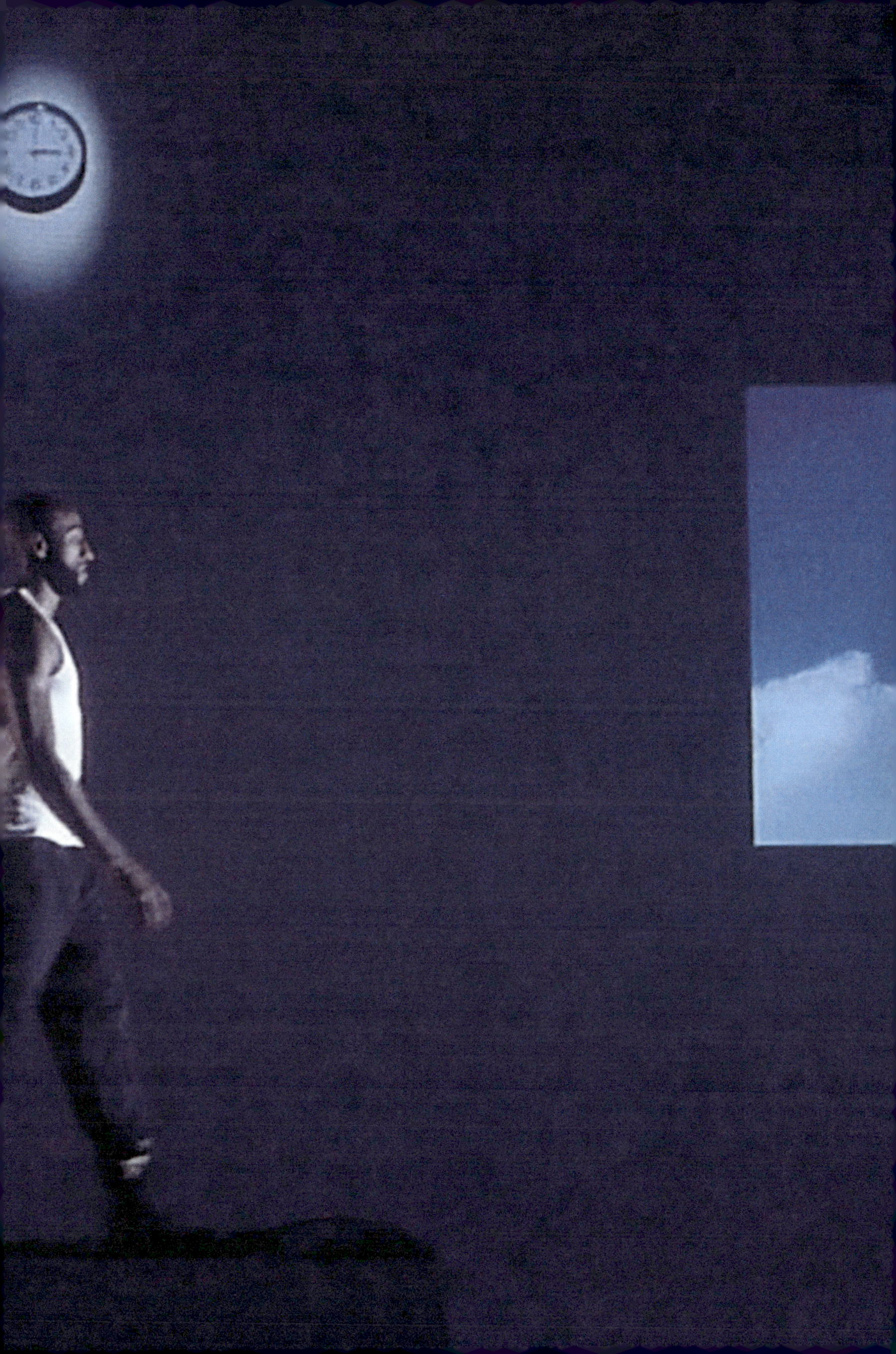

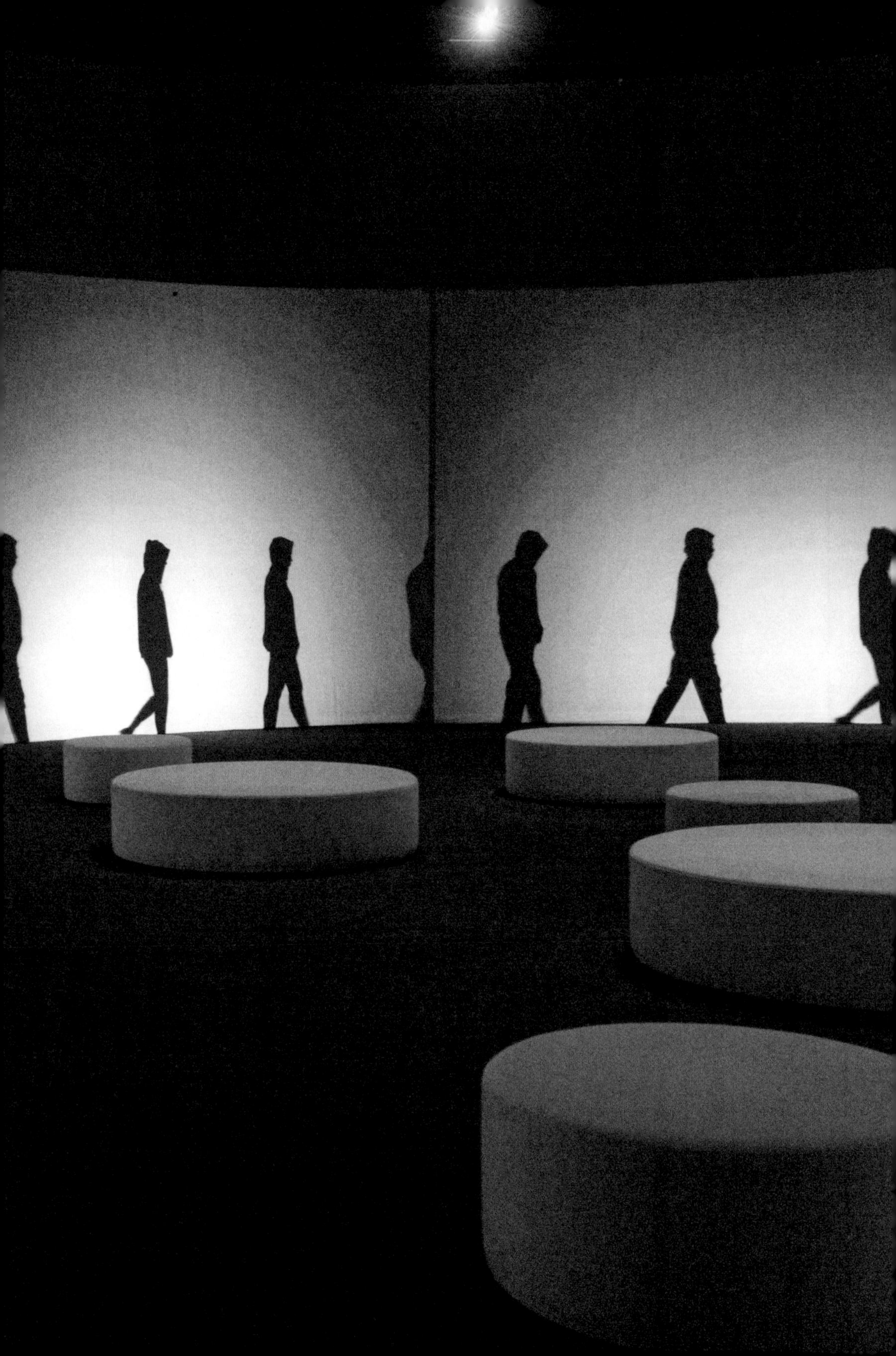

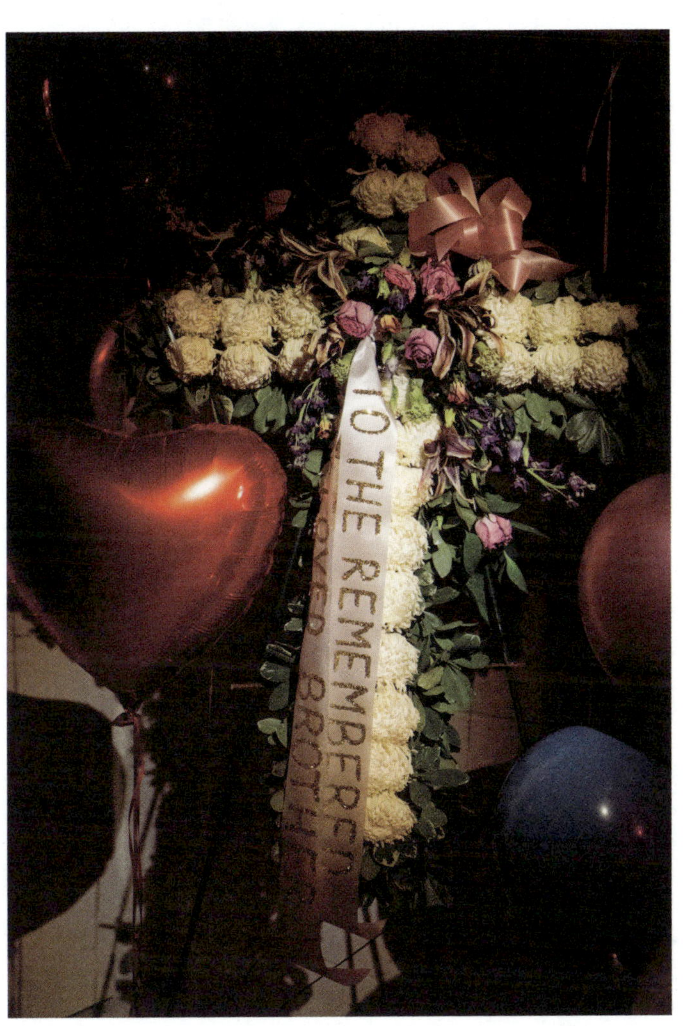
TO THE REMEMBERED

Architecture and Power

Crystal Bridges Museum of American Art
'Carrie Mae Weems on Identity, Relationships & More'
Crystal Bridges Distinguished Speaker Lecture
8 December 2017

The core questions of my life, and probably also of your life, are fairly consistent. What changes over time is simply how you enter the discussion now; how you frame the work now; how you frame your questions now; how you frame your point of reference now. But the core question, I think, is always the same, which is actually a sort of existential idea, but one that is true.

My core question revolves around the question of dismantling power: How do you unlock it? How do you unpack it? It's the power around race, power around class, power around work, power around ownership, power around distribution, power around institutions, power around museums, power around intimacy, right? We're all negotiating levels of power, no matter how you shake it.

How do you enter it? How do *I* enter it? This is my essential question. In looking at the systems of slavery, an American system—not a Negro system or a Black system, but an American system—how do we deconstruct power? I thought it might be important to look at the architecture of slavery—but always, of course, blending and bending and using language as a means to undercut, to build on, to moderate, to intensify, or to add another layer of idea and description to the process.

The power of architecture is extraordinary—the power of places that we are, or are not, invited into. Architecture defines *for* us. It tells us what a building means and to whom it belongs.

I remember living near certain buildings I never felt comfortable entering—I couldn't even figure out how to get into them! For instance, Columbia University, which sits on the edge of Harlem—I didn't know how to get into the building! The architecture was laid out in such a way that it told me I didn't belong there!

But it's not necessarily true of all buildings that we *read*—that we read with our skin and with our bodies. We *know*, right? And so, when we talk about certain institutions, how do people know if they can go into a building? What is on the outside of a building that invites us in, that tells us that it's open to us, that we're free to enter, regardless of where we come from? I think this is an important idea.

•

Portland Art Museum
'Carrie Mae Weems: An Artist Reflects'
3 February 2013

I was awarded the Rome Prize maybe in 2005/2006. All that year, I walked and walked and walked and walked and walked, trying to understand the structure of this city—the role of the church, the role of the square, the role of the pavilion: What do they mean? At some point, I began to understand the role of architecture—and the power of architecture.

Italy marks the beginning of empire; it marks the beginning of the state, where the individual seems so small in comparison to the architecture, so small that they are practically resting in the arms of the state. This idea of being enveloped in the arms of the state was something that I felt consistently as I moved around this extraordinary, beautiful, baroque Renaissance city—very, very powerful.

Hitler wrote about the way in which an architecture needed to function so that the individual would feel at the mercy of the state. Speer built *long* pathways made of marble, so that every single time your foot hit that stone, you knew you were in the wake of power! He wanted you to tremble in the wake of power. Mussolini, of course, felt the same. They all built an architecture that, in one way or another, reflects power. That interests me.

As I was finishing up my year in Rome, I began standing in front of museums. In an important way, I use my own self—my own body—to mark what a space might mean; what's inside and what's outside. It was a simple but elegant idea. What was really funny about being Black in Rome was that people kept asking me what I was doing there! And I'm not only talking about strangers. I'd run into people that I've known for years, people who go to Rome once or twice a year, and *they* would ask *me* what I was doing there! It was fascinating.

Every place I go now, I stand in front of museums. I usually bring my camera. I stand in front of these museums, and I think about them, and I ponder them. It's an act of engagement; it's a performance; it's a meditation. It's a way for me to understand an architecture and experience what that architecture might mean to a body that is similar to my own.

This is the work I've been doing. I continue to stand in front of museums. I love them—but I do question them. I can count the Black women artists that I know on a hand and a half, and I can count the ones who have had major exhibitions on one hand alone.

I'm aware of the conditions and circumstances under which I live. I understand what's going on. I know that museums *are* changing, and I know that museums that are *not* changing need to, so that we can understand what Black artists are doing as human beings! We are all deeply connected. As much as we think that we move along parallel lines, we intersect every step of the way, and I care about this intersection. I've decided it's the one thing that I am going to be pursuing until the bitter end.

For years, I begged anyone who would listen to recognise that a significant demographic shift was taking place in America, that this was something that should be paid attention to, and that it would come to matter in ways that one couldn't begin to imagine. Since 1984, in every lecture I've delivered, I attempted to alert museums, cultural institutions, and universities that this major shift was coming. I warned them to pay attention, challenged them to shore themselves up, to get out in front of this shift. I taught classes and organised convenings on the subject, but few seemed to care or to listen.

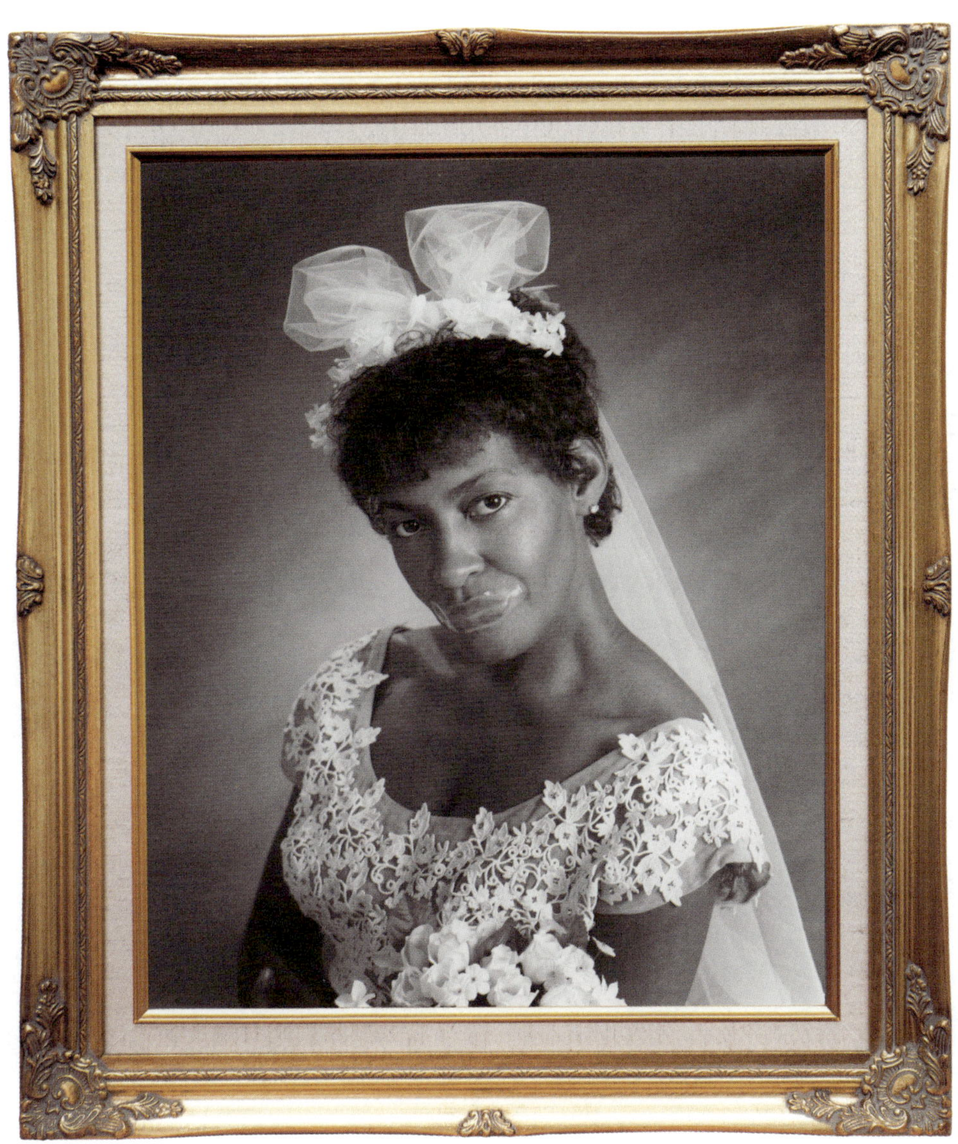

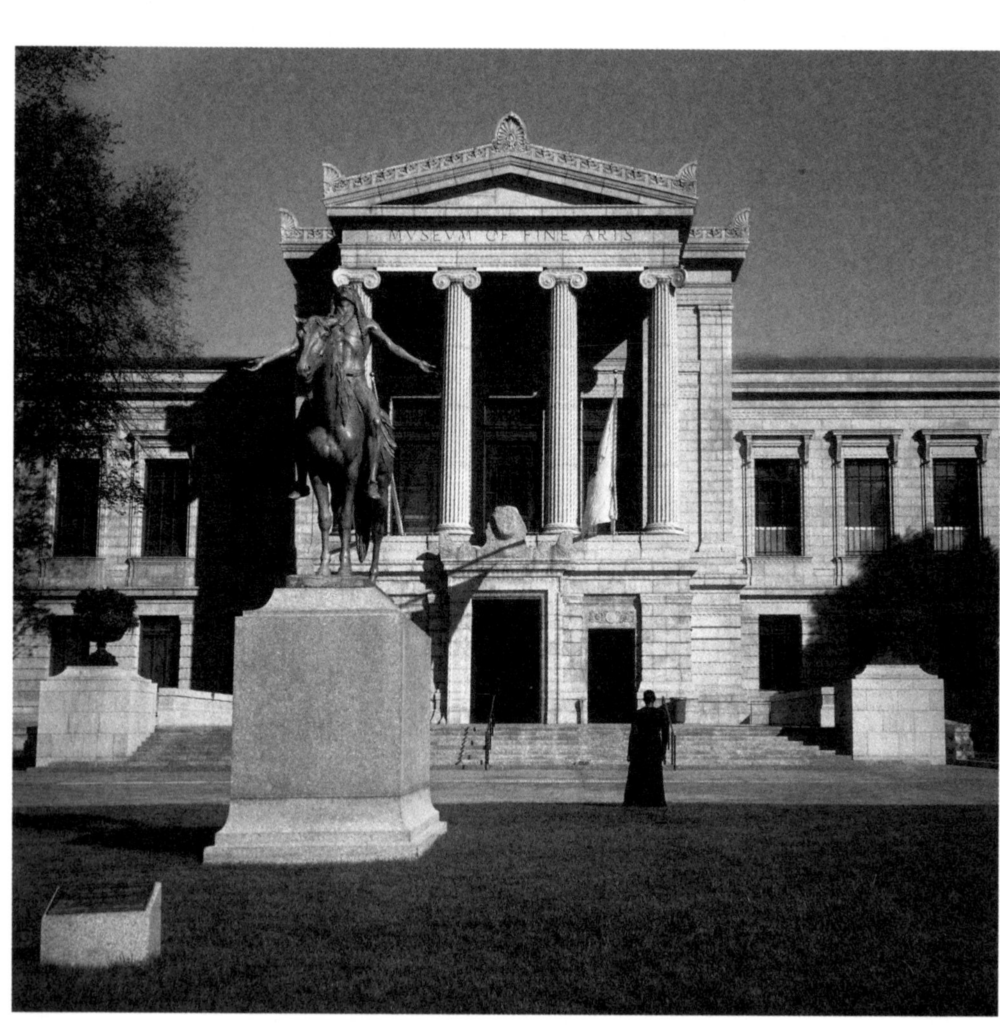
MVSEVM OF FINE ARTS

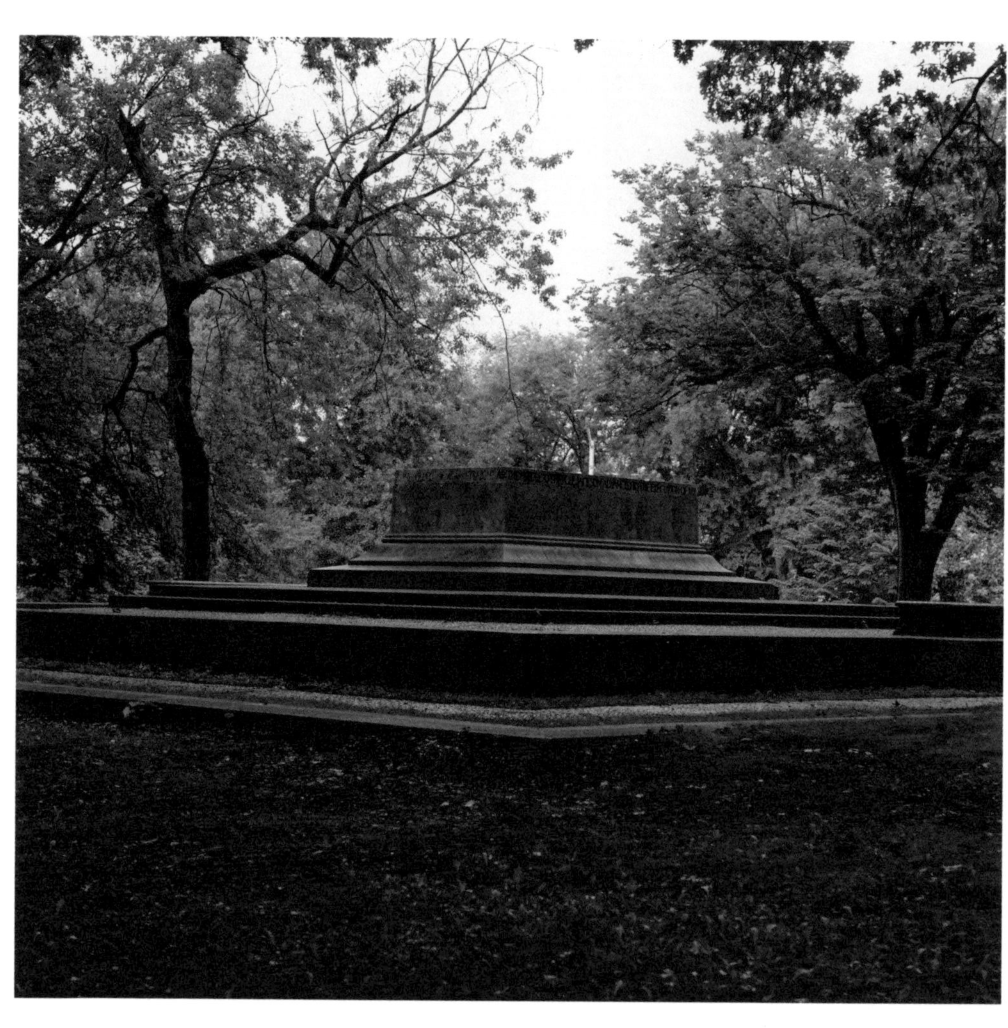

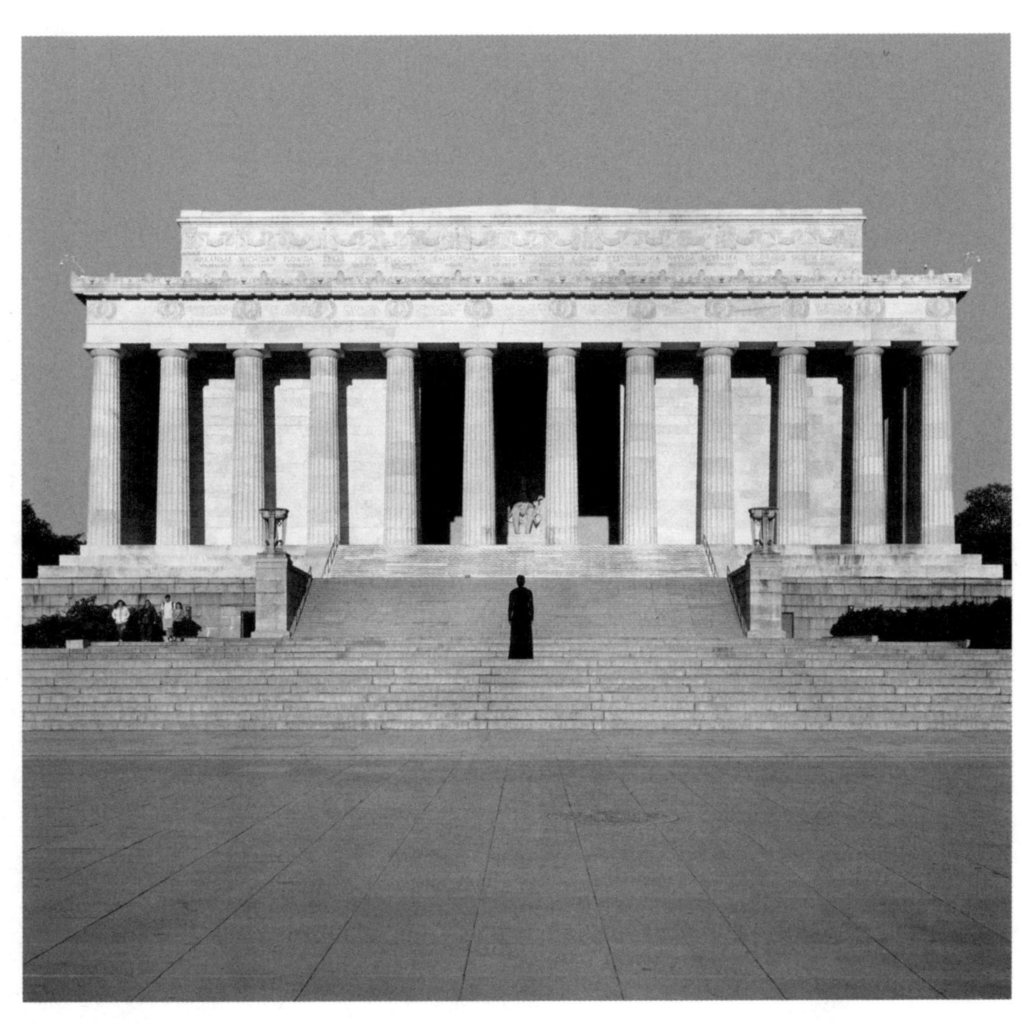
ARKANSAS MICHIGAN FLORIDA TEXAS IOWA

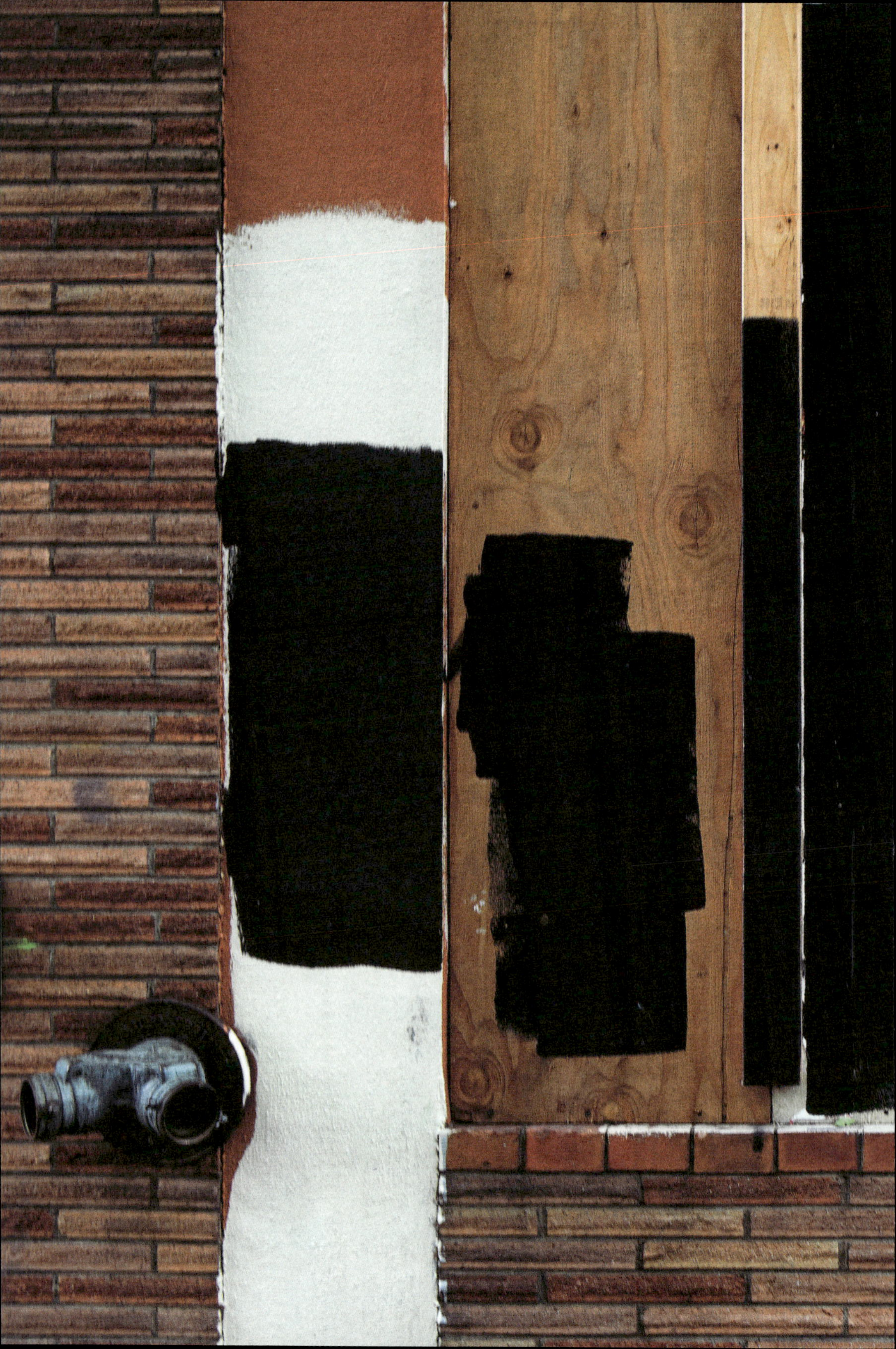

Carrie Mae Weems

Becoming an Artist
2019

Terence Nance

TERENCE NANCE: The first thought that I had, that I can remember, is people trying to call me by my name, and thinking to myself, 'Who is Terence?'

CARRIE MAE WEEMS: Oh, how interesting! How fascinating. I love that. Who is Terence?

TN: Like, not who is Terence, but who are they talking about?

CMW: Yeah! That is so interesting. I knew from a very young age that I would be an artist—that I respond to the world in an imaginative way. Lately, I've been asking myself this question: What is your aesthetic range, Carrie? What is it? What does it look like? There are many influences coming from so many sources, but what is your shit? Really, what is it? And how do you articulate it?

I've been thinking about what's happening in popular culture, the terms of the culture, the way in which it works, the way in which it functions.

For forty years, fifty years, I've been mining this material and thinking, where are the African American bodies and African American aesthetics and African American ideas, away from whiteness? Where are those things located? How will they be incorporated inside of a system that has historically excluded, for the most part, brown bodies?

I've been thinking about it for a very long time. I've made many works around it, written a lot about it. I used to go through *The New York Times*—the Sunday section—and just read, looking for any representation of Blackness, and there was nothing there. As much as I appreciate what's happened in the world in terms of the arts, there was no representation of Blackness in any form! It was just stunning to me.

Finally, apart from what's happening within contemporary culture, these institutions are beginning to realise the significance of what's coming—What do we do? How do we respond? How does the Hammer respond? How does UTA respond? How does Hollywood respond? Finally, universities and museums and institutions are realising, 'Oh, my God! If we don't open these doors, we will be completely irrelevant.'

A part of what's happened to our circumstance in America is that we have become Americans as much as we are African Americans. The complexities of our cultural projection have been so ripped and so torn, so taken and so buried and so erased, that you have to dig to really discover not about your Blackness as such, but your true self. If you play to you, to a deeper understanding of self, what you allow the viewer to do is to walk into your process—not backtracking and backing up into theirs.

In photography there's the Zone System from I to X. Within the European tradition things look best, and scale looks best, above Zone V, which is going towards the lighter end of the scale. Roy DeCarava always pushed towards the bottom end of the scale, towards things that were dark, so that initially, people at the Museum of Modern Art and all of these sorts of institutions, which are primarily, of course, run by white men, they would look at the work, and they would say, 'It's so dark'. The intention was completely misunderstood.

I come back to themes of power constantly in my life. I push aside all the other things that I'm looking at and thinking about, and I get down to the core of the thing, really trying to figure out how you unpack the dynamics of power and its ability to either control you or that you, in some way, control.

The thing that interests me is, how do you get to the truth? It's not just through the thing. It's not really about the photograph, but rather, it's the construction of the photograph. That's the interesting thing—it's not the film; it's the construction of the film. It's the narrative that resides within the film that speaks to us. It's the story, it's the imagination that scratches towards its humanity, that's the interesting thing.

TN: What do you make of what you are facing now as a woman?

CMW: I've been paying attention to what it means to be a woman, what it means to be a woman artist, for a really long time, and when I really looked across the landscape of my life, I realised that very few men have ever really supported me. It blew my mind!

They'll take my ideas, they'll use my ideas, but they will not use me! And that's pretty deep. So these ideas about the ways in which women—minorities—might be undervalued is reflected in the work. It's talked about in the work, it's negotiated in the work, and it's really important.

But, as they say, to change reality you have to start with reality. Based on the scale of your ability to be self-critical, to look at it, to be aware of how you might be an accomplice in your own victimisation, where are you? *All* of that stuff becomes imperative to look at in terms of how we negotiate the realities of our lives.

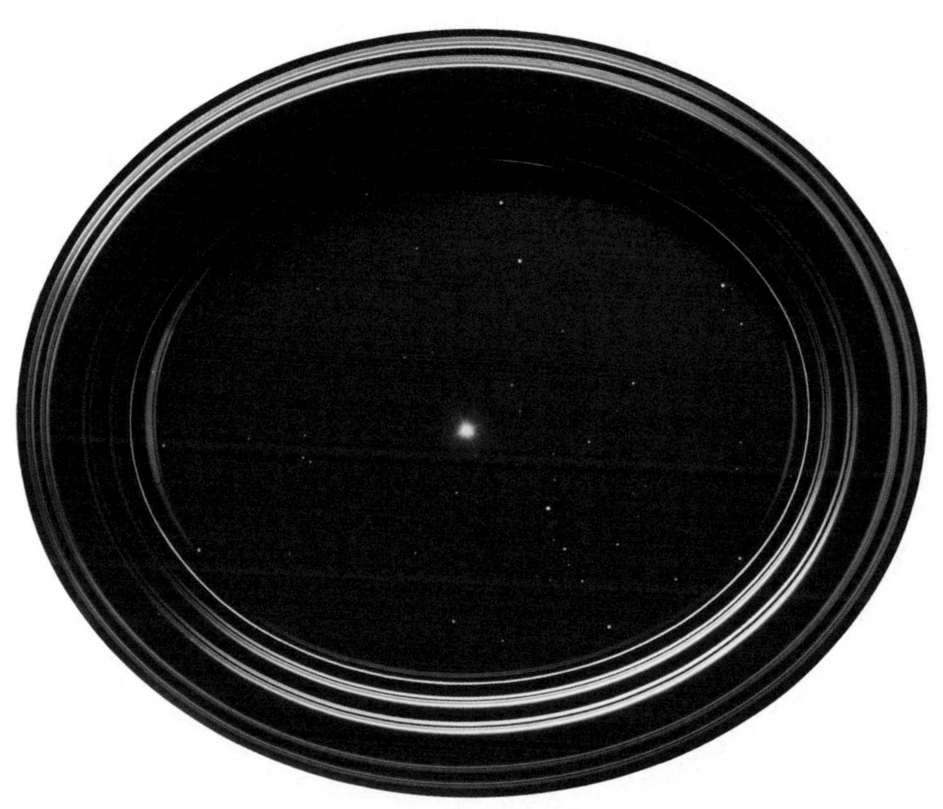

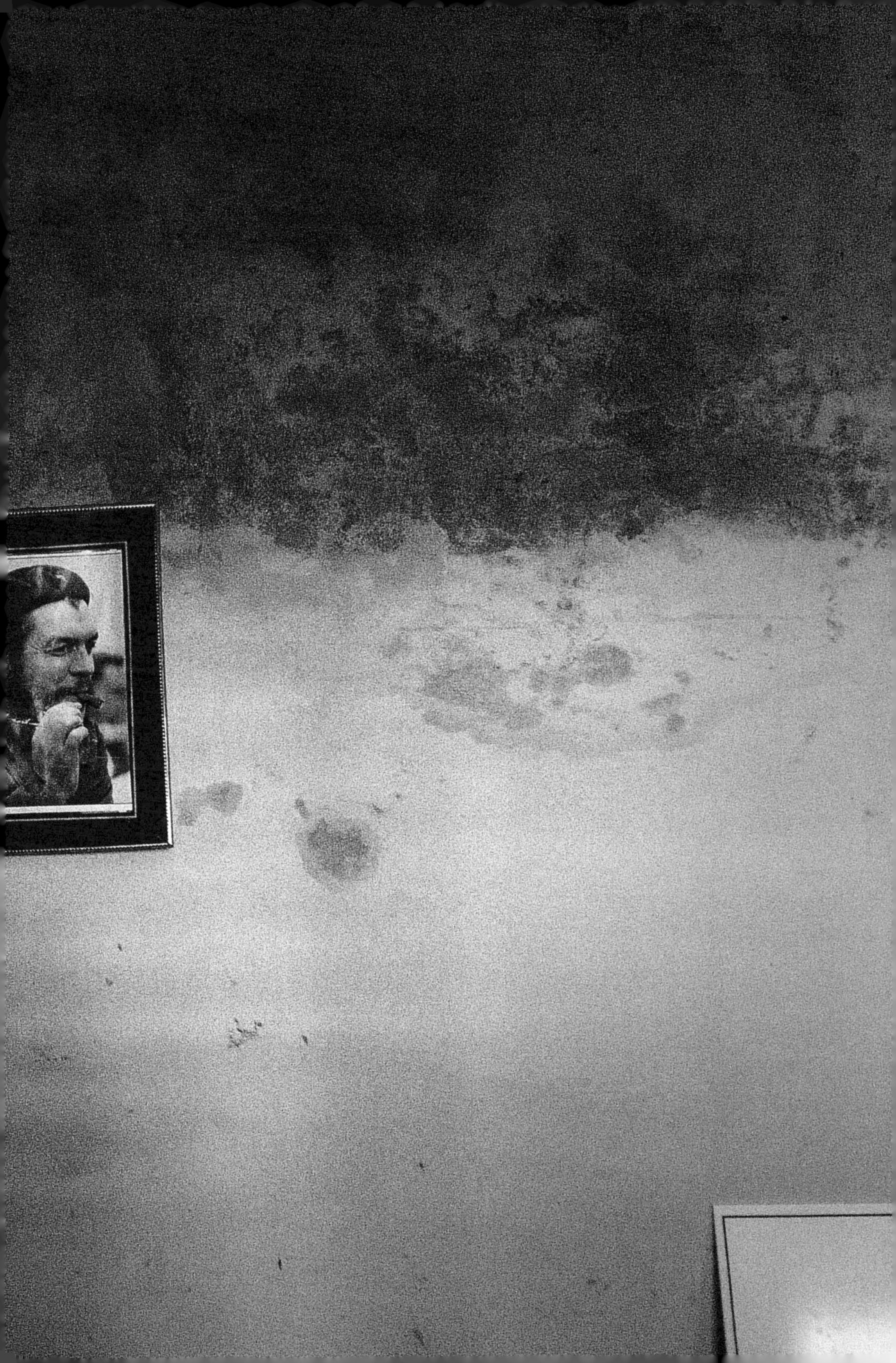

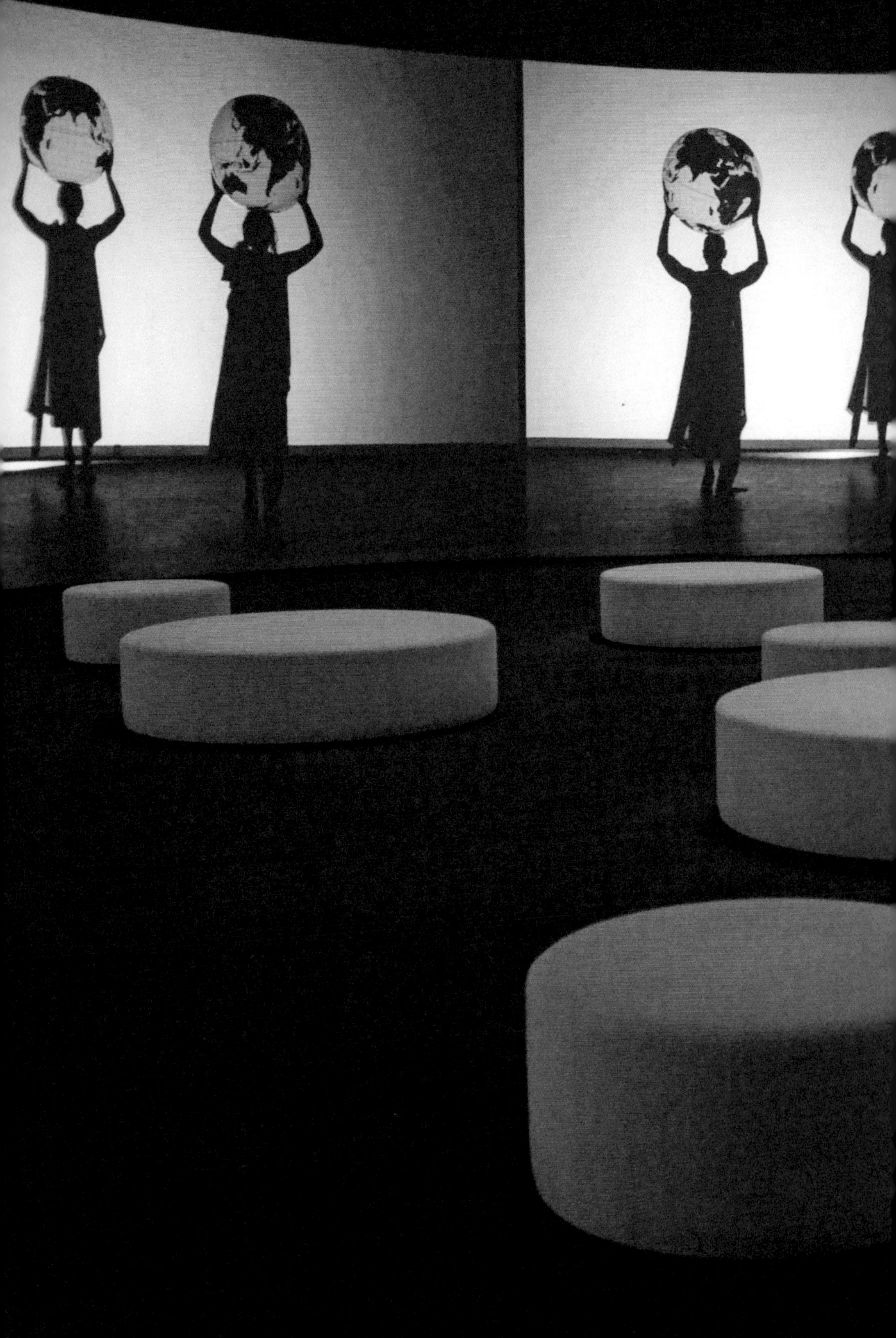

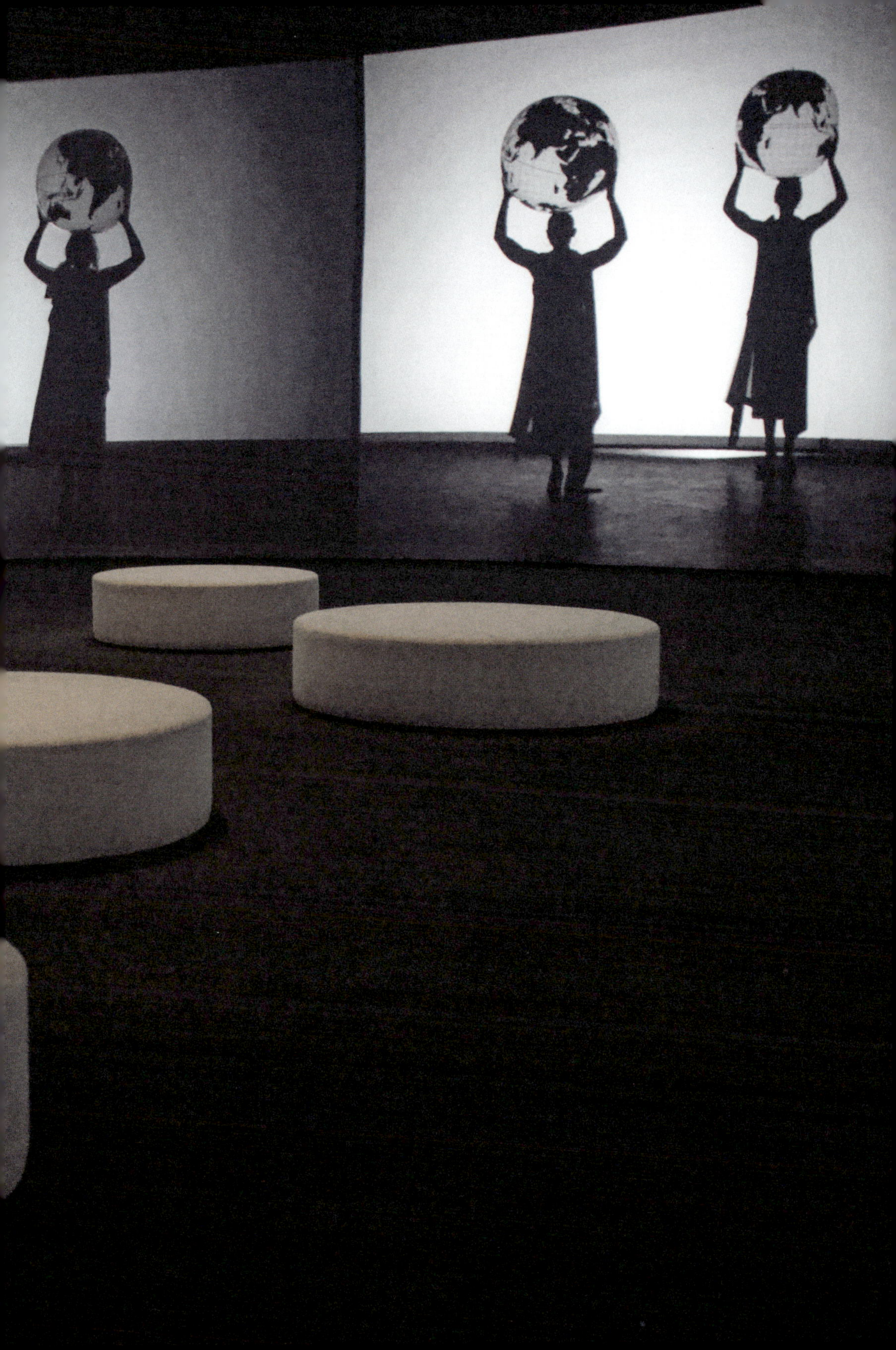

Art for Social Change

National Museum of Women in the Arts
'Carrie Mae Weems—Can an Artist Inspire Social Change?'
FRESH TALK
15 November 2015

I have an organisation in Syracuse. It's called The Institute of Sound and Style. The Institute was developed for very troubled teenagers in my neighbourhood. Syracuse is one of the poorest communities in the country for Blacks and Latinos. In fact, we are *the* poorest.

Understandably, a lot of things were going on in my volatile neighbourhood. I was teaching classes, actually, on art in social change when a young child was killed. He was two years old, and he was caught up in gangland violence. Just two days ago, his father went to jail for another slaying someplace else. This predatory violence was happening in the neighbourhood, in the community.

There was an outcry. I was upset; everybody I knew was upset. I'm thinking, how do I respond to this? How do I deal with this, as an artist, this crisis in my community? What are the tools that I can bring forth that might actually make a difference?

I had decided to develop a campaign even before I started the Institute. It was called Project Activate. Oprah came to the neighbourhood. It was a very troubling, very trying time—very, very, very complex.

For the Institute of Sound and Style, we invited teenagers. Something we did that I knew would be very important, given that I was living in this really poor community, was that the kids not only needed to be trained, they needed to be paid. They needed to have this as a vocational job. We would introduce them to art, to photography, to music, to recording, to graphic arts and graphic design, etcetera, etcetera, etcetera, and we would pay them.

To raise these funds, I sold a body of work. I thought, this is very cool; I'm going to use this body of work to pay my kids, and I'll use the next body of work to pay the staff working with my kids. To find a group of people who were really wonderful, who could work with us to figure out ingenious ways to partner with people who were around me—other record studios that were in the neighbourhood, producers that were in the neighbourhood, teachers that were in the neighbourhood—just figuring it out takes a lot of work. I go to bed and I think about it; I get up in the morning and I think about it. How do I really affect change in this neighbourhood, and how do I pay these kids, and how do I train them in a systematic way? How do I help them realise their own potential?

So I invited in other people—wonderful writers and poets—to work with my kids. I figured that if I can introduce kids to the thing that they're most interested in, that was a way of cutting through some of the nonsense, right? These were wonderful kids.

You know, I really don't like kids all that much. [*Laughter*] But one way or another, I had to figure out how to deal with them, how to work with them, because I care about them. One of the things they taught me was that you can't simply give up on them, because all day long, these kids are being shunned by a system that doesn't know how to deal with them or doesn't want to deal with them. They're constantly testing you and your own sense of loyalty to them.

One of the first things I did when the violence began in the neighbourhood was to make a series of lawn signs. People came out of their homes and assisted me in putting up these signs. I was making billboards, lawn signs, matchbook covers with statements like, 'Beware the ultimate cost of violence; it may mean your life', and taking them to bodegas and bars and having them passed out by the thousands. It was a really amazing project, and many of these signs are still up today.

My billboard project was a call to my community. It was important to have a conversation with the perpetrators of violence. I understand all the bullshit that we are troubled, but this is predatory, and we need to address it. So I developed a series of conversations that went back and forth between me, the perpetrators, and the community itself, and figured out ingenious ways to make it work. We used electronic billboards as opposed to paper billboards so that we could have a sustained narrative on a single billboard.

We built a safe zone, but people had to know about it. We asked, how do we use our local newspaper—that fixed, old-school medium—in strategic ways? We put those newspapers to work by inserting thousands of informational 'Safe Zone' flyers. On one side of the flyer was printed 'A Safe Zone', and on the other side we included phone numbers for various social agencies, information that would be useful to the people who so often lacked access to the resources they needed.

These were simple but important strategies. Creating a safe place, a safe zone that kids knew that they could go into, was important. Put this in your newspaper. Put this in your window. Put this up as a sign. This is now a strategy that people are using in Harlem as well.

We are responsible for the life of our own community, for answering the call to arms for the community. To stop the violence it is necessary to reclaim our community.

It was important to step up and to speak out. We couldn't keep playing this sort of double-standard game. You couldn't not want the police when you needed the police, and want the police when you didn't want the police, right? You had to have a concerted way in which you were negotiating these ideas and, of course, the idea that one needed to remember to dream.

I'm going to finish up by just talking very briefly about several other important artists doing amazing things (for those of you who don't know)—and this is very interesting too.

I know a lot of women who are doing, in some form or fashion, work that is similar to my own, people like Amalia Mesa-Bains and Suzanne Lacy. We all work hard; we are very dedicated in the way that we are caretakers in a very particular kind of way to kids.

And then there are the boys. There are the guys who are out here doing very interesting things as well. There's Rick Lowe and his Project Row Houses. Project Row Houses was started twenty, twenty-five years ago. Rick Lowe had worked as an architect and decided that he really wanted to do a project in Houston where he focused the energy of this area. He received a small grant, sold some work, built out all of the houses within the Tenth Ward, and then invited, in a very controlled and select way, a group of people to live in this community that had been repurposed and redesigned and redeveloped by him. An absolutely wonderful project and a fine artist.

Then there's somebody like Mark Bradford, who's established a remarkable programme in South Los Angeles called Art + Practice, one of the first of its kind where he has purchased a block of buildings in the Leimert Park neighbourhood. This area, actually, was developed by the Olmsted Brothers, the sons of the famous Central Park designer.

Mark Bradford—his mother used to do my hair. Her salon was around the corner from my studio. Mark's new space has been going now for several years, and he's working with Eileen Norton. They too are training young people in their community, doing vocational training, working with psychologists, psychoanalysts even, and urban planners, to develop this incredible location—absolutely beautiful.

The last person is Theaster Gates, who has developed a whole series of structures in Dorchester on the South Side of Chicago—extraordinary work, amazing project.

It's been fascinating to watch these major artists who are now doing these significant projects in their own communities and in their neighbourhoods, buying up entire blocks of houses, repurposing them, redeveloping them, and thinking about really smart and innovative ways to have a major impact in the neighbourhoods in which they're located.

These ideas—these ideas of innovation that artists are involved in, and the relationship of social change that I work on with Mark Bradford, with Rick Lowe, with Theaster Gates—all of us work together in order to think about creative ways in which we bring our understanding, our unique vision, our passion to the practice of art as the agency for change.

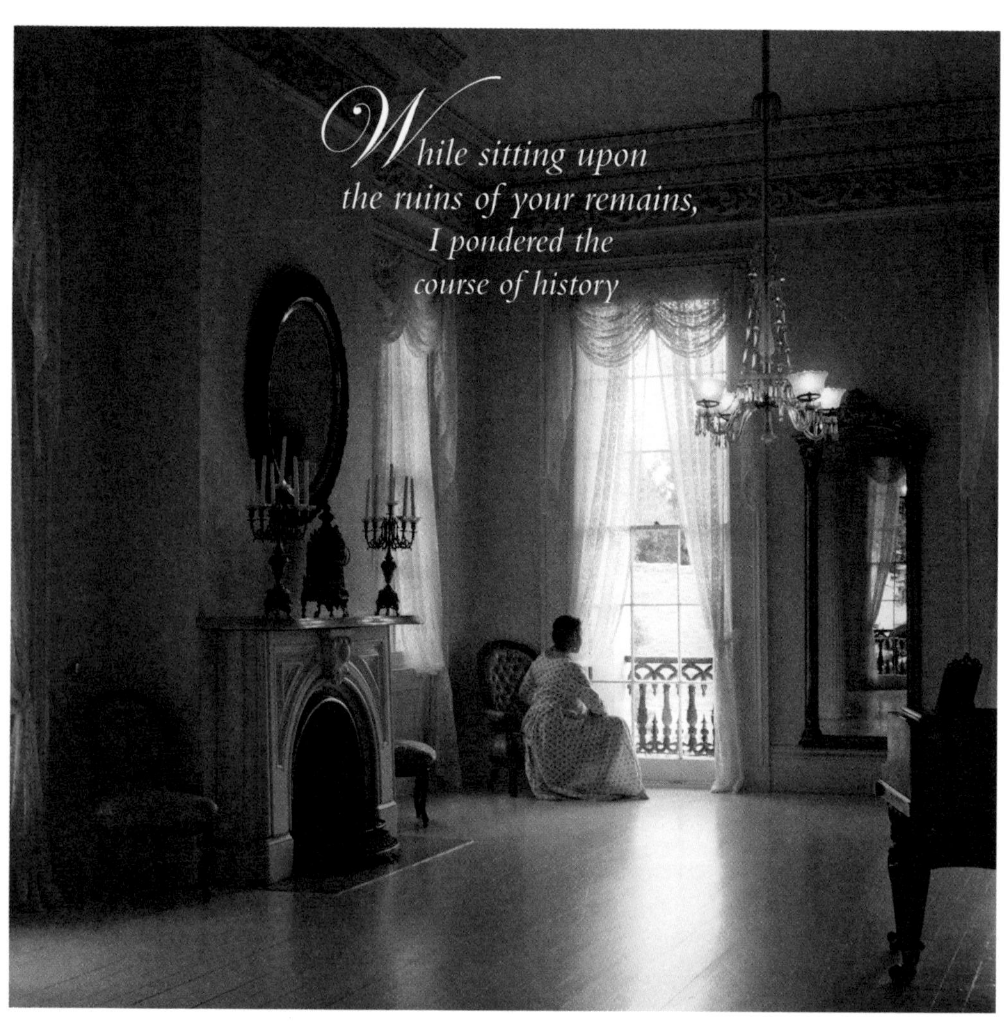
While sitting upon
the ruins of your remains,
I pondered the
course of history

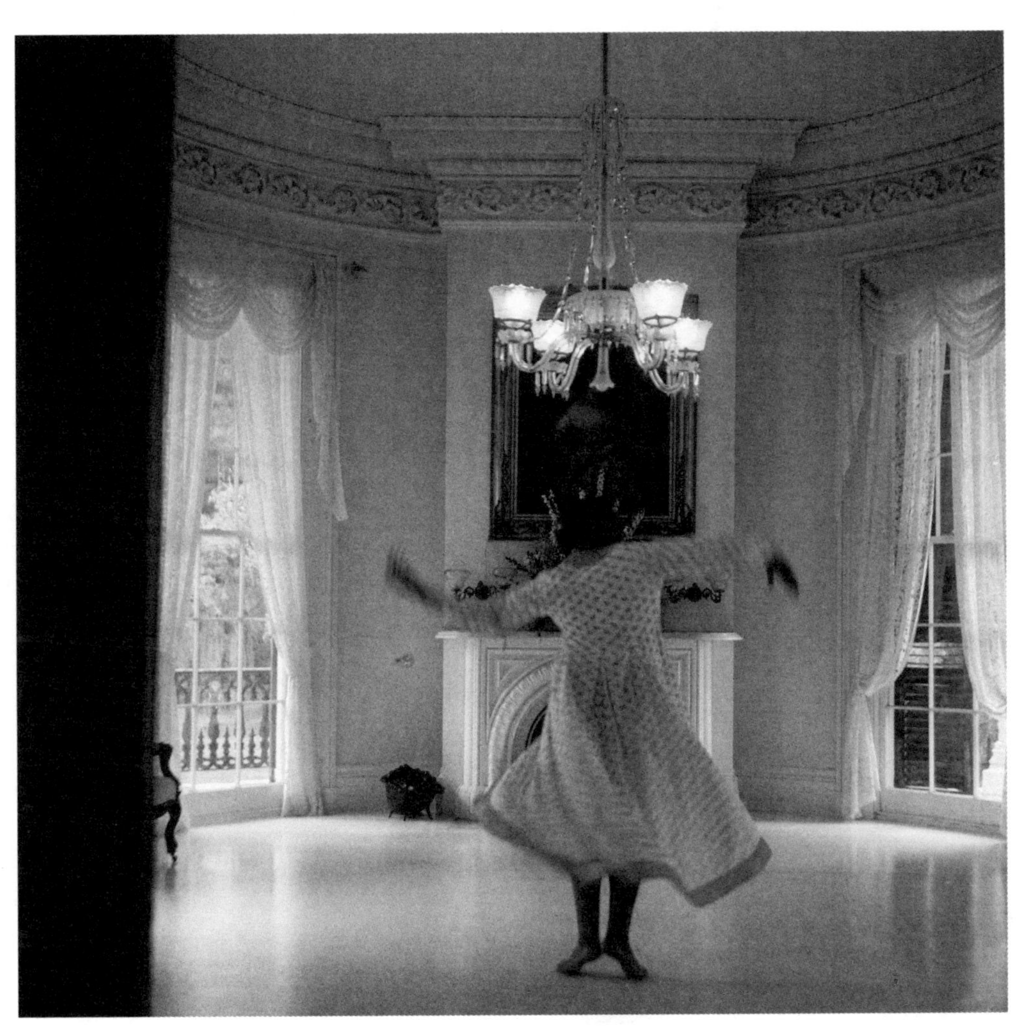

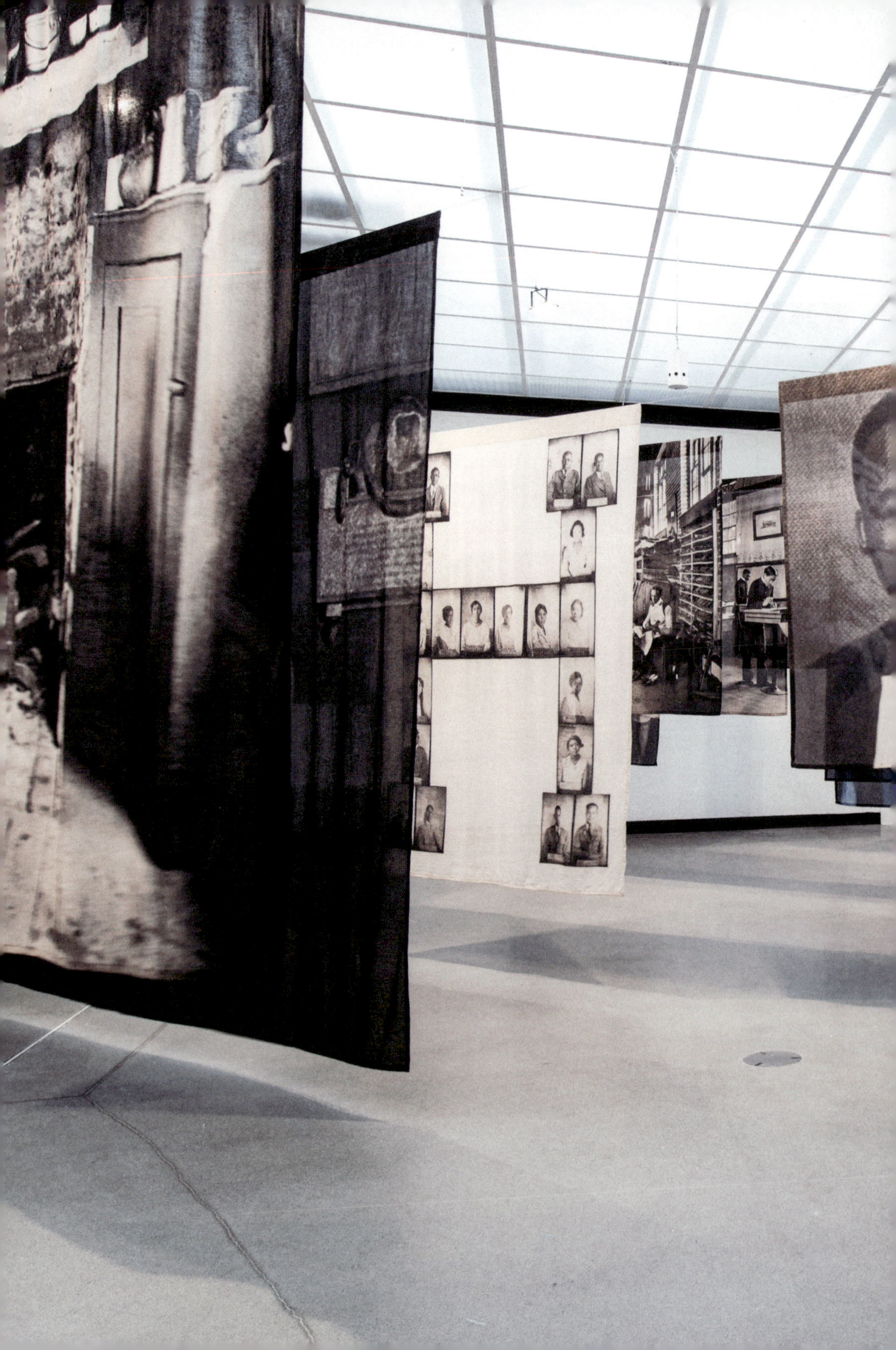

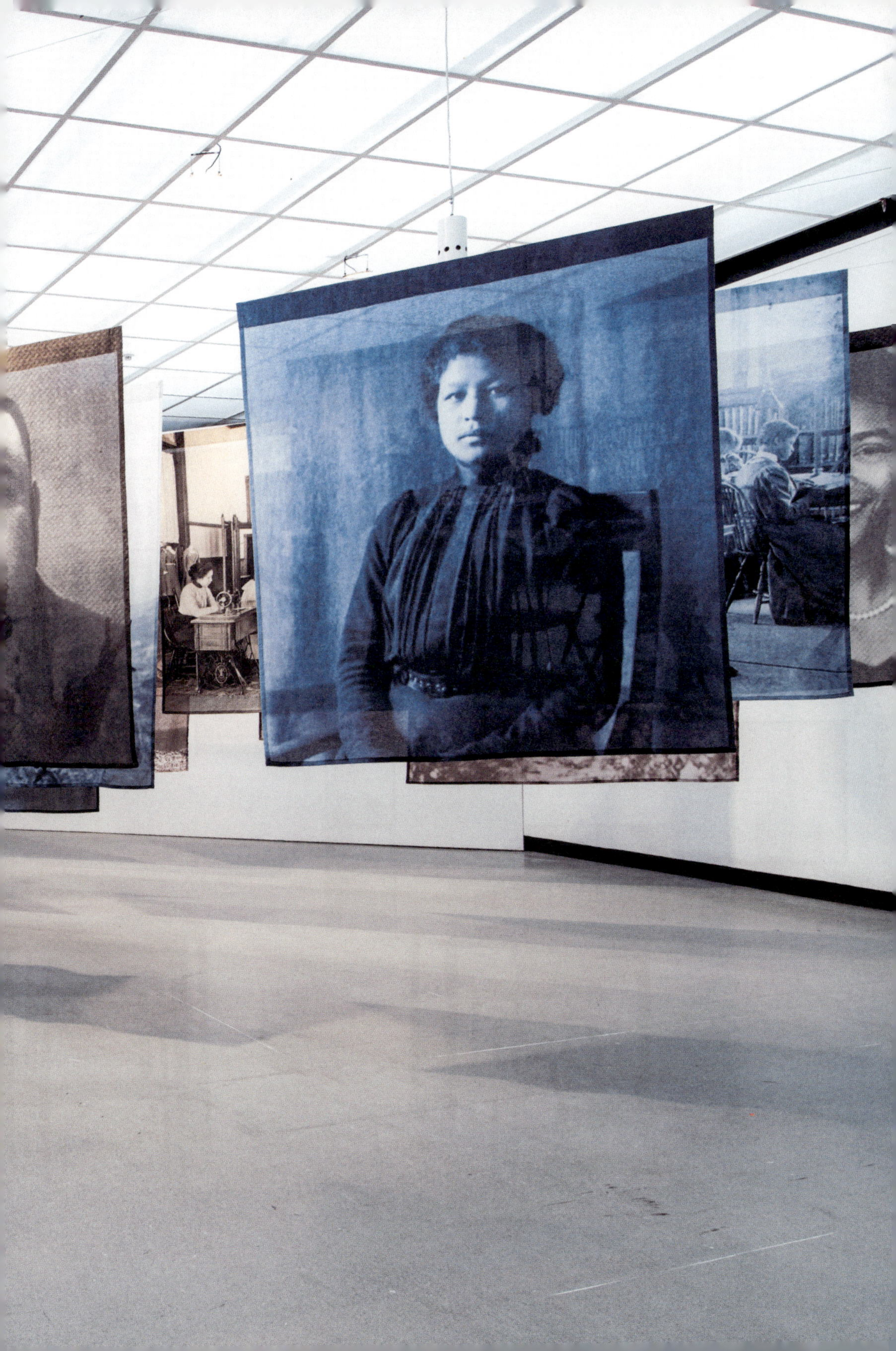

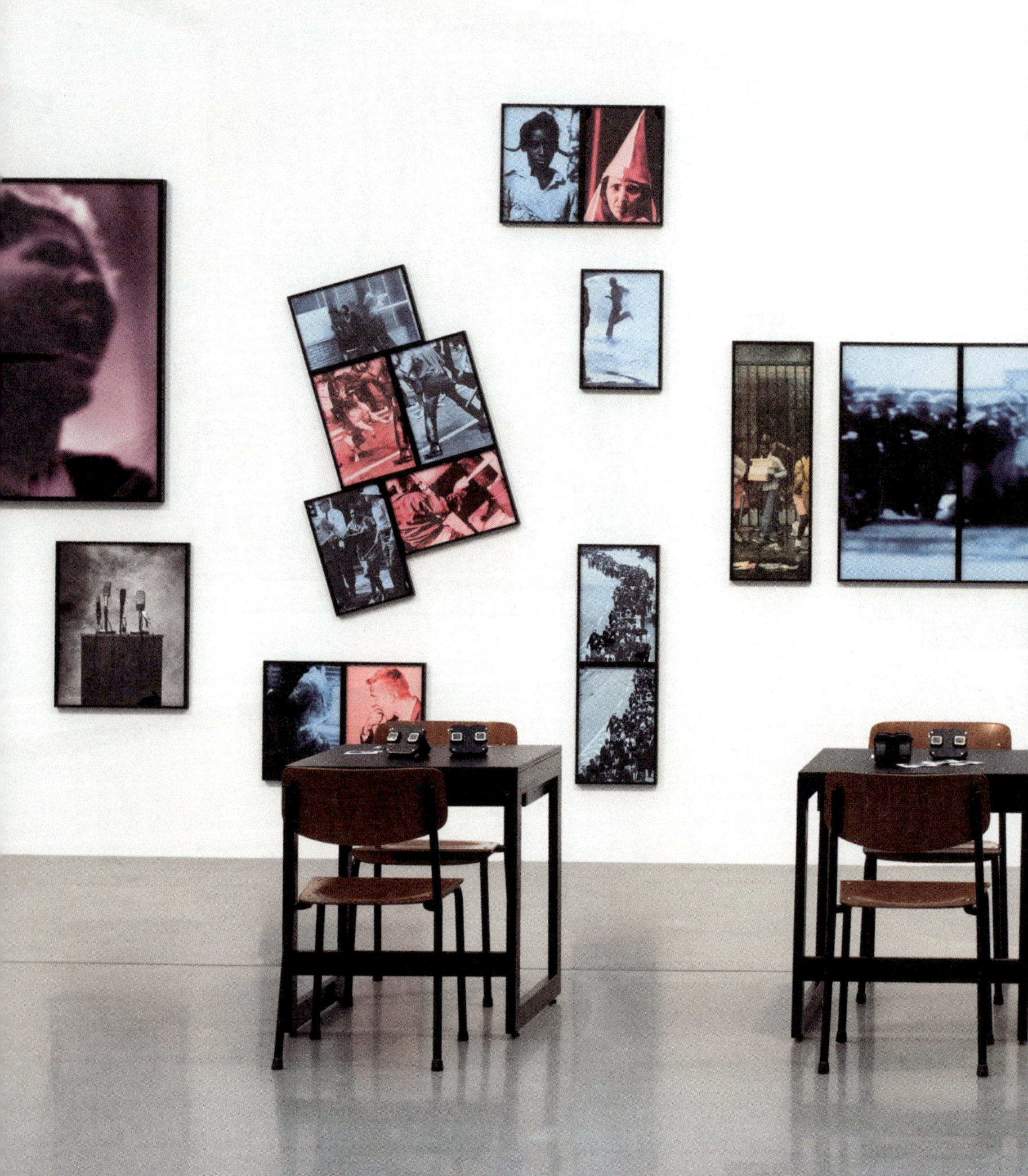

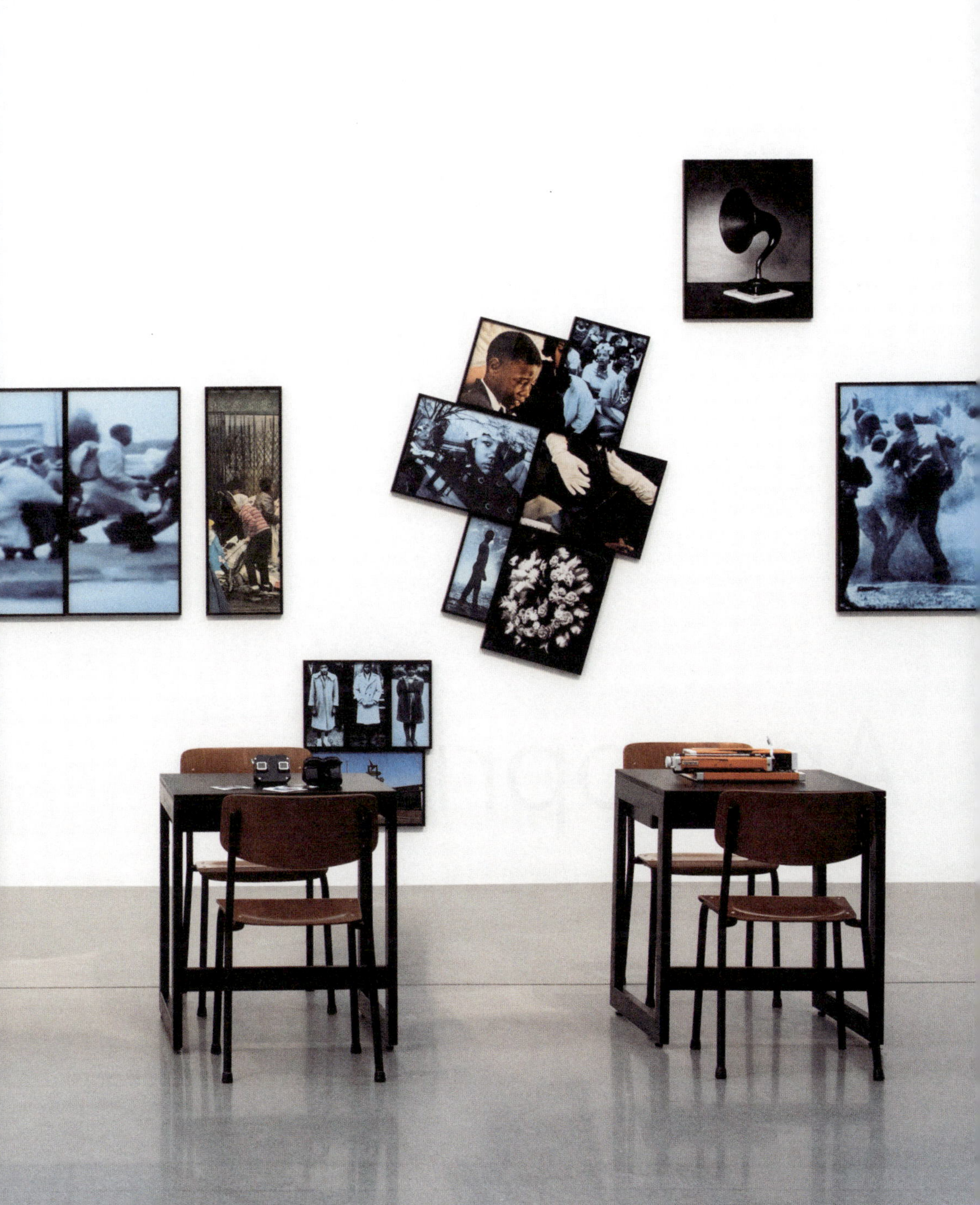

Appropriation and Influence

Guggenheim Museum
'Artist Talk: Carrie Mae Weems',
Reflections on Artistic License
19 November 2019

Carrie Mae Weems, 'Compassion',
in *Art21: Art in the Twenty-First Century 5*,
2009

Appropriation is sometimes the act of stealing.
Sometimes it's an exploration.
Sometimes it's a comparison, a contrast.
Sometimes it's an act of negotiation.
Sometimes appropriation is the marriage of a single idea coming together to form yet another set of ideas.
Sometimes it's an attack on the form itself—on the very act of appropriation.
Sometimes it's simply a hand well played.
Sometimes it's a rip-off.
Sometimes it's a theft.
Sometimes it's a praise song.

Sometimes it's a kind of critical intervention—a disruption, a questioning of ownership, of worrying the line and troubling space.

Sometimes it's getting something that you would not necessarily have otherwise, of underscoring that which has come before, of echoing the past and of charting the future.

It's a dynamic form. Most of us, in one way or another, have been involved in the act of appropriation.

I've done several projects that looked at issues of appropriation, and I've always thought that it was a legitimate use of material, though I can certainly understand that artists would be upset about that. So I've had to negotiate for the use of material. I've had controversies around my work, always, and I think it's actually critically important. Harvard University was going to sue me at one point for using the images of women and men who were enslaved. I thought, 'This is really fascinating. I think you should sue me. This issue of who owns the rights to these images of slaves would be a very interesting thing to play out in public debate. You may be right legally, but I think this is perhaps also a moral question. And maybe we might have to talk about the moral questions that surround your issue of copyright of these particular images.' It was fascinating....

Then there are ideas about compassion—what you sacrifice for compassion, what you give up, what you choose not to live with so that you can express that. But we all sacrifice something for our compassion in some way. We're giving up something so that something else larger can happen, so that something bigger than you can take place. Sometimes we sacrifice our families. Sometimes we sacrifice other levels of interpersonal communication to allow for that larger relationship with questions that move and shape the world. And I'm not being naïve or sentimental or dramatic about it, but I think that I've sacrificed an enormous amount of interpersonal comfort to pursue aspects of compassion, to look at them and to say, 'Yes, I will step up to this. I want this too. And if I want this in this time, in this moment, then certain things have to be sacrificed (because I don't know how to do it all).' Sometimes you sacrifice too much. You find yourself out on a limb and not quite knowing how to get back down the tree. But it's the space that you're in because you have taken the risk. I'm not unaware of the sacrifices and, at times, whom your compassion hurts. As the work is complicated, so is this complicated.

One of the reasons the exhibition *Constructing History: A Requiem to Mark the Moment* (2008) came about was because of this question of appropriation. I didn't want to have to appropriate anybody's material; I just wanted to revisit this history. And so I thought, 'I have to make it myself, and I have to make it in my own way. I have to rise above all of those restrictions and make something that I really want to make, giving a nod to all of those photographers who have come before me.'

I've spent a long time digging in the complex soil of race and racism. I've spent so much time looking at it, thinking about it, troubled over it, obsessed by it. And it still matters to me in a profound way. I really do wonder about this new movement that we're in—what it might mean to have had an African American man become the president of the United States—particularly given that the lives of Black people in the United States have been shattered in an extraordinary way. That's simply the truth of the matter—that the brutal effect of racism on Blacks, on people of colour but on African Americans particularly, has been astounding. It's horrific what has happened to us here, and I know that it still matters and will always matter to me. Yet I know that somehow I have to also free myself from the yoke of it, from the despair of it—that somehow I have to put that aside for the moment, because there are indeed other parts of life and other parts of my existence that also really matter, that need to be explored, and that to a certain extent allow me to retool and face the horror of what has happened with renewed energy and renewed understanding and possibility.

I knew that *Requiem* was going to be extremely demanding, and I wanted to concentrate on building the image and allowing myself the room to do that without trying to wear six different hats. I didn't want to tax myself in that way. What was important was to find the appropriate stand-ins who could physically deliver in the way that I thought was important and necessary. And for the first time I discovered another body and a type that understood gesture and movement in a certain way. There are literally photographs I have where I couldn't quite tell who it was standing in that photograph, she or I. It's like, 'Oh, wait a minute, is that *me*?' It was wonderful to discover that, yes, actually I can have somebody stand in not just for me but for the archetype that I'm trying to get across.

Recapping the last forty years of my own life—beginning with 1968 and ending with 2008, and all those amazing and horrific events, assassinations, brutal acts—has implications and great significance for us all. Now part of that can be closed for me. I've gone back and I've revisited those assassinations. I've revisited the civil rights movement. I have looked at it in any number of ways through any number of works. For me this piece, while certainly not perfect, is an interesting place to pause. It's beautifully articulated—both the video and the twenty photographs that accompany it. It's compassionate but not sentimental, because there is nothing sentimental about reviewing the assassination of King or Evers or the Kennedys, Bobby and John. There's something really tough about it, and I'm happy that I was able to move across that emotional terrain and say, 'If I can just finish this, if I can cap this part of my life off, I think I might be able to move forward'. Maybe we've all reached a kind of threshold and a new gateway to pass through. I think that Obama's election offers us another way of imagining ourselves as a people and as Americans. Maybe it's in that juncture that I could begin to imagine that all the horrific things that have happened to Black people are reconciled through this one swift act. Do you understand what I'm trying to get at? That not all of this has been in vain; that indeed there are some other ways to *be*—and that maybe it really points to the declining significance of race. What we're really up against is not so much that race anymore is the main issue that needs to be negotiated, but rather that the question of class needs to be illuminated. Race and class have always, for me, been deeply linked.

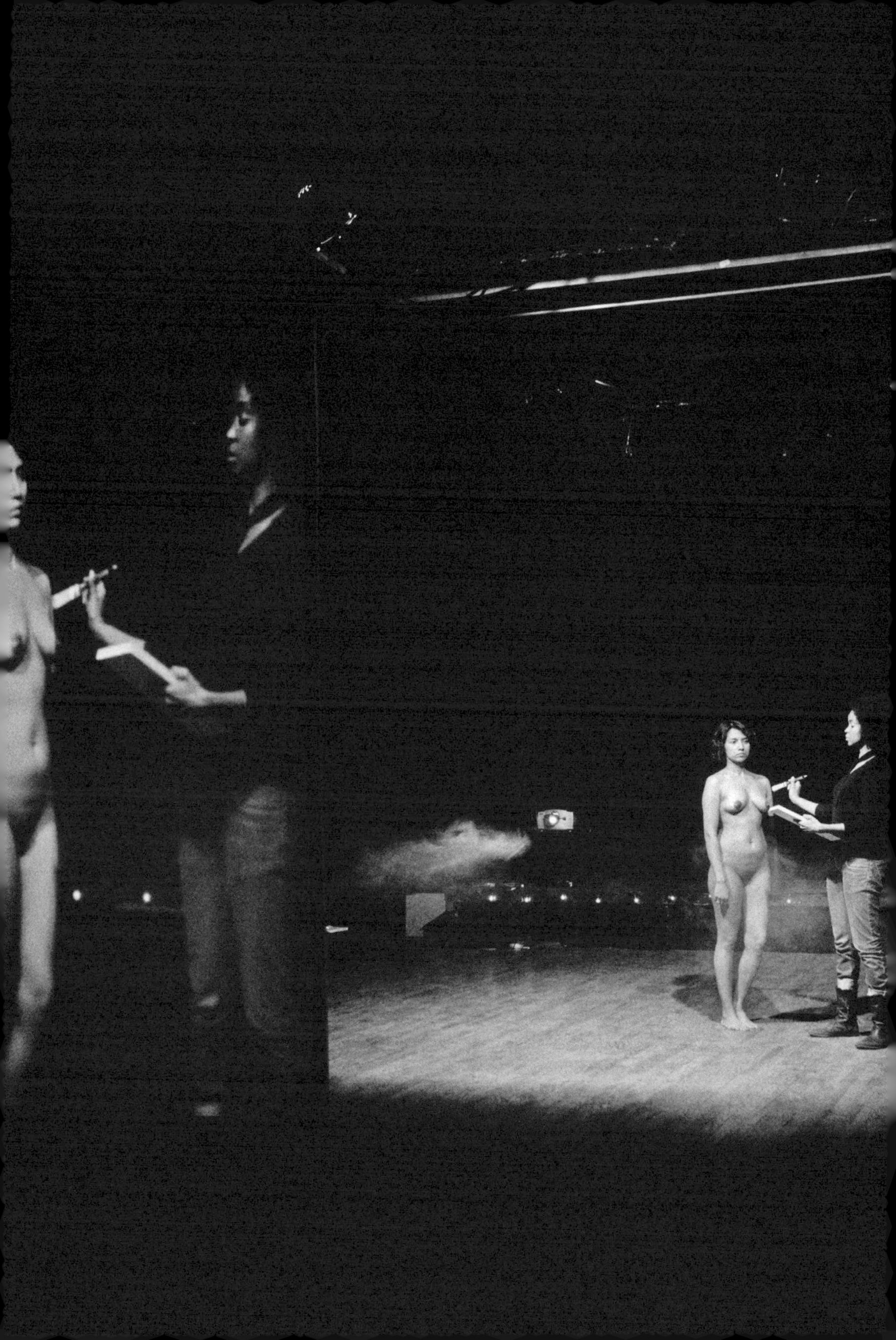

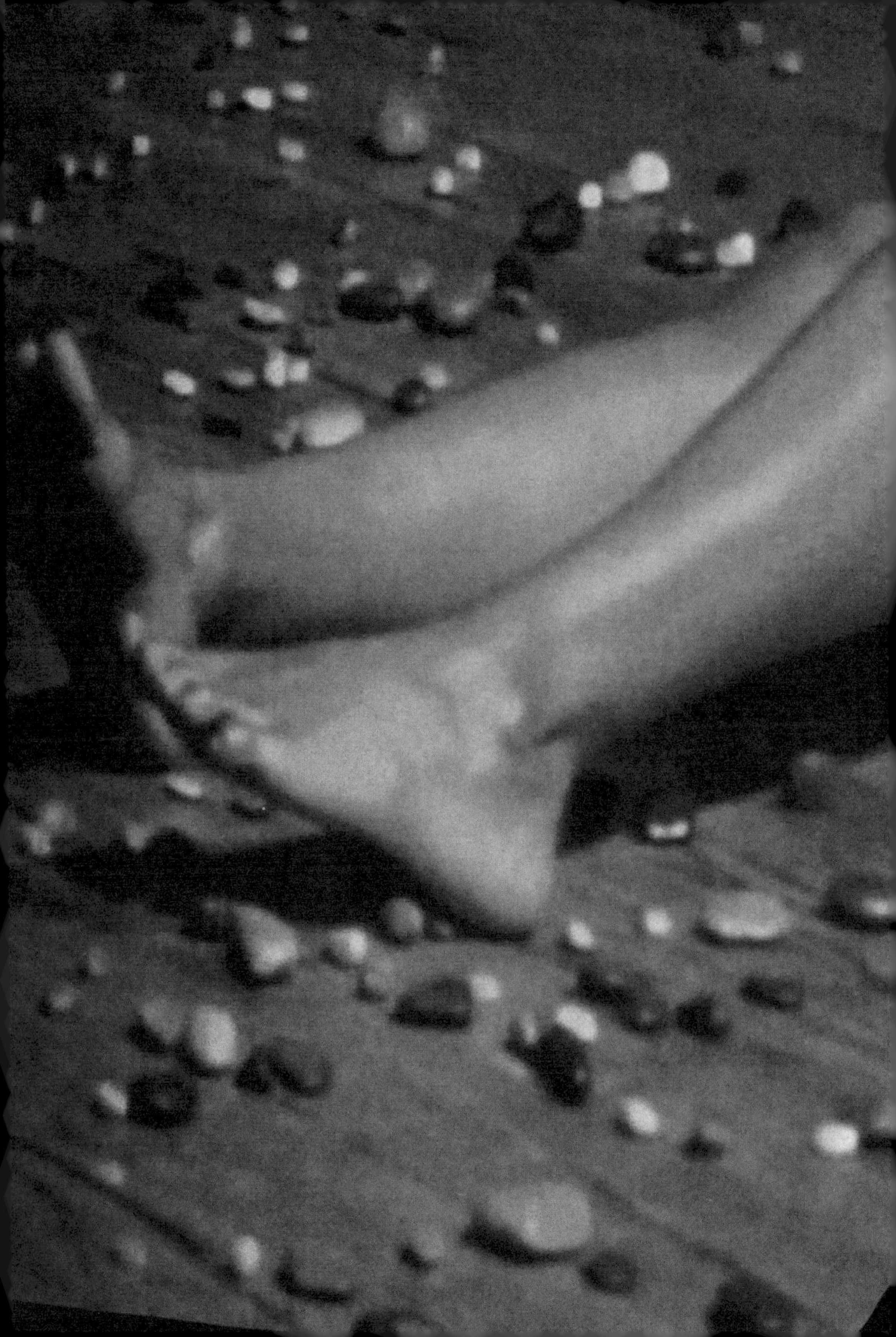

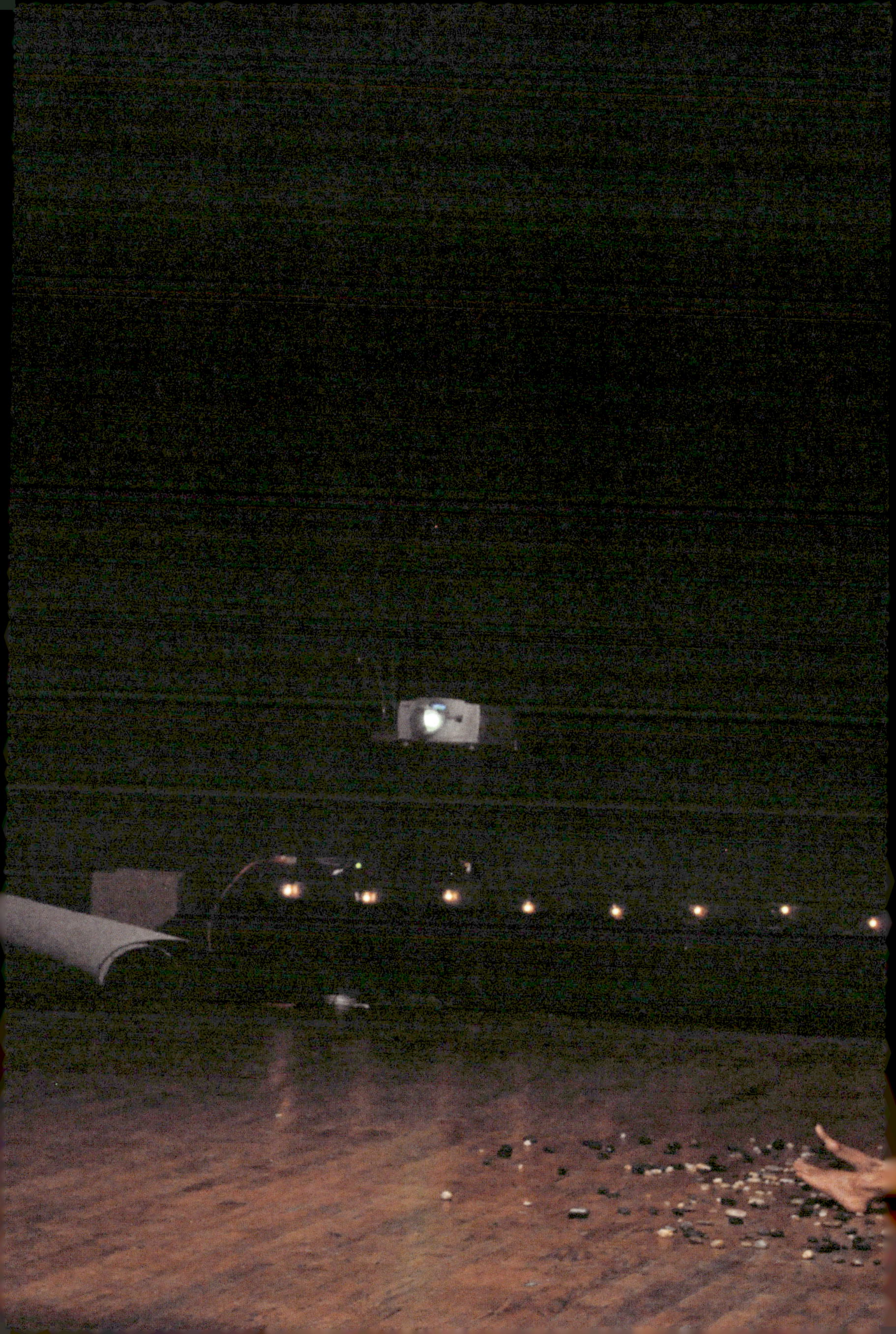

Carrie Mae Weems

On Music, Machinery, and Meeting
2021–2

DJ Spooky
Nona Hendryx
Hans Ulrich Obrist

Conversation with
DJ Spooky
2021

DJ SPOOKY: I would love to hear: How do you get started when you wake up in the morning? It seems like photography is a dimensional process with you. Do you want to riff for a second on that—the part of the process that becomes the work?

CARRIE MAE WEEMS: Much of my process is actually rooted in music, so I start most mornings listening to music.

I have a particular playlist. In the last eight or nine years, I start every morning—almost every morning—listening to 'Ode to Life' by Don Pullen, followed by Stevie Wonder's 'Love's in Need of Love Today'—which I always dance to—followed by Marley's 'Could You Be Loved', followed by the World Saxophone Quartet's 'Come Sunday', and followed by Pharoah Sanders's 'You've Got to Have Freedom', and Louis Armstrong's 'Stardust'. In the afternoon, I settle into Frank Ocean and Alice Coltrane in combination.

It's my thirty-five-minute wake-up ritual. Music is my anchor. Music made by extraordinary artists holds me. Visual artists are also important to me, but musicians top the list.

I'm not a singer by any stretch of the imagination, but I've come to understand that I actually sing my words; it's how I use my voice. I focus on tone, colour, and the melodic qualities of my voice, and this is shaped by my love of song and the influence of music on my life.

Probably more than anything, I am concerned with how to *align* my thinking with the complicated world around me, how to merge my thinking of the world with the realities of the world. It's a song, a sound. Sound is the way we make use of language, and language is the medium through which we construct the world.

All work takes time; even bad work takes time. Certain ideas come fast, through the flash of the spirit; but the *flash* is followed by the real work of working it out! First, I try to focus on the meaning of the work. Then I consider its form. Will it be an image-text piece, a photograph, a video, or a performance?

Making work is a process; it's a constant birthing of the new, and it's hard. Anchored in the process is the struggle with the self, the struggle with ideas, the struggle with the purpose, and the struggle with meaning.

I take the work seriously, and the work takes me seriously; it literally kicks my ass.

Even in play, I take it all seriously.

In play, there's tremendous room for seriousness.

•

Conversation with
Nona Hendryx and Hans Ulrich Obrist
2022

HANS ULRICH OBRIST: I thought we could begin with the question of how it all began. How did you meet each other?

NONA HENDRYX: I met Carrie through Carl Hancock Rux—another amazing artist. If you ever hear Carl speak, you'll never forget it. He has an incredible bass voice. Carl introduced me to Carrie because I told him how much I loved Carrie's work and about the impression her *Kitchen Table Series* had on me, and how it stayed with me. A choreographer for Alvin Ailey created another piece around the kitchen table—two couples on a stage, divided by a wall, and they danced and moved between. It reminded me of Carrie's series, *Kitchen Table*, and I always wanted to bring them together—this particular dance and Carrie's images. I asked Carrie, and she said 'yes', and we turned Joe's Pub into an amazing space for the project.

CARRIE MAE WEEMS: I've known about Nona for years through her work with Patti LaBelle. I knew her amazing voice, but I didn't know *her*. Then I saw the taped memorial service for the poet Sekou Sundiata, and I saw this badass sister standing in the centre of the floor, surrounded by other musicians, but she was the one holding it down. It was Nona, and I thought, 'That's who I want to work with!'

Carl Hancock introduced us. One day he called saying that Nona wanted to talk to me about the *Kitchen Table Series*. I was stunned—I couldn't believe it! The person I wanted to work with wanted to work with me. It was a dream come true!

I mean, there are terrific artists out there, but you can't work with just anybody. So when you find someone you *can* work with, and you are *simpatico*, you hold on, because it's rare. It's a gift!

NH: Yes. When we were doing *Refrigerated Dreams*, Carrie and I had a lot of time to talk about our lives, about family, about society, how we feel about being a woman, and how you are as a woman in the world. We just talked about everything, and that is not always the way artists speak with each other. We talked about George Floyd, about how incredible it is that a person who was not on a path to change the world actually did change the world. These are the conversations we have, and out of it is born the work that we do.

CMW: It's through collaboration that you extend your range and voice. It offers something you don't have, but need. The link between the song we just heard, 'Water Water' [written by Lynn Nottage], and your notion of Afrofuturism is intricately connected. The music, along with the implicit meaning of the song, helps us to speak in multiple languages and multiple tongues, because you're actually singing through the truths as you feel it—the lyrics: *Water, Water, holding me back… how do I get to the other side?* Water then is the barrier and the carrier of dreams hoped for and futures imagined.

In the United States, hundreds of Black men died before George Floyd—specifically when Obama was in office. Indeed, there was an escalation of violence directed against Black men *because* Barack Obama was in office. In fact, the number of deaths declined after his term ended. But George Floyd's murder was the straw that broke the camel's back. His prime-time killing unleashed micro-explosions felt around the world—explosions throughout culture, throughout institutions, throughout our societies. Finally, Black, white, and everyone in between were indisputably and irrefutably made aware of the Black man's burden. The systematic, bald-faced, persistent violence directed against people of colour (particularly men of colour) was on TV, and because of the pandemic lockdown, we were all watching! We all witnessed—at once and as one—an unimagined horror.

HUO: You said once, Carrie, that *Grace Notes* began with a deep desire to get at what was troubling you. It examines the wider social implications of tension at work in communities across America.

CMW: *Grace Notes* was commissioned for the Spoleto Festival by Sarah Lewis and centres on the killing of the Emanuel Nine, Trayvon Martin, Eric Garner, and all the others—an impossibly long list of victims. My question was how to create a work that could, in some small way, ask just the right questions, in just that right way, that would move us forward. It's deeply troubling to know that you are despised, considered less than; how to address the problem with a sense of compassion—a sense of grace—was crucial. The language, colour, and tone had to be just right. And the question that I struggled with then and now is the meaning of grace.

Developing the project took more than a year. My musical collaborators, James Newton, Craig Harris, Geri Allen, and Jawwaad Taylor, are all remarkable musicians and composers, but not singers. I needed a singer's singer, one who could write, compose, and sing.

I knew it had to be Nona. But because of her schedule, I was afraid she'd say NO. Finally I summoned the courage to call her, and she immediately understood what I was after. Forty-eight hours later, she sent me the first draft of the song.

After that, we worked together on the lyrics, making a few minor changes... This morning I found myself singing the song, paying special attention to the lyrics. There's extraordinary emotion in the music. It's haunted by the ghosts of the spirit, but it isn't a spiritual. It has similar elements, but it's not a spiritual.

Nona, can you talk a little bit about how you developed the lyrics?

NH: You asked me to write about grace, and you played me recordings of different conversations you had with your mother about grace. I listened. I listen to voices, and, as a writer—and having been a part of Patti LaBelle and the Bluebells, I've always written for Patti's voice, so Patti's voice is in my head as I'm writing—your voice is in my head as I am writing, as I am thinking. You may not be singing, but your voice is in my head. Your mother's voice stayed in my head as I was writing the song.

The question you asked was, What does 'grace' mean?, and I tried to answer it in song. A song, or singing, is when you cannot any longer say just in words what something means—what something feels like. That is why people moan [*singing a moan-like sound*]; that is why people yell, because they can no longer find words to say what it is that they want, what they are feeling. Words like 'trust and believe in what you can see'—when you are down on your knees—what do you say when life pierces your heart? That's what I was responding to when you were talking about the moment when someone doesn't know whether they're going to live or die—that is a moment of grace.

I love working with Carrie because she is very musical. I know you say, 'Oh, I can't sing', but, yes, you can sing. I could set your voice to music—as

I have. That is where the song came from. Your mother mostly inspired it.

CMW: My mother is extraordinary.

HUO: Carrie, you have been telling us in such a wonderful way how music expands your practice. I wanted to ask Nona how the dialogue with Carrie and with different visual artists expands your own practice.

NH: My first love was poetry. It was the first thing I responded to as a human in terms of something outside of myself. I'm a huge fan of Shakespeare, and of many of the poets from the past. Poetry was something where I found I was able to say more as opposed to just speaking a sentence. In the *Kitchen Table Series*, Carrie, your text was very influential for me because I recognised the people that you were talking about. I recognised my aunts, my uncles, my brothers, my father, my mother.

When you give me guidance about a musical composition, I'm clear about what it is I'm supposed to be doing. You are precise in your words—your chosen words—and that, for me, informs how I want to express music, because it's clear. A lot of people aren't clear. They just want you to write something, but Carrie is always specific.

HUO: Carrie, what is the process in a project like *Grace Notes*? How do you collaborate on such a programme, because you said beautifully that you extend, mutually, your vocabularies?

CMW: Nona and I are very much alike. We come from similar backgrounds and families, so we speak the same language.

From the very beginning of working on *Grace Notes*, I knew it would be a collaboration; it was too big for one person. I needed and wanted to work with other talented artists who weren't afraid to work with other talented artists. Collaboration requires a certain set of skills. You have to be open, or it doesn't work. It's through collaboration that you extend your voice, range, and capacity—it provides you with something you wouldn't have otherwise. In a performance like *Grace Notes*, collaboration is key. When I heard Nona's voice, I knew I'd found what I'd been searching for. But the hardest thing for me, as a first-time director, was to ask her to change some of the lyrics in *Grace*.

Something I find important—the magic of collaboration—is being open to possibilities. Drawing from all the facets of my life has helped me to learn about myself, and by extension, because of the collaboration, about you.

HUO: When I invited you both, I had to promise that we would have enough time to talk about the future—so this is the moment now that we have to switch. Can we talk about how *Dream Machine* began?

CMW: Yes. Nona is going to talk about the extraordinary project she's been working on. Nona is an Afrofuturist and has been working with notions of Afrofuturism for a number of years. She's worked with the likes of Sun Ra, but even the Bluebells were futurist.

I'm not as advanced. My future project is the one I'm actually working on now, and happens to be connected to my first major project, *Family Pictures and Stories*. I've been working on the same project all my life. It's about trying to figure out a way of entering. When and where do I enter? How do I get in there, now, around that circle of things? And every entry point is another way of attacking that thing. I think that, for me, it is just rooted in [*long pause*] a kind of desperate search for the truth as I see it.

So... I never knew my grandfather, my father's father. He was a union organiser for the Southern Tenant Farmers Union. Because of this involvement, he was attacked, beaten, and left for dead. We never saw him, never met him. I saw a photograph of him for the first time only several years ago. My sister, after searching for years, found a photograph of him in his lawyer's office in Chicago, preparing to sue the state of Arkansas for his mistreatment and separation from his family. But that suit was never brought forth.

I'm hoping to continue my grandfather's suit! We're organising a series of trials around truth, reconciliation, and reparations that argues the case of my grandfather and whether or not my family, by law, has the right to sue the state of Arkansas for his mistreatment. So, in the name of Frank Weems, the entire Weems family, and under the UN charter on human rights, we are hoping to sue the state of Arkansas for his mistreatment and permanent separation from his family.

That's what I'm working on [*applause*], and this is linked to Nona's work. Who owns the future? Can the future be designed? Besides AI—artificial intelligence—what will it take? What work has to be done, and by whom?

History moves forward with stops and starts, but nonetheless it moves forward. This links us to the *Dream Machine*. Who will be involved in this future? Who will be involved with AI? Who will be involved with future technology? What will be the voices that we hear, and how will we hear them? What will be most pronounced?

We're at a point of inflection and confluence that presents an extraordinary opportunity, and if we use it right, then something extraordinary can come out of it. If we use it wrongly, then we're doomed.

With that, I turn it over to Nona.

NH: Thank you! Carrie, your project links very much to *Dream Machine*, which evolved out of my work as an ambassador at Berklee College of Music in Boston and Boston Conservatory, and then Berklee NYC in New York.

It evolved through my passion for technology—electronics to begin with, but then technology, science fiction, and the future. Taking what you're doing now, Carrie, in a sense reclaiming the past in the present for the future, is what *Dream Machine* is about, as an installation that will be in New York in 2024. It has three parts: AI, AR, and VR.

The AI features BINA48, which is the only African American female android, designed by Martine Rothblatt and based on her wife, Bina Rothblatt. For me, BINA48 is Eve of the future, and what information BINA48 gets to know, who gets to share with BINA48, who BINA48 gets to be in conversation with, will inform our future.

For me, because I care so deeply about how we shape our future—that AI is here; it is us; we are AI—I think we need to be very careful about what we do, how we inform artificial intelligence. You have your refrigerators that tell you when to put more food in it; you have all the technologies we are living with. Many people say, 'Oh, AI! Cyborgs! Oh, we don't…'. But we already have it!

I think it's really important that we have an African American female AI. If all goes to hell, there will be information from multiple people, multiple places. In terms of your grandfather, this is knowledge that must be there so that, in the future, when AI is making decisions about what will be, who will be, how it will be, we need to have sentient beings that have access to feelings. I'm about bringing feeling to the AI, the human, that is just an extension of us.

Further, the project has an AR component—augmented reality—and that also looks at the land upon which we reside, the land of the Native American, the Indigenous people—and that many of the places that are art institutions in this country need to be cleansed in terms of a spiritual activation, musical, artistic cleansing. So, part of the AI is a ritual walk and how that happens with music that is bringing the spirit back, raising the spirit up. The AR portion is to bring visuals from the past and the present, but to shape them as we would like to engage with them in an AR way. You're in the present, we're here, but we're projecting what we would like to see.

The third part is virtual, which is the Loop Master, who represents an artist, Vernon Reid, from a band called Living Colour. We created a VR—virtual reality—experience for Vernon, and it's in the *Dream Machine* experience, and it's five scenes, five levels. You travel, you arrive… As a dreamer, you come and you pass through the arrival of the playground, the forest of the ancestors, which is where you learn about what influences an artist. It could be a Carrie Mae Weems experience. You travel through, and you end up in a concert, a concert of the artist. They could be in London, or they could be anywhere in the world. They respond to the virtual space, and they are performing live. It is not video. This is happening real time—you are there, together with the artist.

This is the type of future work that I'm doing. Carrie, of course I'm hoping that we will collaborate with BINA48. To me, it is very important that this AI gets to have Carrie Mae ask questions, share thoughts, and maybe talk about your grandfather and some of those things, because that's important, that we pass on these legacies.

CMW: What's fascinating is that, not only is Nona working with AI technology, but we all know that we are in for *something* unique, unplanned, unknown, and unimagined. All the major tech firms—from Meta to Google to Apple—along with scientists, engineers, artists, etcetera—are desperate to solve the problems related to the virtual world, what it's going to be, how it can be used, and why should people be excited by it, because they aren't at the moment. But enormous sums of cash—billions—are on the line. It's extraordinary stuff. But the technology is well beyond our limited capacity.

Recently, I was working with a group of young tech professionals on the future of VR who were all fired the day after we spoke. They talked about the extraordinary advances being made, that VR was the future and such, and I said, 'I'm sorry that you didn't understand your future!' [*Laughter*] 'I'm sorry you didn't *see* it yesterday.' You know what I mean? Because it happened that fast!

HUO: We can immensely look forward to these new collaborations. It is incredible to imagine Carrie in conversation with BINA48 because conversations, Carrie, play such a central role in your work.

•

Conversation with
Hans Ulrich Obrist
2022

HUO: Conversation is a medium for you.

CMW: Using conversation and bringing people together around conversation has been a part of my practice now for many years. A lot of it grew out of my deep curiosity, but also out of my endless concern that people should be brought together in a certain kind of way.

When I had my retrospective exhibition at the Guggenheim Museum in New York in 2014, I immediately began thinking about the shape of the programming. Panels often tend to be fairly didactic, straight ahead thirty- or forty-minute conversations, jammed with four or five people on a single panel, with each one attempting to develop a position or an idea that's never fully realised because there's not enough time. It's the worst type of programming, so I avoid it. I'm more interested in providing a platform and space for artists to think more broadly and share their ideas. Then I can spend my time orchestrating the flow of the various presentations so they work in concert with one another and build on one another. That's the fun stuff, the magic. But getting there takes an enormous amount of time—many months of thinking, rethinking, planning.

For instance, by providing shape to specific themes that elevate across any number of events, I can pull together a rhythm of words, ideas, presentations—a rhythm of meaning, a rhythm of *language*—that evolves over the course of an hour, a day, two days, three days, so that by the end, the artists and the audience have had a total experience.

Wagner talked about *Gesamtkunstwerk*—a 'total work of art', a total experience. I am interested in the total experience, and convenings are a total experience, an experience of listening and talking, of deep engagement with an artist around a set of ideas. I think it's important, and I love doing them. Now I've done three or four, and they have become models for the way in which convenings might happen. There's tremendous satisfaction in knowing that I've crafted a new model of engagement.

HUO: The *Gesamtkunstwerk* aspect that you mentioned is interesting, but you leave a lot of space for people. It's not overwhelming.

CMW: This is where trust comes in; you have to trust the people you've invited to present. You trust them to deliver on the promises that they've made to themselves and to their own production. My job as I see it is simply to carefully orchestrate every aspect of the presentations. Who comes first? Who comes second? Who comes last? Who speaks for fifteen minutes? Who speaks for thirty minutes? Who speaks for an hour? And I make these decisions based on what I know, what I imagine, and what I want to see and hear from artists.

In living artists, living out their work, living out their practice, how do I craft another intellectual experience to engage the emotions, the heart, and the mind in the process of negotiating this thing we call life?

It's been a meaningful way to think about my practice. Indeed, I think of it as being just as important as the photographs, films, and installations I make.

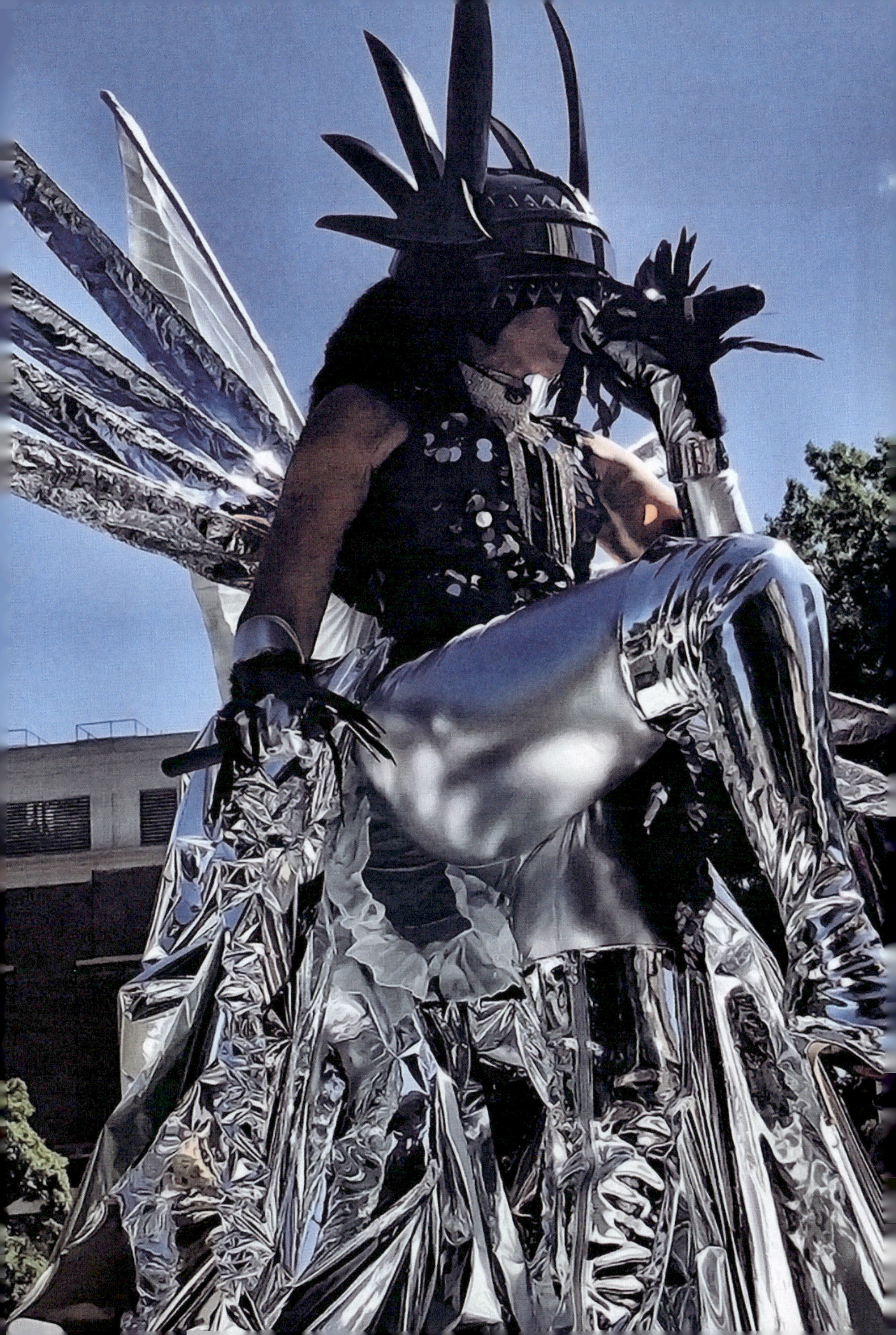

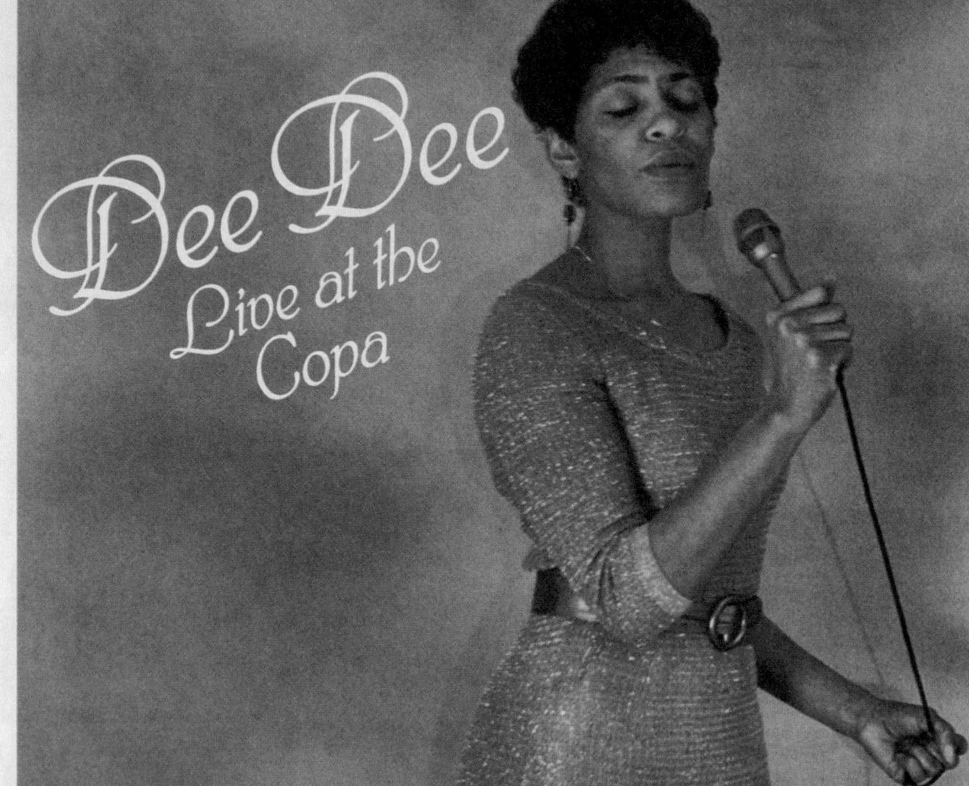
Dee Dee
Live at the
Copa
If You Should Lose Me

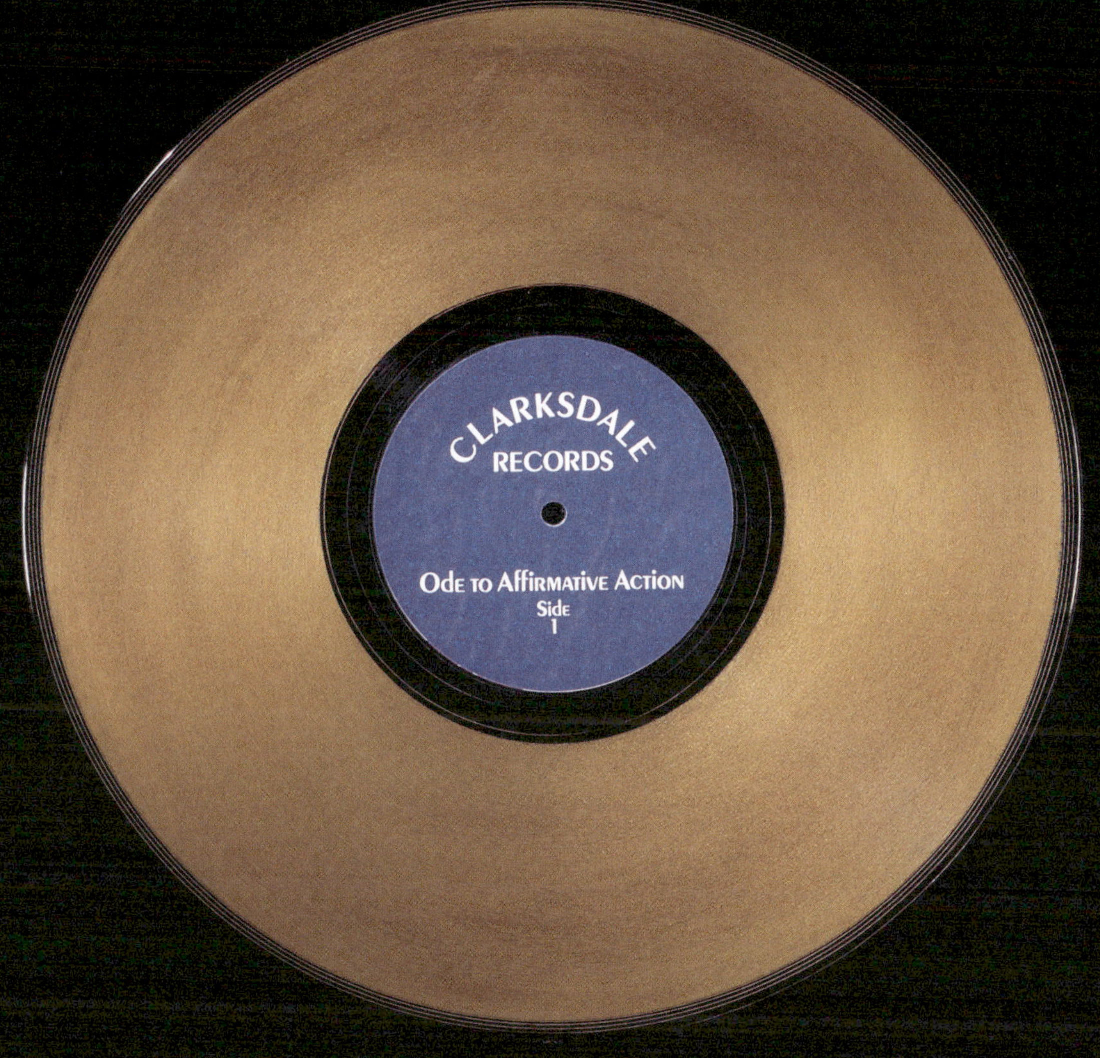
CLARKSDALE
RECORDS
Ode to Affirmative Action
Side
1

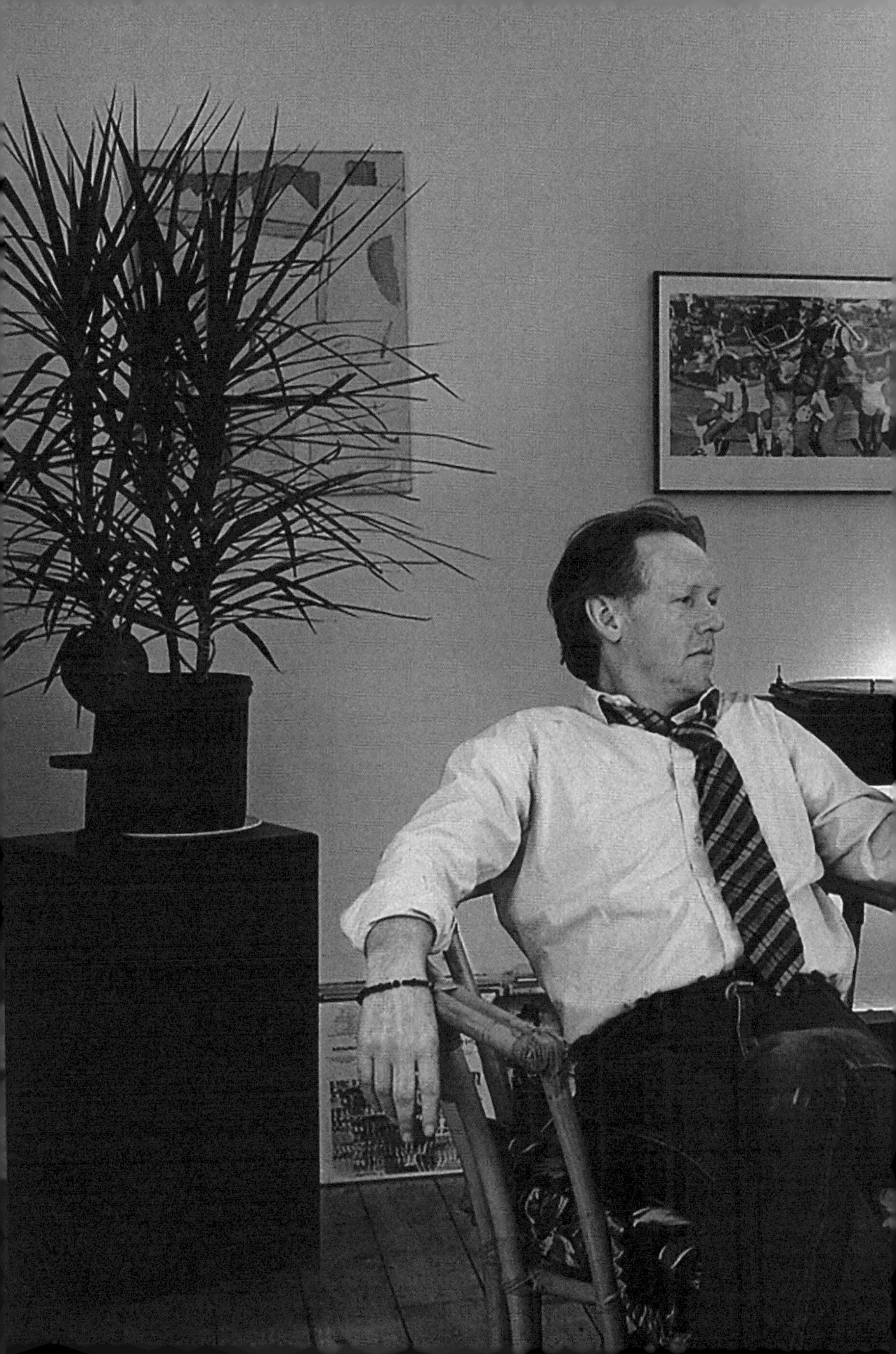

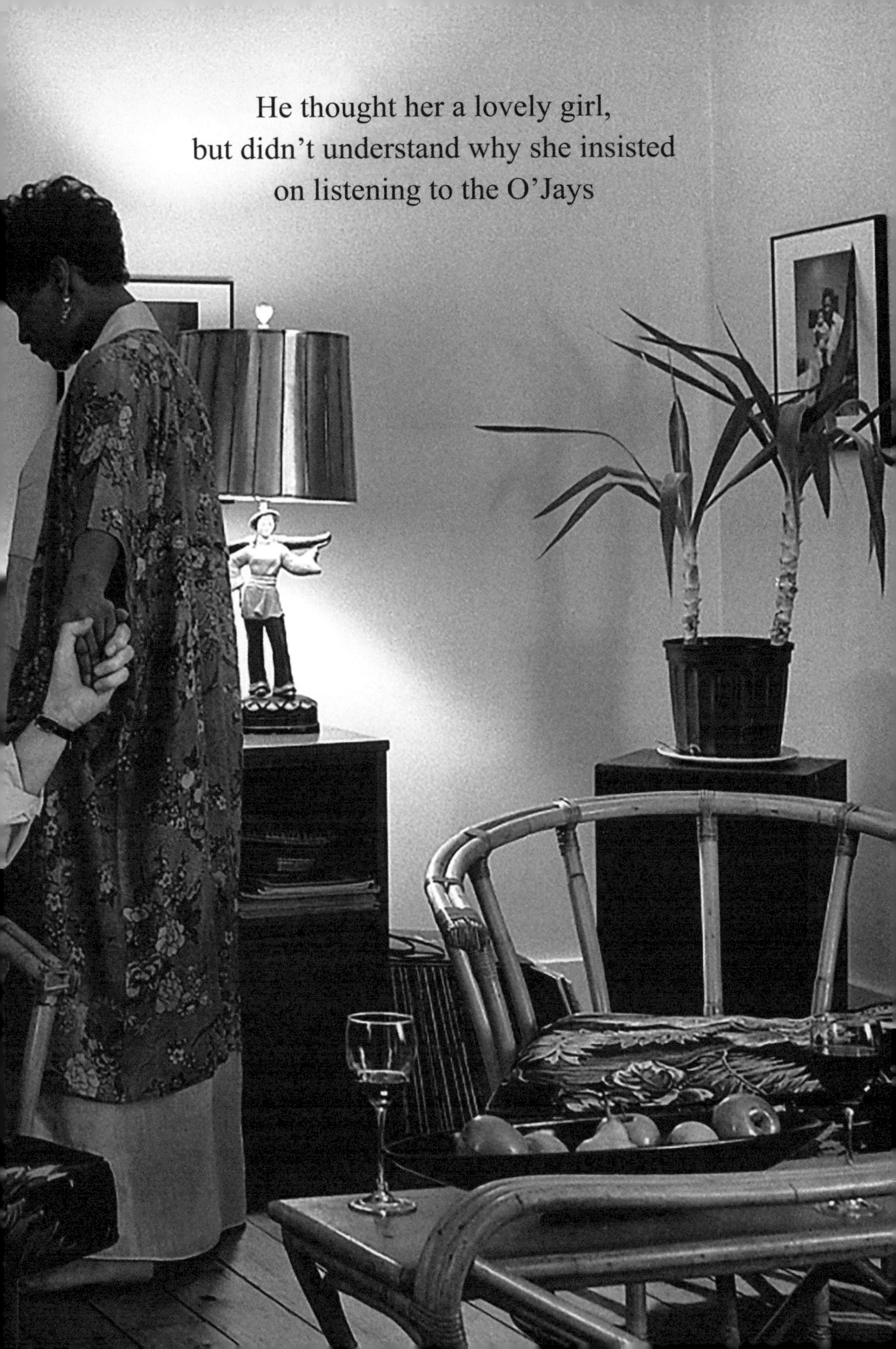

He thought her a lovely girl,
but didn't understand why she insisted
on listening to the O'Jays

As Told to Faye Hirsch

Home

Six or seven months ago, I'd been on the road for a while, travelling a lot. I just could not wait to get home: to wake up in my own bed, be in my own sheets, bathe in my own tub, smoke in my own living room. To be with all the furniture and art that I live with, all the stuff that I've accumulated over the years, that holds a certain kind of meaning for me. In some ways, home is my muse. It's the space that allows for deep contemplation and reflection, the place where you can go to smell yourself, to nourish and replenish yourself, to protect yourself. Home gives me the four walls that I need between me and the rest of the immediate world.

I could never leave my home for good, could never be rootless. I can go out on the limb quite far, but I have to have someplace to scurry back to, to make a nest of the ideas and pieces of material that I've acquired while out there, to sink into. As a visual artist, there are times I must leave; I have to travel. If I'm working on museums as a subject, I'm looking at museums all over the world—not in Syracuse, my primary home, where there's only one. But I need to get home to be able to understand what I've seen out there. So there's home, but there's also the psychological space that home creates.

Why I wanted—no, needed—to be home on this particular occasion: I was dying to hear really good music, to listen to extraordinary voices. I got back from wherever I had been at around three o'clock in the afternoon and went into my kitchen, pulled out my computer, and pulled up my music. I'm interested in all kinds of music and all kinds of singing voices. From three o'clock in the afternoon until about two in the morning I just sat in one place listening to them; from Sarah Vaughan to Frank Sinatra to Aretha Franklin; or Aretha Franklin remixing Glen Campbell, then back to Glen Campbell so I could rethink Aretha. The thing that became clear to me in this moment, maybe for the first time, was that the really great singers, almost without exception, usually only sang. They seldom played piano or did a song-and-dance act. The great singers mostly just sang.

How do you get close to the bone in your work? You don't do it by trying to be a jack-of-all-trades. You can only do it by sinking deep into the structure of the thing. I'm just a photographer, a visual artist, mining the same territory again and again and again, in hopes of getting closer in my lifetime to the full nature of my own voice and the complexity of being alive.

This 'sounding out' is my deepest muse, if you want to call it that—how things are made to sound in the world, and how close you can get to the authentic, complex soundings of the world. I have been listening to Louis Armstrong for forty-five years, and still, every time I hear him, the places he is able to take us in our own imaginations blows my mind. The music delivers us to the deepest part of ourselves. So the question is, will I ever be able to come close even to an approximation of that?

Though you are seeing your own work all the time, it's difficult to truly see it. How can you, since you're always making it? My own work endlessly surprises me. I think, 'I made that? Hmmm... not bad for a girl!' With the Guggenheim survey up, I'm learning a great deal about myself. I don't think of myself as a great artist by any stretch of the imagination. I've seen great art, and my work is not that. I do, however, have a unique voice. I'm aware that it's situated in a very particular space in the art world and that it's been very important—that a lot of people have paid attention to it. From the way the photographs are structured in, say, the *Kitchen Table Series* (1990) to the way I've used language in that and other series, such as *Africa* (1993) or *From Here I Saw What Happened and I Cried* (1995–6), I've figured out how to use voice and language with the image in a rather individual and meaningful way.

Men and women have come to me as a result of their encounters with my work over the years. The work presents the possibility of generating certain kinds of dialogue that might not happen otherwise. A couple I know went to see my show. He's Black and she's white. She's a very old friend of mine. They've been dating for seventeen years. She said, 'We came to your show and had conversations like we've never had before.'

Another friend wrote me: 'I'm standing in front of your work and a man is talking to his son for the first time about race.' That is an accomplishment. In conversations like these, you discover your voice in relation to someone that you thought you knew, someone that you know you love.

I'm dying to get home. I have some work I really want to make. I want to be back in my studio and listening to music. Right now, I'm paying attention to radio and television personalities from the past—hosts and announcers. There was such an art to them, from Groucho Marx to Nat King Cole to Steve Allen to Dick Cavett. They were great personalities of voice and sound—and they had such incredible shows! Today, authenticity is not really being looked for. Until the early seventies, you didn't want fifteen singers on the radio who sounded the same. Now that they sound alike is a given. There's been a homogenisation of culture and language and style that has sabotaged the possibility of an authentic voice. Why not really discover your voice, to allow it to speak through—to not be afraid of being different?

I was just given a BET (Black Entertainment Television) award. I was seated next to Aretha Franklin, Berry Gordy was across from me, and Smokey Robinson was behind me. So many of the younger performers were just horrible—so fake that I was embarrassed for them. And then Aretha took the stage and sang 'A Change Is Gonna Come'. Unbelievable. That odour! That depth! You have to be kind of ugly to sing like that—you can't be way up here to get down.

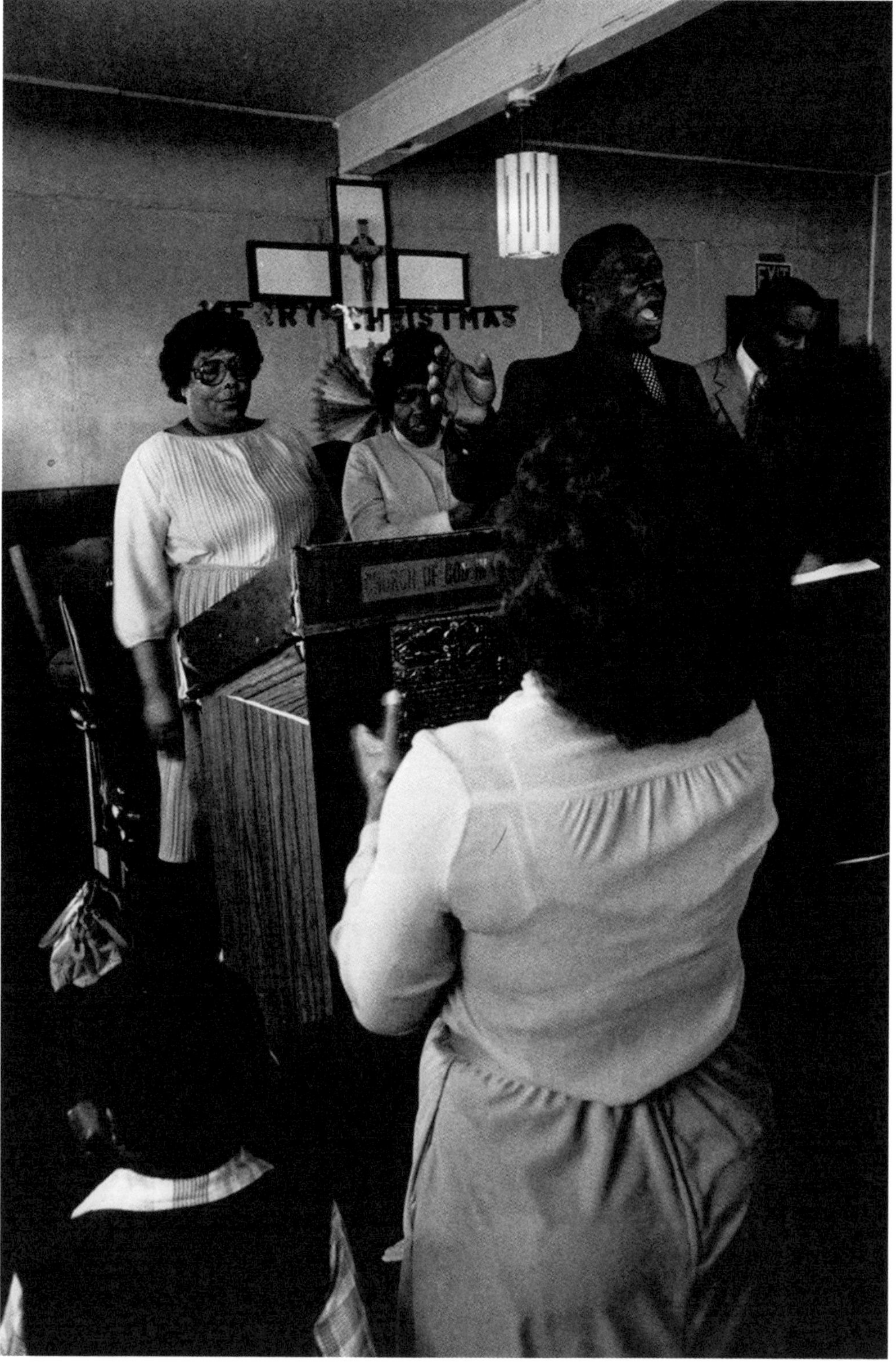

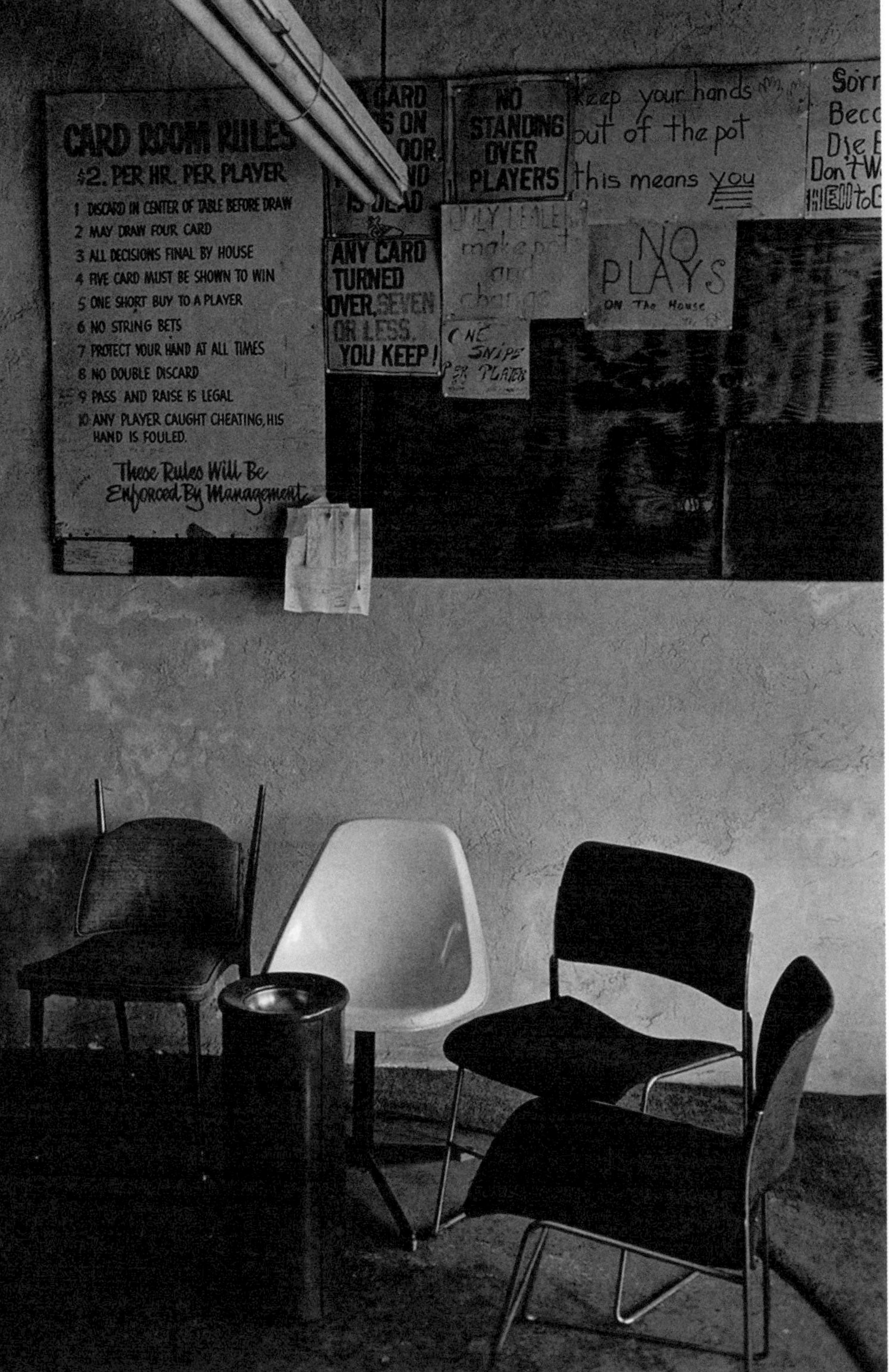
CARD ROOM RULES
$2. PER HR. PER PLAYER
1 DISCARD IN CENTER OF TABLE BEFORE DRAW
2 MAY DRAW FOUR CARD
3 ALL DECISIONS FINAL BY HOUSE
4 FIVE CARD MUST BE SHOWN TO WIN
5 ONE SHORT BUY TO A PLAYER
6 NO STRING BETS
7 PROTECT YOUR HAND AT ALL TIMES
8 NO DOUBLE DISCARD
9 PASS AND RAISE IS LEGAL
10 ANY PLAYER CAUGHT CHEATING, HIS HAND IS FOULED.
These Rules Will Be Enforced By Management
NO STANDING OVER PLAYERS
Keep your hands out of the pot this means you
ANY CARD TURNED OVER, SEVEN OR LESS, YOU KEEP!
NO PLAYS ON The House

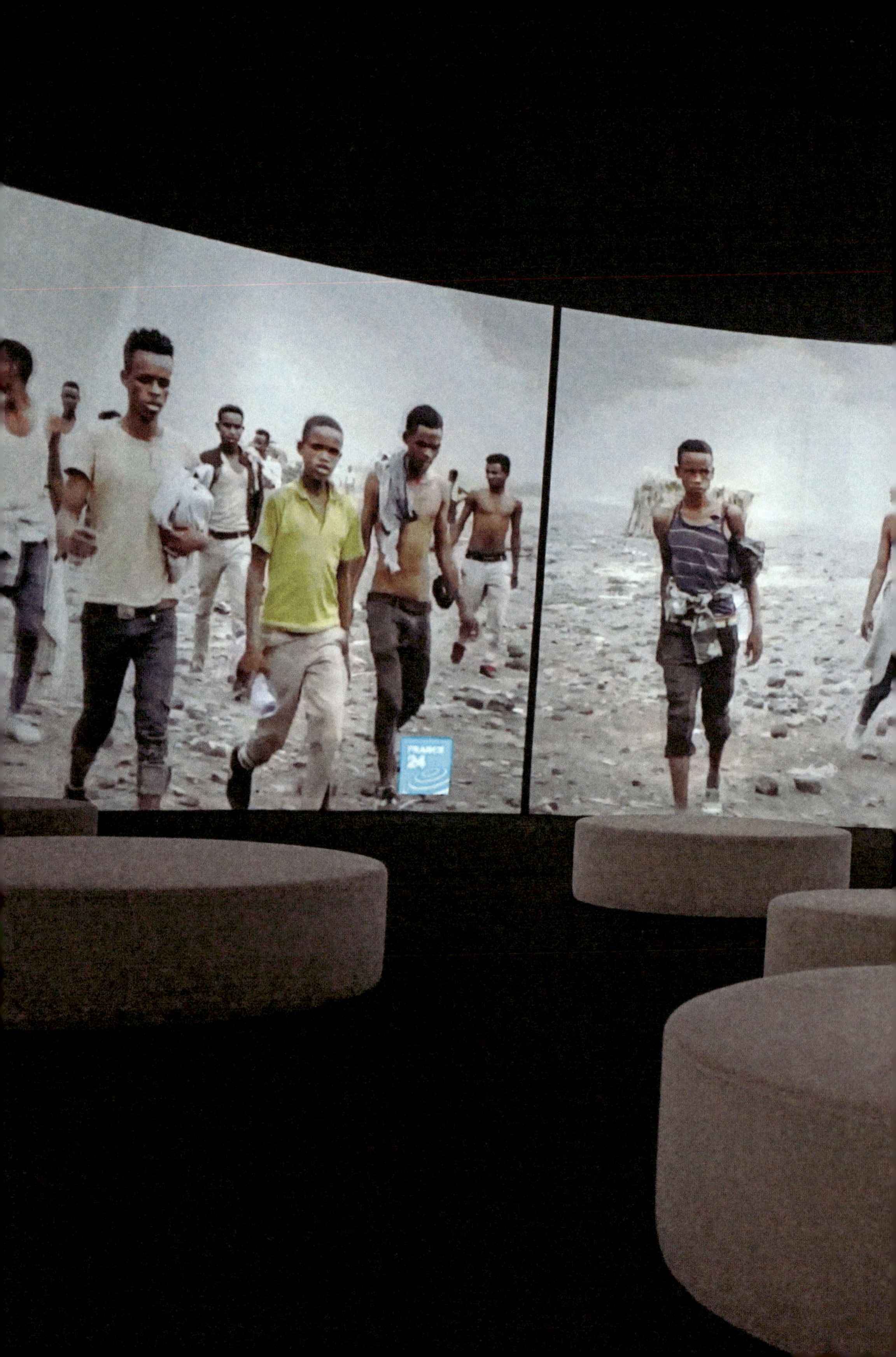
FRANCE 24

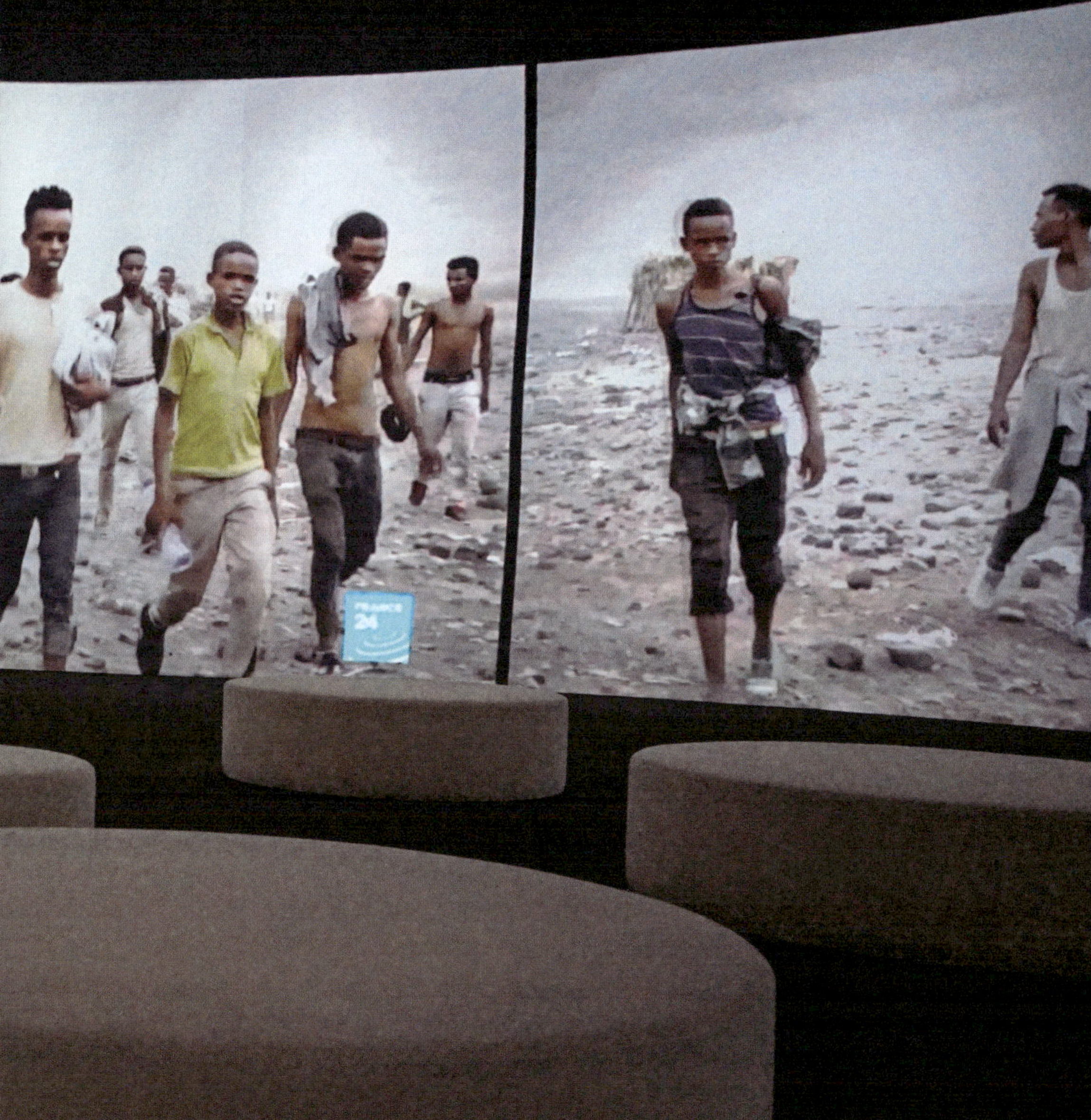

As told to Carrie Mae Weems
by her mother, Carrie Polk

Family Stories

CARRIE MAE WEEMS: What part of Mississippi are you from?
CARRIE POLK: From Clarksdale. Mother was born in Larks, and Papa was born in Silver City.

CMW: What did your family do in Mississippi?
CP: Farm. We sharecropped for Charles Gillet. That one I remember because we were just at the age of remembering.

CMW: Did you live on a plantation?
CP: Oh yeah, we lived on a plantation!

CMW: Were there other families living there too?
CP: Yeah, there was a lot of 'em. Maybe six or seven families on the plantation, maybe more than that. The houses was scattered like. Like our house was over there, and all our land was over there, and you hoed as much land as you wanted to hoe. Then another house was spotted, and they worked so much land, see.

CMW: What was sharecropping like?
CP: You worked a part of the land for yourself and part you worked for the Man. He got half. One bale would go for you and one bale would go for him, see? If you got twenty bales, that mean ten for you and ten for him. But you'd have to pick fifteen hundred to two thousand pounds to get a bale. It depends on how many pounds you got in order to get you a five-hundred-pound bale, ya see, 'cause they take all the seeds outta it, then they weigh the cotton itself. When they take the seeds outta it, they pay you so much money for that, and then at the end of the year they pay you for the bale—the poundage on the bale. And that's the way we did that.

CMW: Was he a fair landlord?
CP: Naw! Some folks just never came out nothin' but in the hole. Say like that. 'Cause my pastor always saying how they worked, and from one year to the next they never came outta the hole. He was always talking about how poor they was. But my daddy was always such a provider, until—really, we never did see no hard times.

People hollering about the hard times in the South, but we always had. Any time of year, if Mother wanted a steak, Daddy could go get her a steak. You see what I mean? Or if it got to that time of evening and we wanted pork chops, Daddy would go get 'em. Daddy always tried to give us things. They provided for us.

So many families in the South didn't try to provide; they didn't can food. They were like the grasshopper. But Mother would can maybe a thousand jars of fruit every year. So all winter our food was stocked up—all winter long. And we would never have to be stingy with eatin'. There was always a-plenty, but some people didn't know how to figure out their money very good and would get real cheated.

But you see, Daddy had such a brain until if they say, I'm gonna pay you, say, twenty cents a pound for the cotton, Daddy had kept all of his tickets, he had figured up all the poundage, and he had figured up everything that he had borrowed from the Man. So when he went up there to settle, he taken a pencil, too! Well, one time ol' man Gillet told Daddy that he had so much and so much coming, and Daddy said, 'Naw, I ain't got so much. You better get your pencil!' Ya see!

But a lots of people wouldn't say nothing. They went on and took it. Whatever he said went; they'd be too scared to argue with the white man, but Daddy let them know, 'You cheaping me!' That last time Gillet told Daddy he was 'too smart' for 'em and he wanted him to leave. So then we moved.

I forgets the place; I don't remember that man at all, but we moved on this plantation. But Daddy worked as a carpenter, 'cause Daddy was a carpenter. Yeah, Daddy could do anything like that, carpentry. He was a freemason; he could build a brick house! So he got the place (the plantation) for Mother, and then he work in town. That way wouldn't nobody say, 'Well, hey, you come', or 'You can't go to town'. And by nobody knowing what Daddy was, nobody would mess with him. And so this is the way Daddy got around. He would do these different things. He worked and saved that money, then he moved, and then we got married. Sadie and I got married.

CMW: How did you meet my daddy (Myrlie Weems)?
CP: On the plantation. On Charles Gillet's plantation. Well, I met him before then. He was on a place called Hanes. He and Mrs. Weems and all them, they lived not far down the road from us, see. Then they moved away; they moved down around Marks; then they moved back into the area where we was, and they had grown up and we had too. So that's how we met. But later on, me and your daddy worked on the same plantation, and he lived in the cotton house. That's where you put the cotton. You pick it and put it in the cotton house. Well, that's where he lived, in the cotton house with his little friend.

CMW: How did Papa and Ozzie meet?
CP: I don't know. Daddy's first marriage was a bad experience. She liked to lay around. He had caught his wife with the other man, so he was free to marry. He knew the man. But Daddy really never talked too much about hisself. I think he preferred to be left out, and his life was shut like.

CMW: Do you think Papa got by 'cause he passed for white?
CP: Well, yeah. Even after we got to Portland, one day a white man asked him how did he feel riding them niggers in his car, and he would come up against those kinds of things, but he always had an answer for 'em, 'cause he never denied that we was his family. That was one thing that he never denied! And you know, when we lived in the South, they had the Jim Crow signs, and you see Daddy would put us behind the sign and he sat in front of the sign. He would do things like that; in a sense he could ride wherever he wanted to ride, because they didn't know, you see. And I guess when he came up he was able to go into a restaurant and eat. Where Black people had to go through the back doors, he was able to go right in and eat his meals, you see.

CMW: Did you know Papa's mother or father?
CP: No, 'cause his mother had died. But she had three kids: Papa, Katie, and Joe. Joe and Papa are half-brothers; they have different fathers. But Joe's daddy didn't like Papa, so Uncle Kelly raised him. Daddy is the oldest. And I think because Daddy is crossed-breed that the man didn't like him, so Uncle Kelly

raised Daddy. Katie died young, so I never knew her, but Joe is still alive and lives right outside Clarksdale.

CMW: Did Papa ever meet his father?
CP: Oh yeah, Daddy knew his daddy; oh yeah, oh yeah! They tell me that old man still lives in Clarksdale, tell me he still have a plantation. He knew who he was! Uncle Kelly knew who he was too, but they wouldn't tell nobody.

CMW: I heard he was a Jew from Chicago?
CP: I don't know about Chicago, but I feel he was a Jew.

CMW: Why do you think that?
CP: Because when I worked at the Bardys, the only thing that Daddy ever really came up and told me—the Bardys were Jews—he came up and told me, he said, 'Baby, you know, these are our people.' So that gave me the clue that he was Jewish. And then, you see, Daddy travelled with Jews, and in Clarksdale those Jews—those old Jews—knows Daddy, they knows who he is, you see. He was a travelling salesman with Jews.

But the way I understand it, his father was a travelling salesman too. But in later years the old man had a plantation. But he could have been a travelling salesman and had a plantation too. And I always felt that he had a connection with the gins—the gin mills—that's what they do to the cotton, okay? Because Daddy could work at one gin mill, and if they made him mad at that one, he could just walk away from them and go to the next one over there and go to work. So he worked from one gin mill to the next, and whichever one he went to they wouldn't turn him down. I have a feeling that his father had something to do with them mills. I might be wrong about it, but I really do.

CMW: Did you ever ask Papa about his father?
CP: Let me tell ya somethin': I think that he always felt that he really didn't want us to really know. And he had his reasons. See, I think that his daddy had a family, and he wouldn't tell white people what he was. But I have a feeling that those Jews knew. But like them different plantations that we moved on, this is what he had the advantage of. See, Daddy was a smart thinker. He had the advantage enough to know that as long as

they didn't know whether he was Black or white, he could get what he wanted. And he wouldn't let no white man come up and tell us nothing. 'If ya got anything to say ya, say it to me. But my children, ya ain't got nothin' to do with them.' Well, ya see, nobody else could do like that. And even if they had asked him what he was, he wouldn't tell 'em. So he left all of us like that.

CMW: What was Grandmomma Ozzie like?
CP: Wasteful, very wasteful. But she was strong. Mother was a person who did not play with her children, but she was a friend to her children, you know? You could talk to her. She was very easy to talk to, and her whole mind was kinda settled around her kids.

Like she'd set out her best china and silver and feed us, or cook one of these great big dinners and invite all her children over and stretch out her table and just service 'em! This is the type of person she was—if it was good enough for her, it was good enough for her kids. And anything that she had, if it was good enough for anybody else, it was most certainly good enough for her kids to have. And she didn't believe in her kids being the last ones eats. If they couldn't sit down and eat it along with you, you sure wasn't gonna put your feet up under the table.

Wasteful, very wasteful lady. And a very free-spirit person, free! And I don't know of no one like her. Her and Daddy either. And I don't know of no one who disliked her. You know Johnny, the one who had the cleaners, and his wife, she always wants me to come and see her. And whenever I see her, she say, 'Ain't nobody else like Ozzie. I don't know, I just miss her!'

CMW: Did Great-Grandmomma Bessie live on Charles Gillet's plantation too?
CP: No, they lived on a different plantation, and her husband was a dairyman; he worked at the dairy. They lived at Rich. That's the only place I know'd Momma to live was at Rich. I know'd they moved to other places, but for years they stayed on this plantation, and Momma was a midwife. See, Momma delivered Jerome and all them. She was a sweet woman. And her husband's name was Joshua. Oh, he was a lot of fun. He and I, we would have it! And that's where I got the nickname 'Mule'.

Stubborn, honey! That's where I got that name from. And I like grapes, and they tell me he'd just go out and get garbs of grapes and just bring 'em to me, sit me down and just let me eat off them grapes.

CMW: Did Papa and Ozzie go to school?
CP: Papa had sixteen years. He went to, as far as I can tell, the eighth grade. Then he went back and started all over. He went through school twice up to the eighth grade. What he missed out on the first time, he picked up on the second go-around. Mother, I believe, went up to the ninth grade.

CMW: What about you?
CP: I started the ninth grade, then I dropped out. I got married. Daddy was there when I got married, but he was out here (in Portland) when Sadie got married.

CMW: Do you ever think you got married too young?
CP: Yep! Sure I did. I think lots of us got married too young. We didn't even think about it until later—years later.

•

My father said he remembers being just a little boy when a gang of white men armed with shotguns and looking evil surrounded their house one morning and called out Granddaddy Weems. They told him if he kept doing what he was doing that he'd be a sorry nigger 'cause they'd hang him for sure. You see, my grandfather was a political sorta guy, involved in organising coloured people. Daddy said he was like Martin Luther King. When it came to speaking, he could talk that talk, and the white folks both feared and hated him, wanted him outta town and soon.

Well, the way I hear it, they succeeded, because one night Granddaddy Weems left the house going to one of the organising meetings and wasn't heard from again for a very long time—years in fact. Everybody thought for sure the white folks had gotten hold of him and cooked him. Maybe they tried; nobody knows for sure. But way after a while, somehow or another, Grandfather Weems contacted the family and let it be known that he was safe and living in Chicago.

Daddy saw his father only once after that. He says that he wanted to see his father so bad that he went to Chicago looking for him. Didn't have no phone number, no address—just stalked the streets in the coloured section of town looking. 'And I found him, too. I was walking down the street and saw this man that looked just like my daddy going into a pool hall, and I followed him in. I walked up to him, and before I could ask him his name, he told me, "Yeah, I'm your daddy", and we hugged and kissed right there in the pool hall. Ain't never seen him again.'

I never met Grandmomma Weems, but my cousin Pat lived with her for a long time and says that she was a wonderful person—easy. She died back in the early 1970s from cancer of the uterus, an illness she didn't believe she had. Pat says, 'But I think Grandmomma would have been alive today, 'cause when I graduated high school in 1967, they had diagnosed her as having cancer of the uterus. But she said, "Naw, I don't wanta go for it! Naw, momma ain't got no cancer; they just wanta cut on me." So she just laid around and didn't go. She probably would have been alive today if she had had that surgery.'

I asked Daddy to tell me about when he kidnapped his momma off a plantation in Memphis, but he said he didn't want to talk about it 'cause it was too many details. But Alice told me that Mattie Jean, my cousin who was living with my grandmother back then, told her that the white man wouldn't let them go 'cause they owed him money. But every year they owed him more money, ya know. They were caught up in the sharecropping system and couldn't get out. Well, anyway, one night my daddy came for them. It was wintertime, and it was raining cats and dogs, and they had to move and move fast. They didn't even have time to dress. They just run through the night in their nightclothes and barefoot, hightailing it on outta there.

My father has seven brothers and one sister, and I think because their father left them when they were all just small kids, they felt that they could do the same thing. I tell you, the Weems brothers are a strange lot.

Now, for all I know, all of them, with the exception of my father and his brother, Clarence, have been married two or three times and have more kids in and outside of marriage than the law allows. He had one brother named Claybourne who constantly beat his women. He'd take 'em in the woods, beat them, and threaten to throw 'em off bridges and stuff: a wild man! But his time had run short. My cousin Pat says, 'Something was bound to happen to him sooner or later, 'cause ain't no woman gonna take all that mess. Ya know, they'll take. They usually get away with it through the years until somebody bring they hat to 'em. I mean, I hate that he's dead and everything, but sooner or later something was bound to happen to him.'

I said, 'I heard some woman killed him.' Pat said, 'That was his wife! They had gotten married! The woman say that ever since he come out here to Clarence's funeral, he had been acting strange and went to losing weight. They had went to this party, and ya know, he drunk beer—he's a natural beer drinker. That's all he drunk, and he had gotten high and threatened to jump on her. Well, he did jump on her. Then he threatened to kill her!'

Ya know, when somebody drunk, ain't no telling what they might do. He mighta really meant it. And I bet ya nine outta ten, it was something that happen at that party. Maybe somebody gave her some attention or something. I bet it was over nothing. So naturally she was gonna protect herself. Like you wouldn't stand up and let somebody kill you if you could help it. It was over a year after Clarence died. It wasn't that long ago.

Now James Weems is also a character, and when you talk about him you just hang your head. One day he just walked off and left his family, then tried to play it off like he'd had amnesia for all them years. Amnesia, girl! In fact it was at Clarence's funeral—first time in over twenty years he'd seen his boys, Jerry and James. After all them years the man tried to play daddy with 'em. Now you know that don't make no kinda sense. Somebody needs to tie that fool up by his toenails and beat him. Amnesia!

Honey, I'm telling you, I don't know what to say about the Weemses, but some of them are so cold—cold dudes.

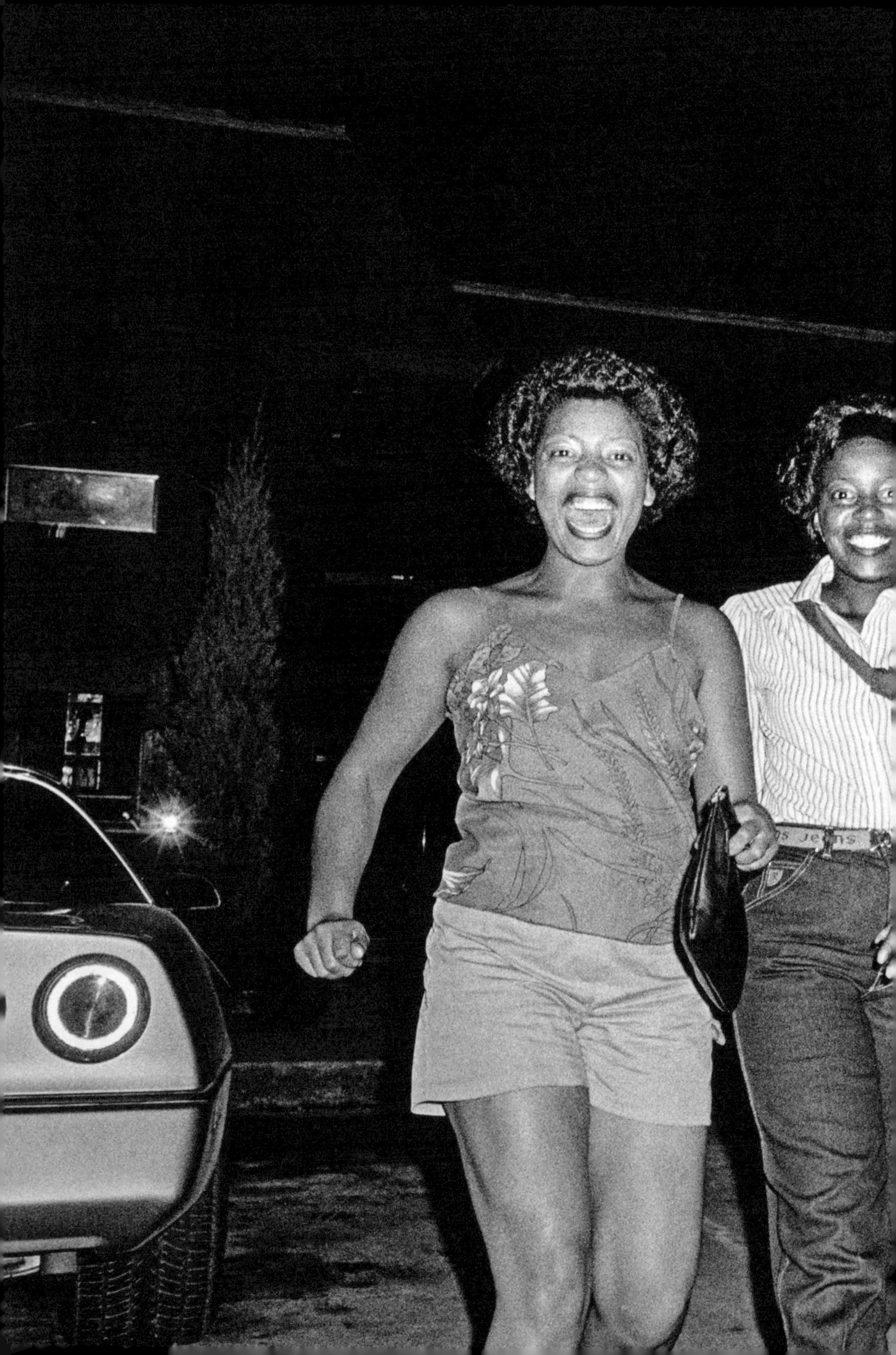

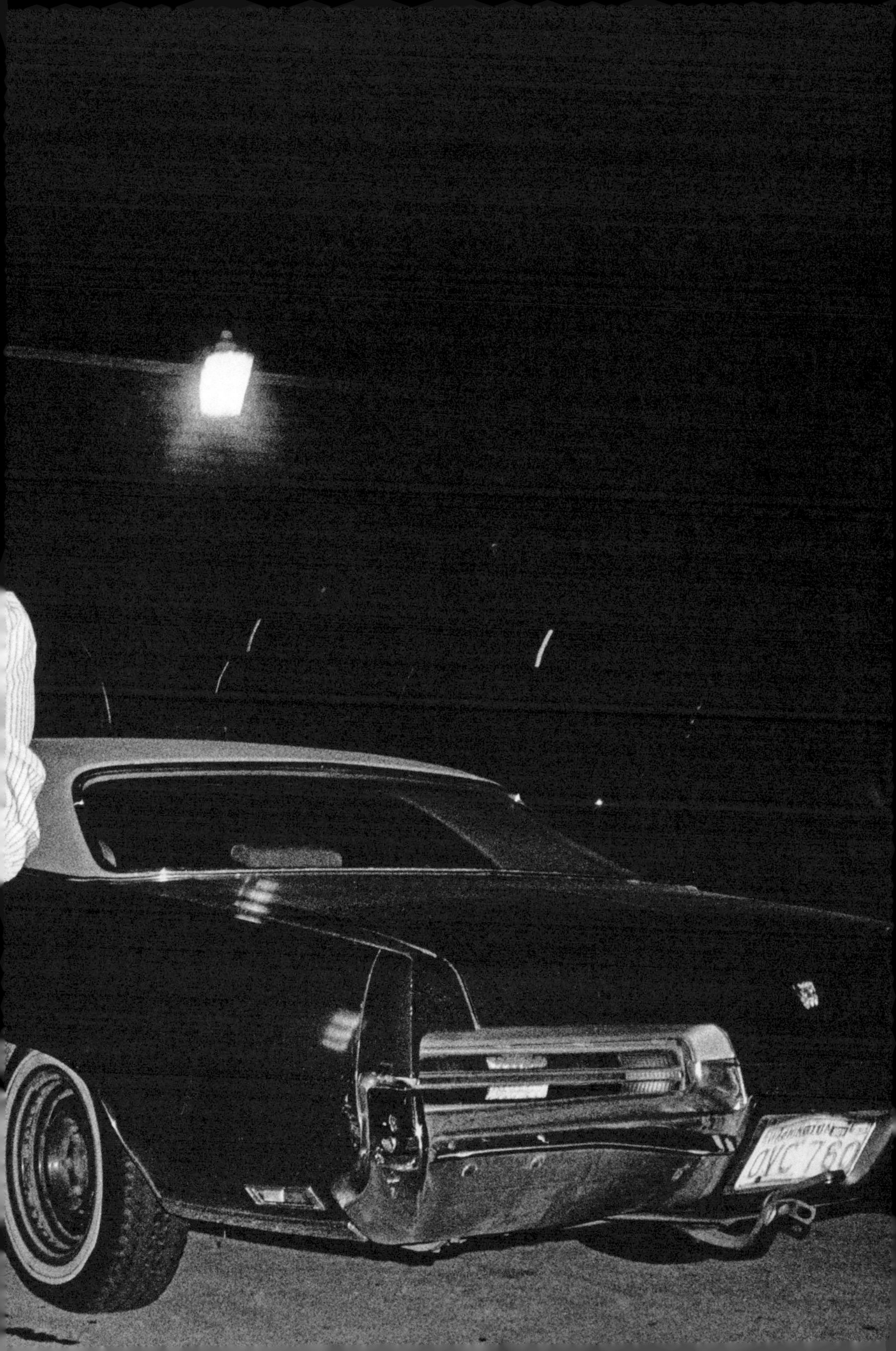
OVC 760

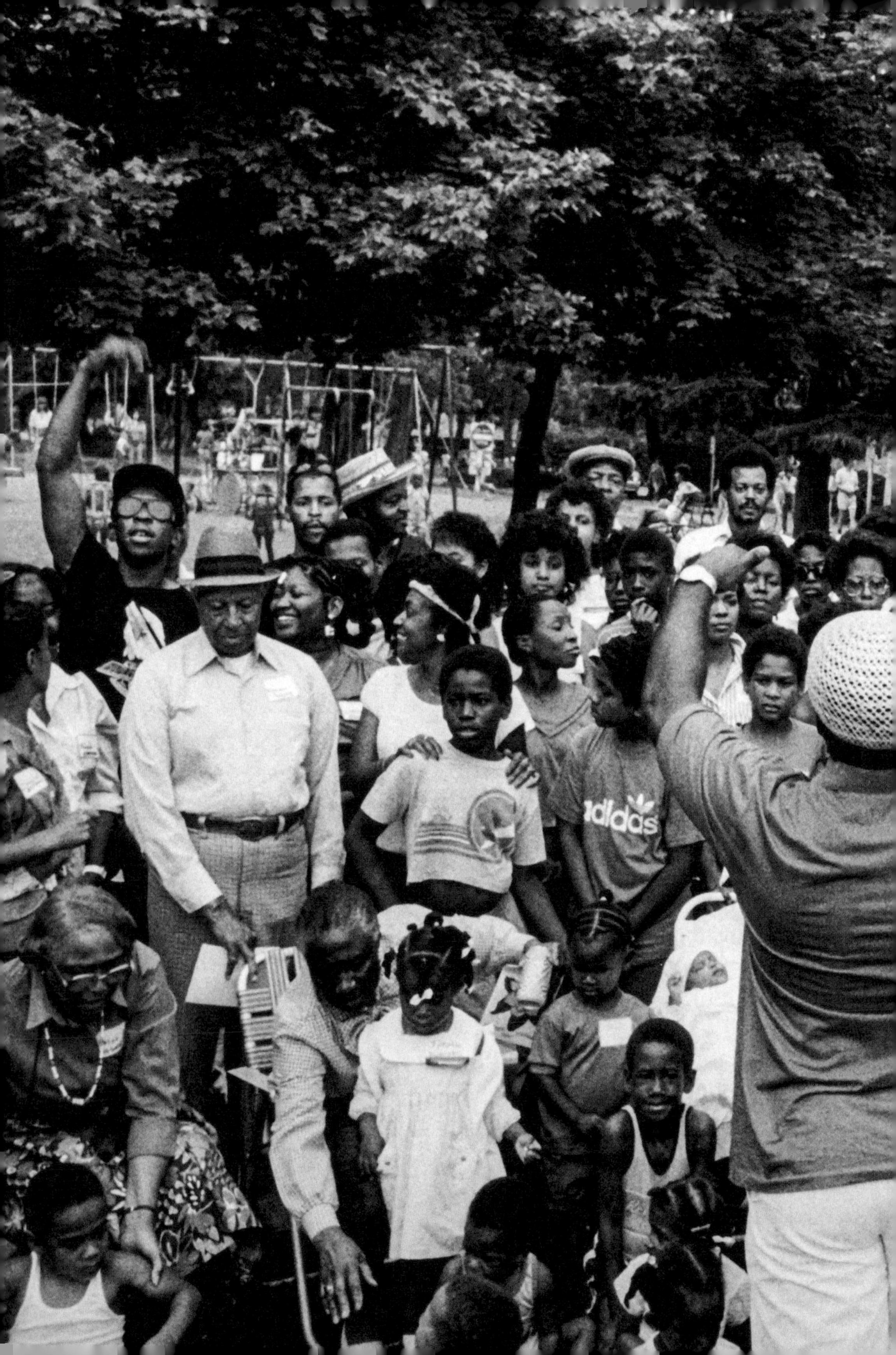
adidas

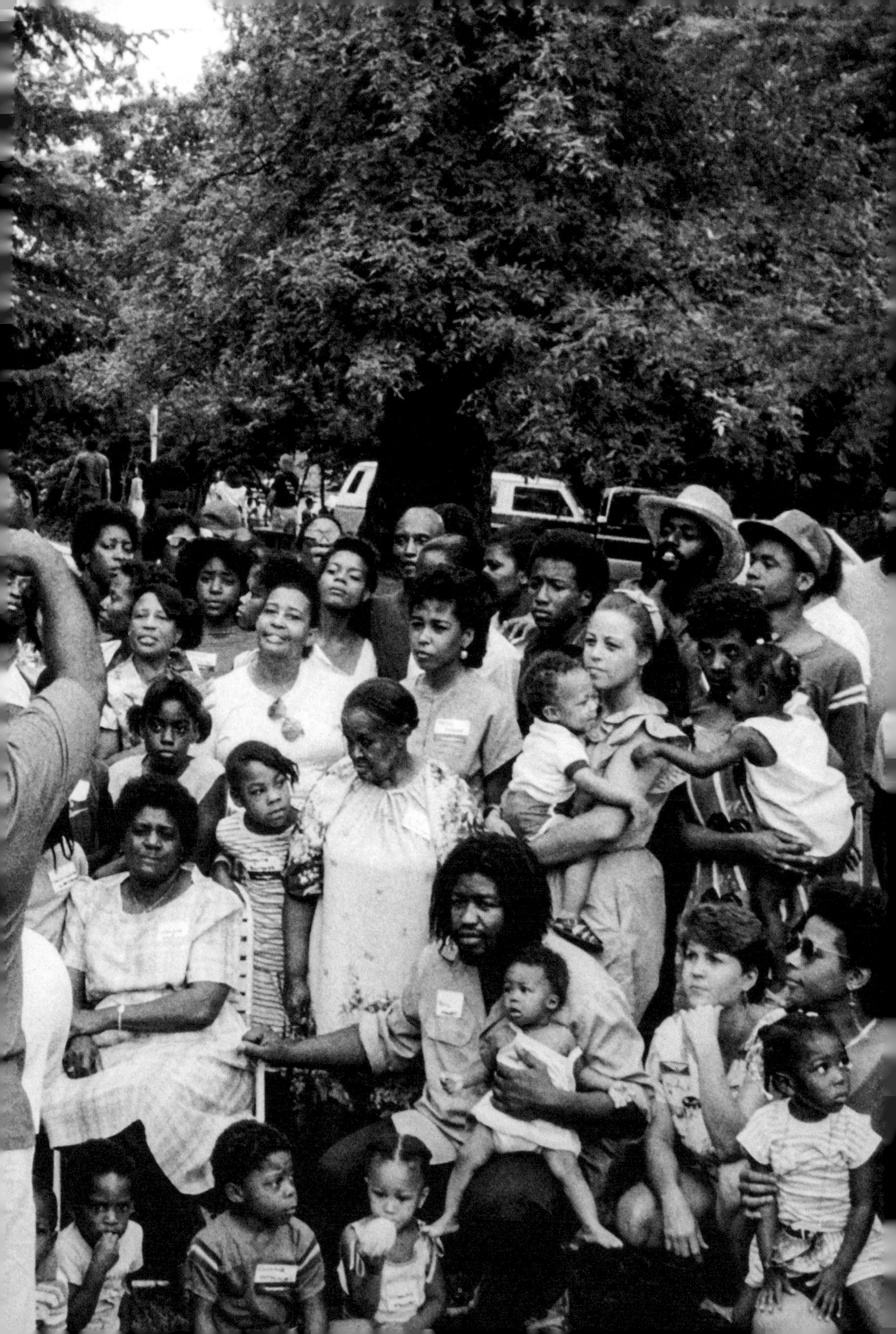

Carrie Mae Weems

Black Love
2014

Theaster Gates

CARRIE MAE WEEMS: I was telling someone the other day that I went to a Good Friday service, which I hadn't done in maybe ever in my life, I don't know. I walked in, and there was a little boy who was, maybe, eight, nine years old, holding it down, holding down the entire service—it was unbelievable—for about five songs.

I was rapt, but I was also thinking about all kinds of things—including James Baldwin. Bill T. Jones has organised an amazing James Baldwin festival that is going on this week [*applause*]—really extraordinary, and lots of artists are torn between being here and being there.

I thought about what Baldwin sacrificed. I thought about his engagements, about this willingness he had to give of himself that was so completely shaped by the church that he had been brought up in—a Pentecostal church, the same church I was brought up in—and that he was able to give extraordinary love and devotion, not only to his community and to the idea and concept of Black people, but really to America; that he really wanted to see a changed place.

There was a contradiction, though. Baldwin was able to give extraordinary love, extraordinary devotion, extraordinary commitments, but he had a very difficult time receiving it.

I see you, similarly, as a man who is able to give extraordinary love, who has decided that you are going to work in this way because it matters, and that it has deep, deep, deep, deep meaning for you. You're giving of yourself to a neighbourhood, to a city, to a state, to a nation. I wonder, to what extent, then, you are able to receive the love offered you.

THEASTER GATES: You know, love is a fuel, and it's not just output that I'm saturated in a net, in a Milky Way, of generosity and love—so much so. Love is so complicated. There has been the love that my mom gave, and then the love of my first love. I feel like I'm still feeding—feasting—on those generous moments. But it is true that there is a way in which we all make certain kinds of sacrifices relative to the things that we feel purposed for, and that, culturally, when you name that—like, if you become a 'this' or a 'that'—then people know that you're committed to this cause, and as a result, there are going to be certain kinds of love that you just won't receive. That ain't me. But I hope that being purposeful doesn't mean that you don't have the capacity to receive.

CMW: Or make space to receive.

TG: But I also think, like my art practice, I don't do anything every day—and so, I understand that I can carry love over seasons and make time to care deeply and go to work. That may not be that I make time to go to work nine to five, and then I receive love six to ten [*laughter*], and I'll feel neglected.

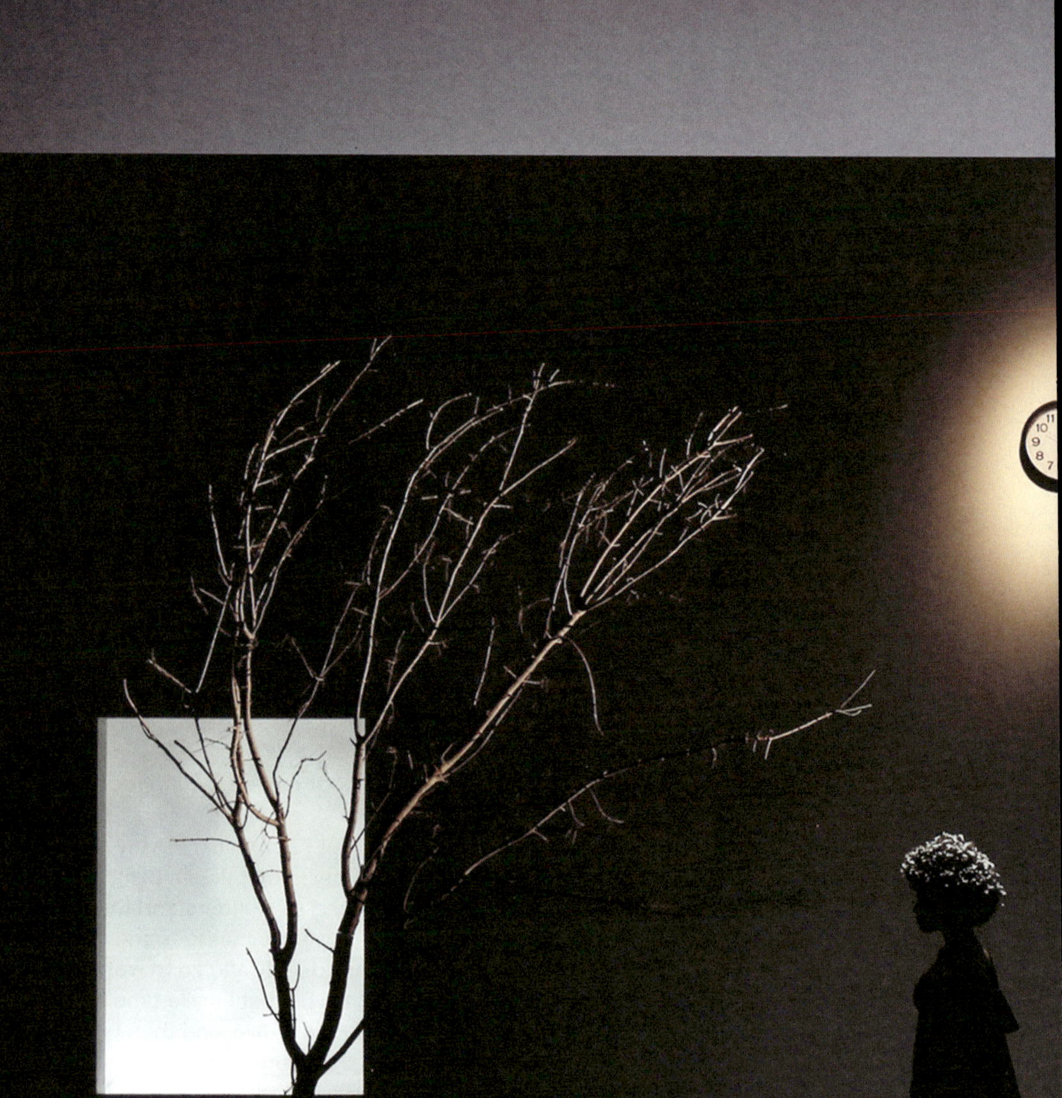

While We Can

While We Can

While we can
Consider the nature of what is and what will be
Consider the ebb and flow of tides,
The bliss of water ebbing at the shore
And the wonders of the world
While we can
Stand for something
Or fall for anything
Consider the slope of a woman's body
And the joy it brings without force

Consider the long days and the restless nights
The vast yearnings of the lonely and the lost
Consider the deep despair of mothers and fathers
When their children die much too soon,

While we can
Consider the meaning of meaning
Consider beauty and all its bounty
Consider the lack of consideration
And the meanness of broken spirits
While we can,
Consider fixing what is broken, damaged, or lost
Within ourselves and around us

While we can
Consider mood indigo, and a love supreme
Anchoring us to the rhythm of life, all its glory
and to a peace yet unknown

Consider the depth of the valley and the height of mountains
And protecting them before they are washed away

Consider saving yourself and some small portion of the world
And consider the wonders of the world
its extraordinary challenges
and consider the evidence of things unseen
the beauty of Grace
Its meaning and its purpose

While we can

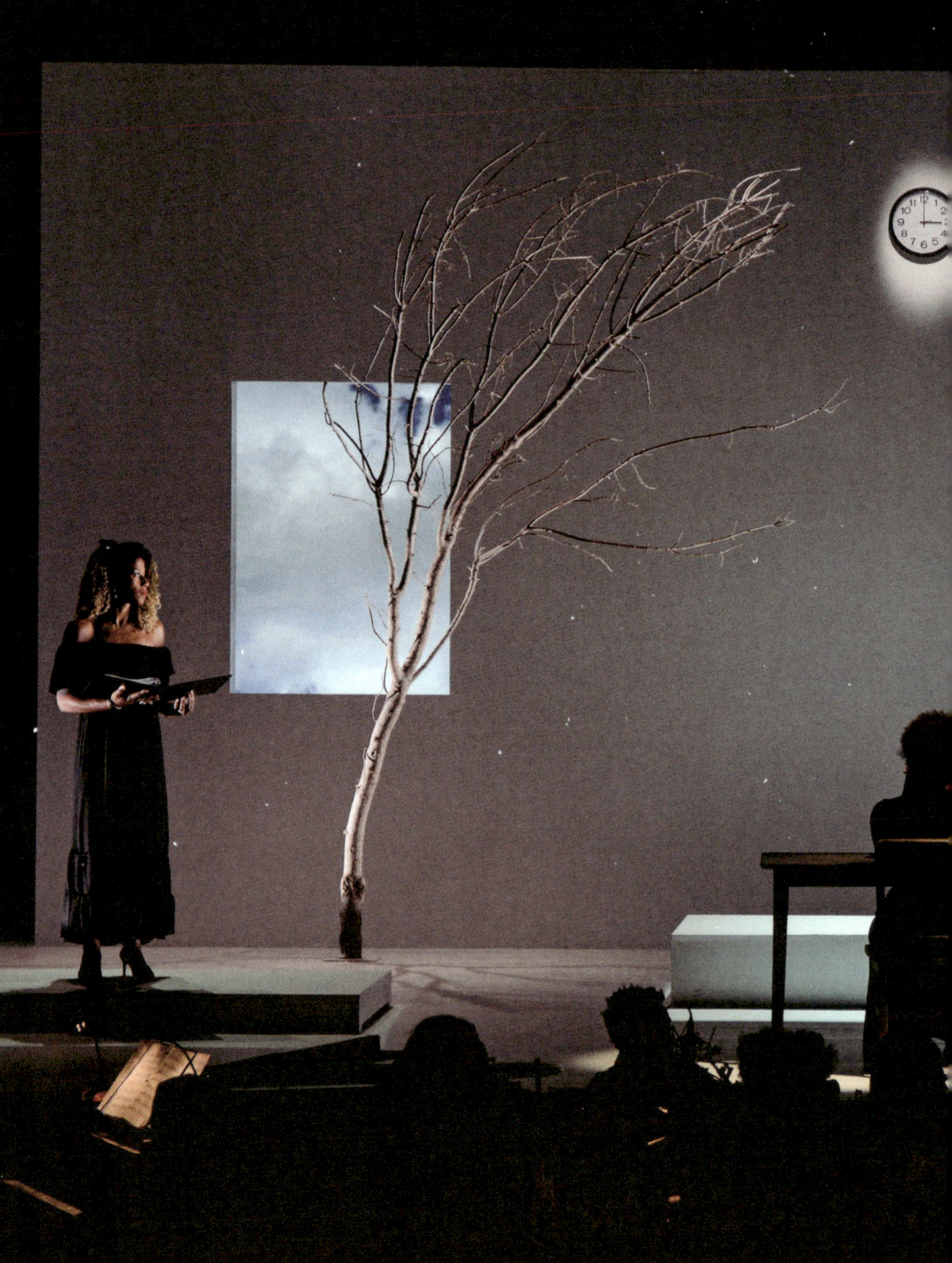

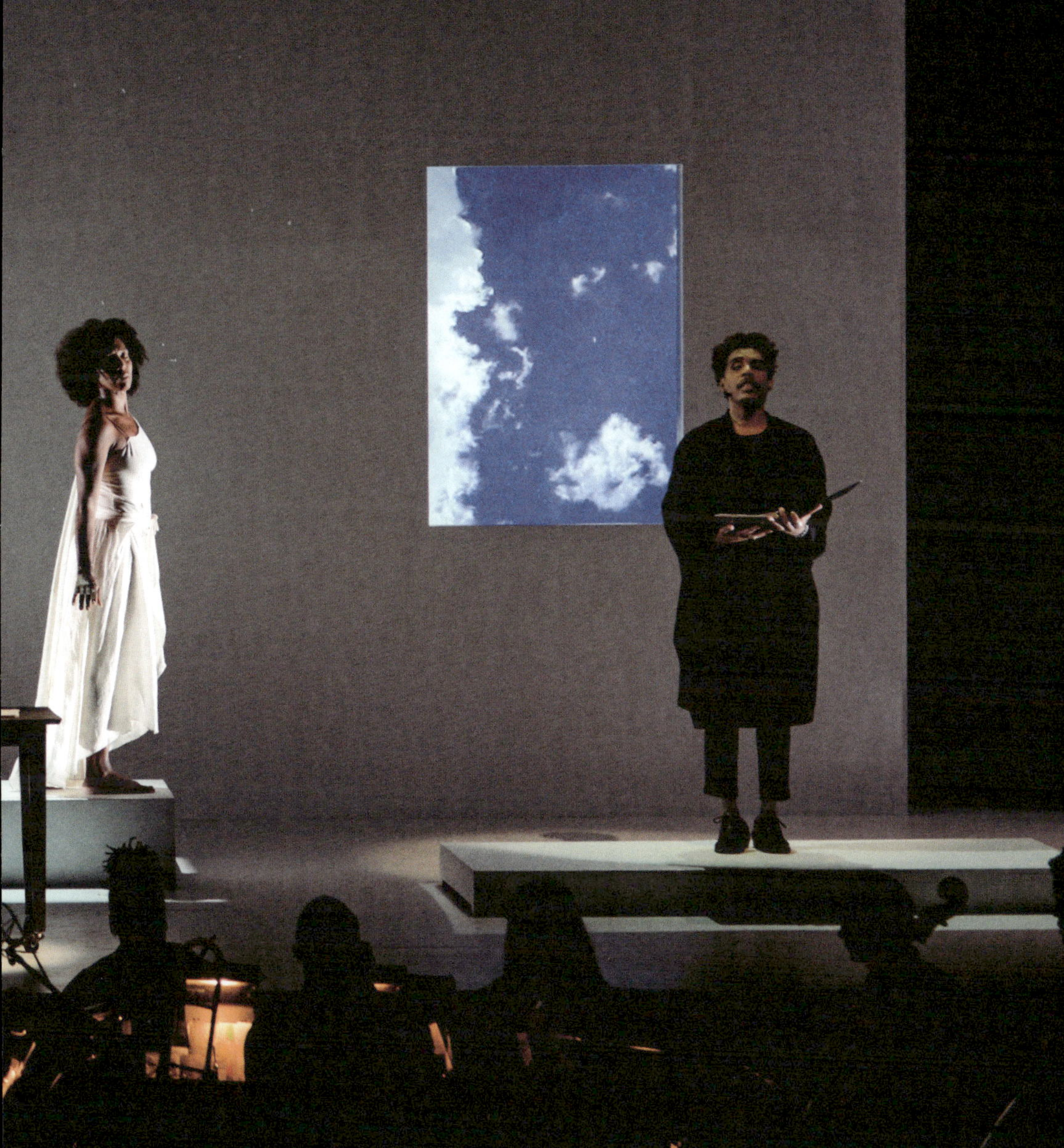

On Grace

Crystal Bridges Museum of American Art
'Carrie Mae Weems on Identity, Relationships & More'
Crystal Bridges Distinguished Speaker Lecture
8 December 2017

Ideas come to me—not really when I'm sitting at my desk, but when I'm lying in bed, that sort of twilight zone between being asleep and awake, or also simply in dreams, when you simply relax. You don't get it when you're trying; you only get it when you relinquish, when you give it up.

A few years ago I was talking to my students in my dream, trying to tell them how they should approach a project, how they should make a project about Obama, our first African American president, and what we might have to say to him in the midst of everything that was going on.

It was a perfectly laid-out dream; it had a beginning, a middle, and an end. It was remarkable! I remember waking up out of that dream, floating over to my computer, and writing to about thirty artists that day, saying, 'We need to thank this man; we have to thank him for his service to the nation.' And amazingly, it turned into a project.

By the end of the day, more than twenty-five artists had responded saying, 'Absolutely, yes.' The plan was to make a beautiful gift box and donate it to the Obama Presidential Library. I want him to know what artists were thinking about during his time in office.

A number of artists replied—musicians, composers, poets—and suddenly I had a wealth of material that became *Grace Notes: Reflections for Now*.

Then, a couple of months ago, I was in bed again, on a hot summer night, tossing and turning. *Grace Notes* had just been performed at the Kennedy Center, but I was still wrestling with the meaning of 'grace'. I fell asleep and had another extraordinary dream. I was standing by the seashore when I saw the formation of a tsunami, a gigantic black wall of water big enough to destroy the world. I started running so I could warn my friends that this wave was coming. And just as I started to run, I looked over, and there was Donald Trump leering at me! And I thought, 'What is he doing here in my dream?'

I run past him, shouting that a wave was coming. Then I saw Martin Puryear's great *Ladder for Booker T. Washington* leading up to the sky, and all of my family and friends were climbing it. They were all singing, 'We're climbing Jacob's Ladder', not as a hymn, but as a protest song. Fabulous!!

This dream rocked me out of my sleep, out of my bed, and I ran out onto the balcony, standing there and sobbing for a long time. But I had my answer. It was a truly extraordinary moment.

This *thing* is coming that threatens to submerge us, but what we have to hold on to, through it all, is our dignity and the core of our humanity—the core of our humanity, along with our insight and our determination to be true to ourselves. When all else fails, what we can hold fast to is our humanity, this unique ability to offer it as a gift to others; to offer it as a gift to strangers, as a gift even to those who are willing to take your life. To them you still offer your humanity, just as the Emanuel Nine offered it to Dylann Roof, who indeed took their lives.

As one of the parishioners said, 'I won't allow him to destroy my faith. *I forgive him.*'

This is the essence of grace.

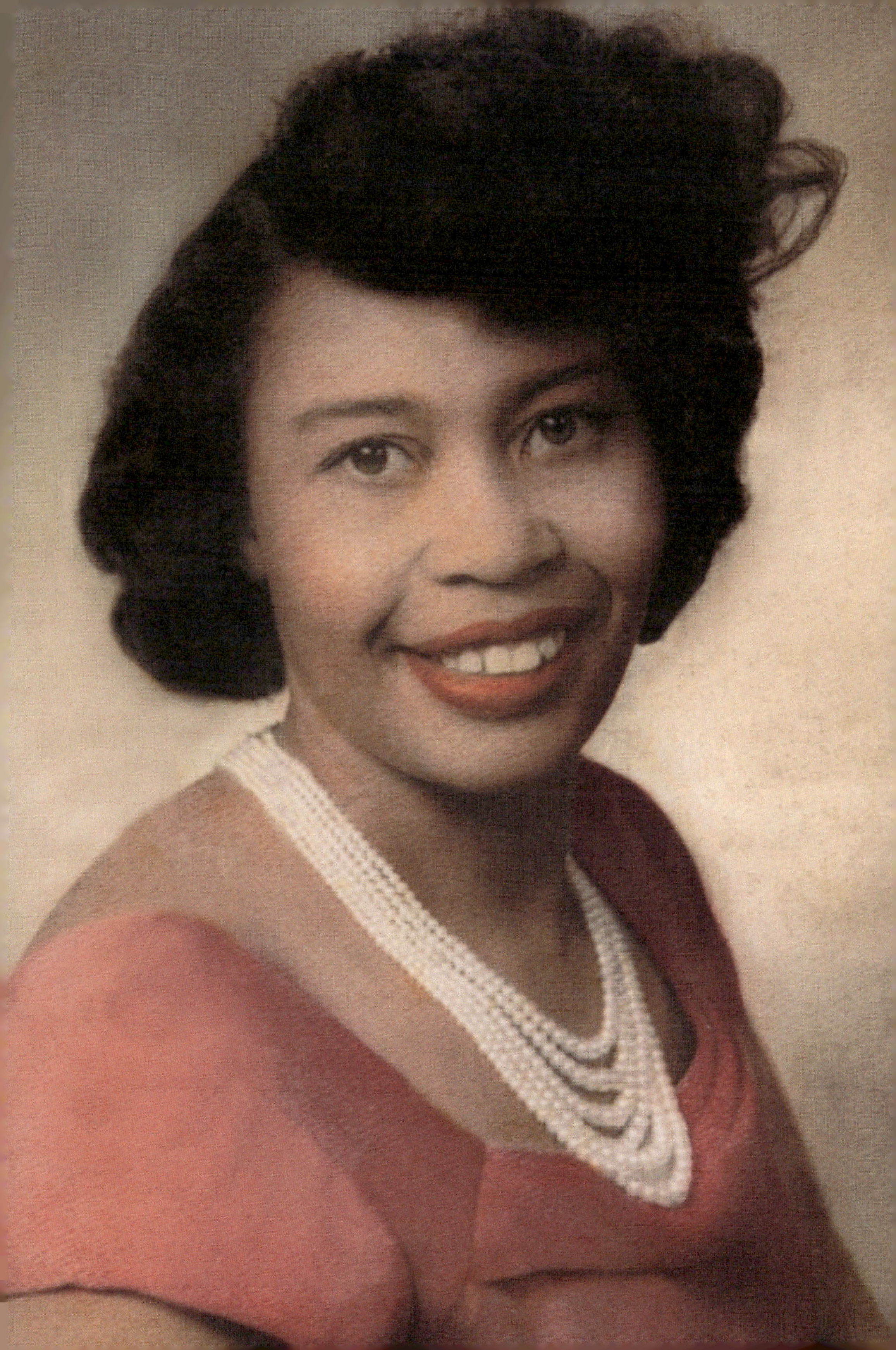

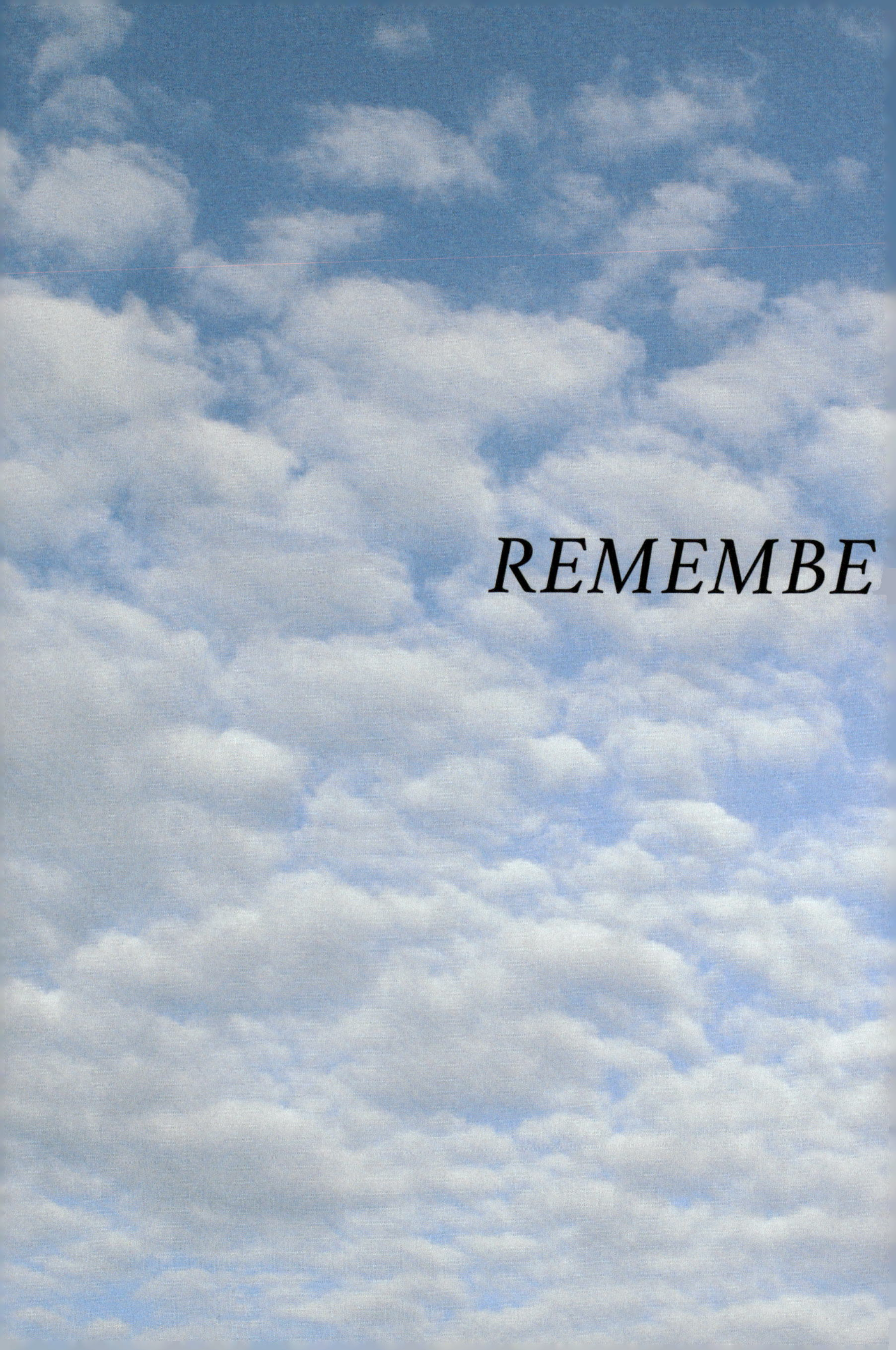

REMEMBE

TO DREAM

Reflections for Now

Afterword

Reflections for Now compiles for the first time Carrie Mae Weems's own words through a diverse and inspiring body of writing. Expanding on ideas raised through Weems's major solo exhibitions at Barbican, London (22 June–3 September 2023) and Kunstmuseum Basel (4 November 2023–17 March 2024), this publication gives insight into the creative mind and production conditions of one of the most significant contemporary artists at work today.

Spanning from the 1980s to the present, the texts collated in this publication explore the artist's long-lasting engagement with language, poetry, and music. Renowned for her singular approach to visual work and imagery, Weems has used words, captions, jokes, poems, prose, and spoken words in her multidisciplinary work across photography, film, performance, and installation. *Reflections for Now* celebrates the artist's own voice alongside the performative qualities of her artistic practice.

Challenging notions of identity through the lenses of memory, space, sound, and image, Weems's words—as personal as they are political—extend a practice that ponders the consequences of long-lasting histories of violence and oppression, as a means to engage multiple communities in a collective reformulation of a shared present.

This constant scrutiny of the past, and a sense of hope and responsibility towards the future, are key in Weems's practice. As she states in relation to the artistic community: 'I am always aware of the people that widened the path for me so that I can work a little easier... and now I have to use my skin and my body to push for an even wider path so that another group of young artists who are coming behind me can work and live, be and produce more easily than ever before.'

Featuring a selection of material including poems and texts emanating from her films, sound works, and performances alongside transcripts of conversations, statements, and lectures, *Reflections for Now* highlights the unique voice of an artist that throughout her career has constantly anticipated her own time. Photographs, installation views, and illustrations from Weems's personal archives were chosen and arranged by the artist like a visual essay interweaving the different forms of writing.

Although each piece was conceived in different circumstances, their arrangement in a sequence brings connections that work together like a score of untold histories. 'It's about encounters and collisions. A meander of words,' Weems says.

Chronicling a unique time in the history of the United States, Weems brings to the page the lyrical and introspective quality of her social thinking. A meditation on living, loving, and mourning, *Reflections for Now* presents the opportunity to engage deeply with Weems's vital contribution to the arts and celebrates the long-overdue recognition of her visionary work in Europe.

When the idea for this book first arose, we wanted to make a publication that would function as a libretto for Weems's exhibitions in London and Basel, echoing the artist's operatic strategies of exhibition-making. For their crucial support and brilliant work in helping us bring this idea to life, we would like to thank Megan King and Amy Kozlowski of Carrie Mae Weems's studio. Our heartfelt thanks are also extended to Jack Shainman, Barbara Thumm, and their respective gallery teams for their complete commitment to the excellence of this book and its associated exhibitions.

As Weems has often remarked, reciprocal influence among artists and creatives is key to the development of the arts. We would like to thank the voices that appear in conversation in this book, including Dawoud Bey, Terence Nance, Paul D. Miller (aka DJ Spooky), Nona Hendryx, Hans Ulrich Obrist, and Theaster Gates, for their generosity in allowing their reflections to be part of these pages.

In this regard, we would like to thank the publications and journals which first featured some of the texts in this book. We are indebted to the pioneering work of *BOMB Magazine*; UTA Artist Space; Art21; *The Brooklyn Rail*; *Art in America*; and MIT Press. We are also grateful to the following institutions for their work in hosting Weems's lectures and conversations: Portland Art Museum (Portland, OR); Crystal Bridges Museum of American Art (Bentonville, AR); National Museum of Women in the Arts (Washington, DC); the Solomon R. Guggenheim Museum (New York City, NY); and Art Basel, particularly Emily Butler, and Serpentine Galleries.

Our foremost thanks go to those at publisher Hatje Cantz who made this project possible: Nicola von Velsen, for her immediate support from the outset, and Adam Jackman and Richard Hagemann for their care, flexibility, and attention to detail. We would also like to express deep gratitude towards Rupert Jenkins, Julie Wolf, and Irene Schaudies for their endless patience and meticulous work in copy-editing this book.

Our ultimate and deepest thanks go to Carrie Mae Weems, for her immense generosity in letting us gather these writings, the trust granted to us to propose this book, and the high spirit of her work that has guided the inception and making of these pages.

The Editors

Contributors

Nona Hendryx

Nona Hendryx is an African American multidisciplinary artist, passionate about music, visual art, and technology. Known for being one third of the music trio Labelle, Hendryx is an Ambassador for Artistry in Music for Berklee College of Music and Boston Conservatory. Hendryx has curated a celebration of Grace Jones at the Park Avenue Armory and an Afrofuturism theatrical performance for the Metropolitan Museum of Art's Temple of Dendur, *Nona Hendryx and Disciples of Sun Ra in the Temple*, among others. Currently she is developing *Dream Machine*, an immersive experience which includes artificial intelligence, augmented reality, and virtual reality to premier in 2024.

DJ Spooky

Paul D. Miller, aka DJ Spooky, is a composer, multimedia artist, and writer whose work blends genres, global culture, and environmental and social issues. Miller has collaborated with an array of recording artists. His 2018 album, *DJ Spooky Presents: Phantom Dancehall*, debuted at #3 on Billboard Reggae. He was the inaugural artist-in-residency at the Metropolitan Museum of Art's The Met Reframed (2012–13). Miller's artwork has appeared in the Whitney Biennial, The Venice Biennial for Architecture, and the Art Basel/Miami fair, among others. His books include the award-winning *Rhythm Science* (2004), *Sound Unbound* (2008), and *The Imaginary App* (2014). His writings have been published by *The Village Voice, The Source*, and *Artforum*. He was the first founding executive editor of *Origin Magazine*.

Dawoud Bey
Dawoud Bey is an American artist, photographer, and educator making work about histories of and people from marginalised communities. Since his initial photographic series, *Harlem, USA* (1975), he has been exhibited at the Art Institute of Chicago, the Barbican Centre, and National Gallery of Art, among others. His recent retrospective exhibition, *Dawoud Bey: An American Project* showed at San Francisco Museum of Modern Art, the Whitney Museum of American Art, the High Museum of Art, and the Museum of Fine Arts Houston. Besides monographic publications, including *Seeing Deeply* (2017) and *Street Portraits* (2021), his critical writings on contemporary art and photography have appeared in a wide range of publications. A MacArthur Fellow, Bey is a professor and Distinguished Artist at Columbia College Chicago, where he has taught since 1998.

Theaster Gates
Theaster Gates is an artist based in Chicago. His work focuses on space theory and land development, sculpture and performance. His projects attempt to instigate the creation of cultural communities by acting as catalysts for social engagement, political and spatial change. Gates has exhibited and performed at Palais de Tokyo, Paris; Kunstmuseum Basel, Switzerland; National Gallery of Art, Washington DC; Whitechapel Gallery, London; and dOCUMENTA (13), Kassel, among others. He was awarded the Artes Mundi 6 prize, the Nasher Prize for Sculpture, and was recipient of the Légion d'Honneur. Gates is a professor at the University of Chicago in the Department of Visual Arts, and serves as the Senior Advisor for Cultural Innovation and Advisor to the Dean.

Hans Ulrich Obrist
Hans Ulrich Obrist is Artistic Director of the Serpentine in London, and Senior Advisor at LUMA Arles. Prior to this, he was the Curator of the Musée d'Art Moderne de la Ville de Paris. Since his first show *World Soup: Küchenausstellung* (The Kitchen Show) in 1991, he has curated more than 350 shows. Obrist's recent publications include *Ways of Curating* (2015), *The Age of Earthquakes* (2015), *Lives of the Artists, Lives of the Architects* (2015), *Mondialité* (2017), *Somewhere Totally Else* (2018), *The Athens Dialogues* (2018), *Maria Lassnig: Letters* (2020), *Entrevistas Brasileiras: Volume 2* (2020), and *140 Ideas for Planet Earth* (2021).

Terence Nance
Terence Nance is an artist, musician, and filmmaker. He wrote, directed, scored, and starred in his first feature film, *An Oversimplification of Her Beauty* (2012). He was a Guggenheim Fellow in 2014 and debuted his Peabody Award-winning television series *Random Acts of Flyness* on HBO in 2018. Nance released his first EP, *Things I Never Had* (2020) under the name Terence Etc. With filmmakers Jenn Nkiru, Bradford Young, Nanette Nelms, and Mishka Brown he formed The Ummah Chroma Creative Partners—a directors' collective and production company, who released *Killing in Thy Name* in collaboration with Rage Against the Machine in 2021. Following the 2022 releases of *Random Acts of Flyness Program II* and his debut album, *Vortex*, Nance is currently working on healing, curiosity, and inter-dimensionality.

Image Captions

Back cover: *The Glenstone*, 2018

p. 3 *Missing Link, Happiness,* from the series *The Louisiana Project*, 2003

p. 4 *Listening Devices*, 2013–14

pp. 6–7 *Untitled (See No Evil, Hear No Evil, Speak No Evil)*, 1995

pp. 8–9 *Untitled (Moab)*, 2021

pp. 10–11 *The Remains of What Is Left Behind*, 2022

pp. 12–13 Detail from *Cyclorama—The Shape of Things, A Video in 7 Parts*, 2021. Installation view from Park Avenue Armory, New York ©Carrie Mae Weems

p. 17 *My Father, Myrlie Weems*, 1984

pp. 20–1 *A Woman Observes, from the series Constructing History*, 2008

pp. 22–3 Detail from *Down Here Below*, 2019

pp. 24–5 *The Considered, See Bergman*, 2012

p. 31 *Scenes & Take (Great Expectations), from the series Scenes & Take*, 2016

p. 37 *By Any Means Necessary,* from the series *And 22 Million Very Tired and Very Angry People*, 1991–2022

pp. 38–9 *Who, What, When, Where*, 1998

pp. 40–1 *Tobacco Worker (Father); Tobacco Worker (Son),* from the series *Dreaming in Cuba*, 2001

p. 45 *Julisa,* from the series *People in Conditions*, 2021

pp. 50–1 *Cyclorama—The Shape of Things, A Video in 7 Parts*, 2021. Installation view from Park Avenue Armory, New York ©Carrie Mae Weems

pp. 52–3 Detail from *Cyclorama—The Shape of Things, A Video in 7 Parts*, 2021. Installation view from Park Avenue Armory, New York ©Carrie Mae Weems

p. 57 *Untitled (Apache Motel, Moab)*, 2021

p. 58–9 Still from 2-channel video *Cornered*, 2012

pp. 60–1 *Untitled (Birmingham Blue)*, 2020

pp. 62–3 *A History of Violence*, 2018

pp. 68–9 *George Floyd Memorial, Minneapolis–St. Paul*, MN, 2021

pp. 70–1 Still from *People of a Darker Hue*, 2016

p. 72 Detail from *Cyclorama—The Shape of Things, A Video in 7 Parts*, 2021. Installation view from Park Avenue Armory, New York ©Carrie Mae Weems

p. 73 Detail from *It's Over—A Diorama*, 2021. Installation view from Park Avenue Armory, New York ©Carrie Mae Weems

p. 79 *Thoughts on Marriage*, 1989

p. 80 *Museum of Fine Arts, Boston,* from the series *Museums*, 2006

p. 81 *British Museum,* from the series *Museums*, 2006

p. 82 *Missing Monument,* from the series *Monuments*, 2000

p. 83 *Echoes for Marian*, 2014

pp. 84–5 *Painting the Town # 7,* from the series *Painting the Town*, 2021

p. 89 Detail of *The North Star*, 2022

pp. 90–1 *Che*, 2018

pp. 92–3 Detail from *Cyclorama—The Shape of Things, A Video in 7 Parts*, 2021. Installation view from Park Avenue Armory, New York ©Carrie Mae Weems

p. 100 *Pondering Your Remains,* from the series *The Louisiana Project*, 2003

p. 101 *A Single's Waltz in Time,* from the series *The Louisiana Project*, 2003

p. 102–3 *The Hampton Project*, 2002. Installation view from Württembergischer Kunstverein Stuttgart ©Hans D. Christ

p. 111 *The Impossible, See Magritte*, from the series *Essay on Equivalents*, 2012

p. 112–13 *The Destroyed, See Mendieta, Legs*, from the series *Essay on Equivalents*, 2012

p. 123 *Nona as the Future*, Kennedy Center Parade, 2019

pp. 124–5 *Ode to Affirmative Action*, 1989

pp. 126–7 *He thought her a lovely girl...*, 1987

pp. 132–3 *Untitled (A Man Stands in the Pulpit); Untitled (House Rules),* from the series *S.E. San Diego*, 1983–5

pp. 134–5 Detail from *Cyclorama—The Shape of Things, A Video in 7 Parts*, 2021. Installation view from Park Avenue Armory, New York ©Carrie Mae Weems

p. 145 Vera Weems and children with evicted Arkansas sharecroppers, January 1936. Photographer: John Vachon. *Untitled photo, possibly related to: Parkin (vicinity), Arkansas. The families of evicted sharecroppers of the Dibble plantation. They were legally evicted the week of January 12, 1936, the plantation having charged that by membership in the Southern Tenant Farmers' Union they were engaging in a conspiracy to retain their homes; this contention granted by the court, the eviction, though at the point of a gun, was quite legal. The pictures were taken just after the evictions before they were moved into the tent colony they later enjoyed.* Retrieved from the Library of Congress

pp. 146–7 *Welcome Home,* from the series *Family Pictures and Stories*, 1978–84

pp. 148–9 *Polk Family Reunion,* from the series *Family Pictures and Stories*, 1978–84

pp. 152–3, 156–7 *Grace Notes: Reflections for Now*, 2016 ©William Struhs

p. 161 *My Mother, Carrie Polk*

pp. 162–3 *Remember to Dream*, 2020

Notes

In reproducing the texts contained in this publication, every effort was made to credit the copyright holders. In those instances where the correct rights holder could not be located, notwithstanding due diligence, Barbican and Kunstmuseum Basel request that any information concerning such rights holders be forwarded in order for corrections to be made in any subsequent editions.

Carrie Mae Weems + Dawoud Bey
pp. 26–30
This interview, *Carrie Mae Weems by Dawoud Bey*, was commissioned by and first published in *BOMB Magazine* No. 108, Summer 2009. © *BOMB Magazine*, New Art Publications, and its Contributors. All rights reserved. The BOMB Digital Archive can be viewed at www.bombmagazine.org.

Becoming an Artist:
Carrie Mae Weems + Terence Nance
pp. 86–8
This is an abridged version of a conversation which took place between Carrie Mae Weems, and Terence Nance for UTA Artist Space's series 'DREAMWEAVERS: In / Conversation' (2019). Directed by Sing J. Lee and Sylvia Zakhary, produced in collaboration with Cultural Council, Swizz Beatz, Lyft Entertainment, and presented by *W Magazine*, the text appears here by permission of Carrie Mae Weems and Terence Nance.

Appropriation and Influence
pp. 106–10
Abridged version of 'Compassion', originally published as part of *Art21: Art in the Twenty-First Century 5* (New York: Art21, Inc., 2009). It appears here courtesy of Art 21 and Carrie Mae Weems.

On Music, Machinery, and Meeting:
Carrie Mae Weems + DJ Spooky,
Nona Hendryx, Hans Ulrich Obrist
pp. 114–22
The conversation between Carrie Mae Weems and Paul D. Miller, aka DJ Spooky, was commissioned by *The Brooklyn Rail* as part of their series 'The-New-Social-Environment #269' and took place in 2021. This excerpt appears here by permission of Carrie Mae Weems and Paul D. Miller.

Originally titled 'Premiere: Carrie Mae Weems, Nona Hendryx, and Hans Ulrich Obrist', this discussion was held as part of Art Basel Miami Beach's Conversations programme, 2022 , as was the following discussion with Hans Ulrich Obrist. (Watch them on artbasel.com.) Both conversations appear here as an excerpt courtesy of Art Basel, Emily Butler (Art Basel Conversations Curator), Carrie Mae Weems, Nona Hendryx, Hans Ulrich Obrist, and Serpentine Galleries.

Home
pp. 128–31
This text was first published as 'Home (As Told to Faye Hirsch)' in *Art in America*, April 2014, 34–35. It appears here courtesy of Carrie Mae Weems.

Family Stories
pp. 136–44
'Family Stories' was originally published in *Blasted Allegories: An Anthology of Writings by Contemporary Artists*, edited by Brian Wallis (Cambridge: MIT Press, 1987, p. 19). It is reproduced here courtesy of Carrie Mae Weems.

Acknowledgements

I sincerely hope that you, the reader, haven't wasted too much of your time wandering through the messy maze of my mind, my half-baked ideas, my incoherent thoughts, scattered musings, and poor use of the King's English. Like a song, much of the text printed here was meant to be heard not written, so much has been lost in translation from sound to sight.

But should you find that you have indeed arrived on this page, please consider this: at the core of all these words is simply a woman in search of ways to disrupt the horrors that stem from the corruption born of power and privilege.

For the space given to share my humble thoughts and images, I wish to thank curators Florence Ostende and Maja Wismer for their shared vision in imagining this publication and exhibition at their respective institutions.

To Rupert Jenkins for his assistance in shaping the text for publication, and the extraordinary design team Paco Lacasta and Paloma Castellanos for this intelligently conceived and beautifully designed publication.

Finally, my deepest gratitude to the relentlessly insightful curatorial assistant Amber Li and the brilliant curator Raúl Muñoz de la Vega, who embraced this project as a labour of love, and without whom this publication simply would not have been possible.

This book is dedicated to those who have endured the systemic violence directed against them and who still stand.

Carrie Mae Weems
April 2023

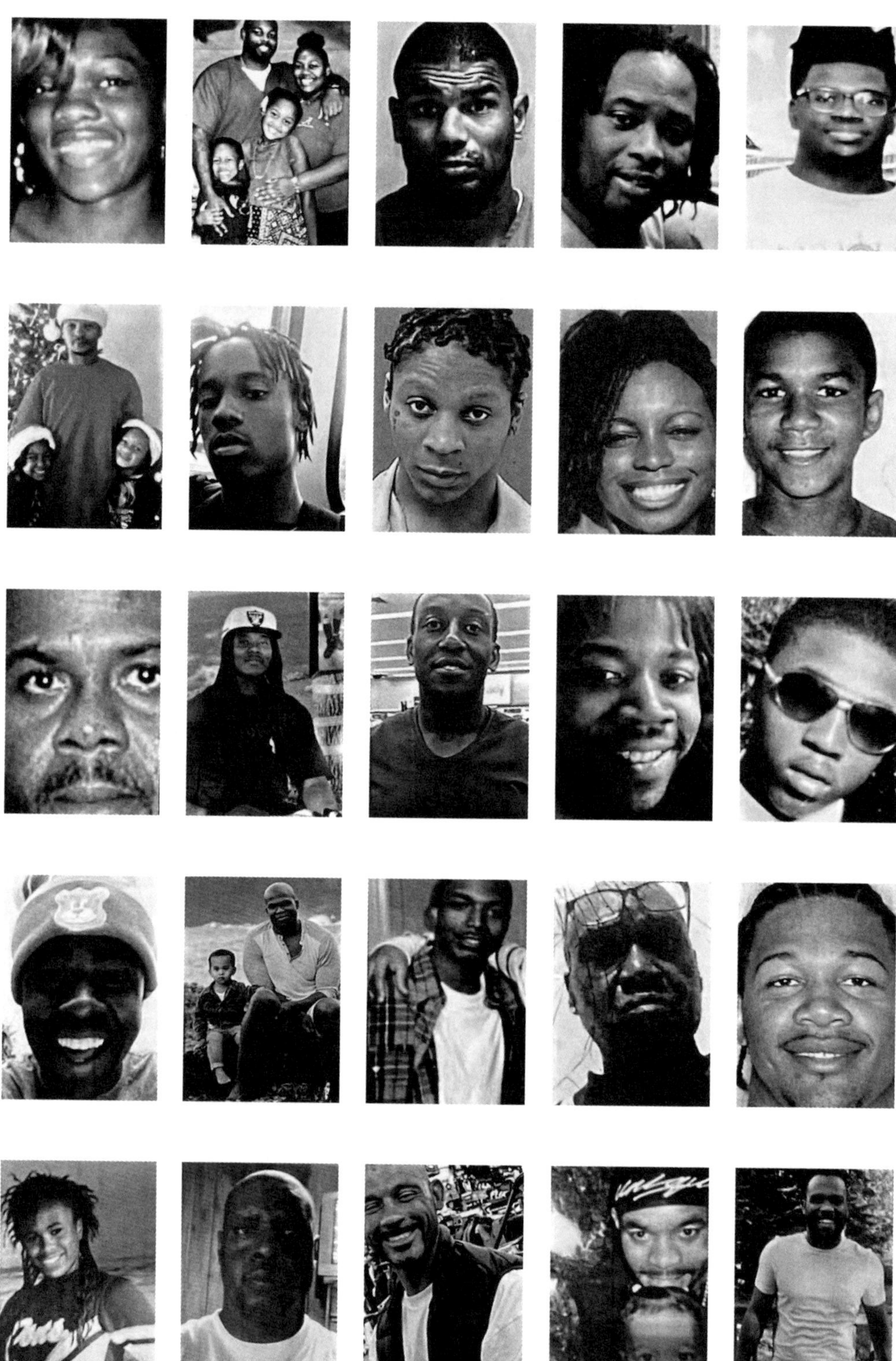

In Loving Memory

Aaron Bailey / Abdul Kamal / Adam Ardett Madison / Adam Trammell / Ahmaud Arbery / Akai Gurley / Albert Joseph Davis / Alexander Jamar Marion / Alexia Christian / Alfred Olango / Allan Feliz / Allen Desdunes / Alonzo Smith / Alteria Woods / Alton Sterling / Andre Gladen / Andre Horton / Andre Larone Murphy Sr. / Andre Maurice Hill / Andrew Depeiza / Anesson Joseph / Anthony Antonio Ford / Anthony Ashford / Anthony Bartley / Anthony Dwayne Harris / Anthony Hill / Anthony Jones / Anthony Marcell Green / Antone G. Black Jr. / Antonio Garcia Jr. / Antonio Johnson / Antronie Scott / Antwon Rose Jr. / Antwun Shumpert / Aries Clark / Armando Frank / Artago Damon Howard / Arteair Porter / Arther McAfee Jr. / Arthur R. Williams Jr. / Arthur Walton Jr. / Arvel Douglas Williams / Ashtian Barnes / Askari Roberts / Asshams Pharoah Manley / Atatiana Jefferson / Balantine Mbegbu / Barry Gedeus / Bennie Branch / Bennie Lee Tignor / Bettie Jones / Bill Jackson / Bishar Hassan / Bobby Gross / Botham Jean / Brandon Jones / Brandon Webster / Brendon Glenn / Breonna Taylor / Brian Keith Day / Brian Easley / Brian Pickett / Briatay McDuffie / Byron Williams / Calin Roquemore / Calvin Toney / Calvon A. Reid / Cameron Hall / Cameron Tillman / Cedric Stanley / Cedrick Chatman / Chad Robertson / Chance David Baker / Channara Tom Pheap / Charleena Chavon Lyles / Charles A. Baker Jr. / Charles David Robinson / Charles K. Goodridge / Charles Roundtree Jr. / Charlin Charles / Charly Leundeu Keunang / Che' Taylor / Chester Jenkins / Chinedu Okobi / Chris McKinley / Christian Taylor / Christopher Alexander Okamoto / Christopher J. Davis / Christopher Jones / Christopher Kalonji / Christopher McCorvey / Christopher Sowell / Christopher Wade / Christopher Whitfield / Cimarron Lamar Lamb / Cindreia Europe / Clifton Armstrong / Clinton Roebexar Allen / Corey Jones / Corey Levert Tanner / Corey Mobley / Cornelius Brown / Cortez Washington / Craig Demps / Cynthia Fields / D'Angelo Reyes Stallworth / D'ettrick Griffin / Dainell Simmons / Dajuan Graham / Dalvin Hollins / Damian Daniels / Danny Thomas / Danny Washington / Dante Parker / Darion Baker / Darrell Banks / Darrell Gatewood / Darrell Lawrence Brown / Darrien Nathaniel Hunt / Darrion Barnhill / Darrius Stewart / Daryll Blair / Dason Peters / Daunte Wright / Daverion Kinard / David Andre Scott / David Felix / David Jones / David Joseph / David McAtee / Daviri Robertson / DeAndre Lloyd Starks / Deaundre Phillips / Deborah Danner / Deion Fludd / Dejuan Guillory / Delrawn Small / Dennis Grigsby / Dennis Plowden / Denzel Brown / Deomain Hayman / DeOntre L. Dorsey / Deravis Caine Rogers / DeRicco Devante Holden / Devin Howell / DeWayne Watkins / Dewboy Lister / Dion Johnson / Dominic Hutchinson / Dominique Clayton / Dominique Franklin Jr. / Dominique Silva / Donald Ivy / Donnell Thompson / Donnie Sanders / Donovan Thomas / Dreasjon Reed / Dustin Keith Glover / Dylan Samuel-Peters / Dyzhawn L. Perkins / Elijah Glay / Elijah McClain / Emantic Fitzgerald Bradford Jr. / Emanuel Jean-Baptiste / Eric Garner / Eric Harris / Eric Reason / Eric Ricks / Ernest Satterwhite / Ervin Edwards / Eugene Williams / Euree Lee Martin / Ezell Ford / Felix Kumi / Frank Shephard / Fred Bradford Jr. / Fred Brown / Freddie Blue / Freddie Carlos Gray Jr. / Gamel Antonio Brown / George Floyd / George Kent Harvey / George Mann / George Robinson / George V. King / Geraldine Townsend / Giovonn Joesph-McDade / Gregory Lewis Towns Jr. / Hallis Kinsey / Herbert Gilbert / Howard Wallace Bowe Jr. / India Beaty / India Kager / Iretha Lilly / Isaiah Lewis / Isaiah Tucker / Jacob Servais / Jacorey Calhoun / Jamar Clark / James Bauduy / James Carney III / James Leatherwood / Janisha Fonville / Jaquyn O'Neill Light / Jason Moland / Jayvis Benjamin / Jean Pedro Pierre / Jeffery B. Lilly Jr. / Jeffrey Ragland / Jenoah Donald / Jerame C. Reid / Jeremey Lake / Jeremy Lett / Jeremy McDole / Jermaine Darden / Jermaine McBean / Jerome Keith Allen / Jerry Brown / Jesse J. Quinton / Jessica Nelson-Williams / Jimmie Montel Sanders / Jimmy Atchison / Joel Acevedo / John Bailon / John Crawford / John T. Wilson III / Jonathan A. Ferrell / Jonathan Price / Jonathan Sanders

/ Jordan Baker / Jordan Edwards / Jordan Michael Griffin / Josef Richardson / Joseph Curtis Mann / Joshua Johnson / Joshua Terrell Crawford / Joshua Wayne Harvey / JR Williams / Juan Markee Jones / Juan May / Julian Dawkins / Julian Edward Roosevelt Lewis / Julius Graves / Junior Prosper / Justin Griffin / Kaldrick Donald / Kanisha Nicole Fuller / Keara Crowder / Keeven Robinson / Kelta O'Neil / Keith Childress / Keith Dutree Collins / Keith Harrison McLeod / Kendall Alexander / Kendra Diggs / Kendrell Antron Watkins / Kendrick Brown / Kenneth Johnson / Keoisha L. Hill / Kevin Bajoie / Kevin Bruce Mason / Kevin Hicks / Kevin Higgenbotham / Kevin L. Duncan / Kevin Leroy Beasley Jr. / Kevin Matthews / Kionte DeShaun Spencer / Korryn Gaines / Kris Jackson / Kurt Andras Reinhold / Kwame Jones / La'Mello Parker / Lajuana Phillips / Lamont Perry / Lamontez Jones / Lana Morris / Landon Nobles / Laquan McDonald / Larry Eugene Jackson Jr. / Larry Jackson Jr. / Lashano J. Gilbert / Lavall Hall / Lavon King / Lawrence Hawkins / Leroy Browning / Leslie Sapp III / Levon Leroy Love / Levonia Riggins / Lindani Myeni / Lionel Gibson / Lionel Morris / Lorenzo Antoine Cruz / Mahlon Edward Summerour / Manuel Elijah Ellis / Marc Brandon Davis / Marcellis Stinnette / Marcus McVae / Marcus-David L. Peters / Mario Clark / Mario Dantoni Bass / Mark Anthony Blocker / Mark Roshawn Adkins / Marlon Brown / Marlon Horton / Marlon Lewis / Marlon S. Woodstock / Marquez Warren / Marquise Jones / Marshall Miles / Marzues Scott / Maurice Holly / Maurice S. Gordon / Meagan Hockaday / Melvin Watkins / Micah Anthony Key / Michael 'Blue' Thomas / Michael Brent Charles Ramos / Michael Brown Jr. / Michael Dean / Michael Eugene Wilson Jr. / Michael Noel / Michael Ricardo Minor / Michael Wilson / Mickel Erich Lewis / Miguel Espinal / Miriam Carey / Montez Dewanye Hambric / Montrell Moss / Muhammad Abdul Muhaymin / Mya Shawatza Hall / Mychael Johnson / Naeschylus Vinzant / Nana Adomako / Natasha McKenna / Nathaniel Harris Pickett / Nicholas Walker / Norman Cooper / Oliver Jarrod Gregoire / Ollie Lee Brooks / O'Shae Terry / Pamela Shantay Turner / Paterson Brown Jr. / Patricia Spivey / Patrick Lynn Warren / Paul Gaston / Paul O'Neal / Peter Gaines / Peter John / Philando Castile / Phillip Gregory White / Quanice Hayes / Quintine Barksdale / Quintonio LeGrier / Raphael Thomas / Rashaun Washington / Raynard Burton / Rayshard Scales / Rayshaun Cole / Reginald L. Moore Sr. / Reginald Williams Jr. / Richard Gregory Davis / Richard Perkins / Ricky Deangelo Hinkle / Ritchie Lee Harbison / Robert D'Lon Harris / Robert Dentmond / Robert Lawrence White / Roderick Ronall Taylor / Ronell Foster / Ronnie Ledesma Jr. / Ross Anthony / Roy Lee Richards / Rumain Brisbon / Ryan L. Stokes / Ryan Twyman / Sabin Marcus Jones / Saheed Vassell / Salvado Ellswood / Samuel David Mallard / Samuel DuBose / Sandra Bland / Shaun Lee Fuhr / Sherida Davis / Sherman Evans / Shermichael Ezeff / Spencer McCain / Stephen Gayle / Stephen Murray / Stephon Clark / Tamir Rice / Tanisha Anderson / Tashii S. Brown / Tawon Boyd / Terence Crutcher / Terrance Moxley / Terrence LeDell Sterling / Terry Price / Thomas Allen / Thomas Lane / Thomas Williams / Thomas Yatsko / Tiano Meton / Tiara Thomas / Tina Marie Davis / Tommie Dale McGlothen Jr. / Tommy J. Yancy Jr. / Tony McDade / Tony Robinson / Torrey Lamar Robinson / Tracy Clyde / Treon Johnson / Trey Ta'Quan Pringle Sr. / Troy Robinson / Trye King / Tyrone Davis / Tyrone West / Vernell Bing / Vernicia Woodard / Victor Emanuel LaRosa / Walter Scott / Warren Ragudo / Warren Scott / Wayne Wheeler / Wendell Celestine Jr. / William Alfred Harvey III / William Chapman / William Howard Green / William Matthew Holmes William Taylor / William Wade Burgess III / Willie James Sams / Willie James Williams / Willie Lamont Sample / Willie Lee Bingham / Willie Neall Harden / Xavier Tyrell Johnson / Yvette Smith

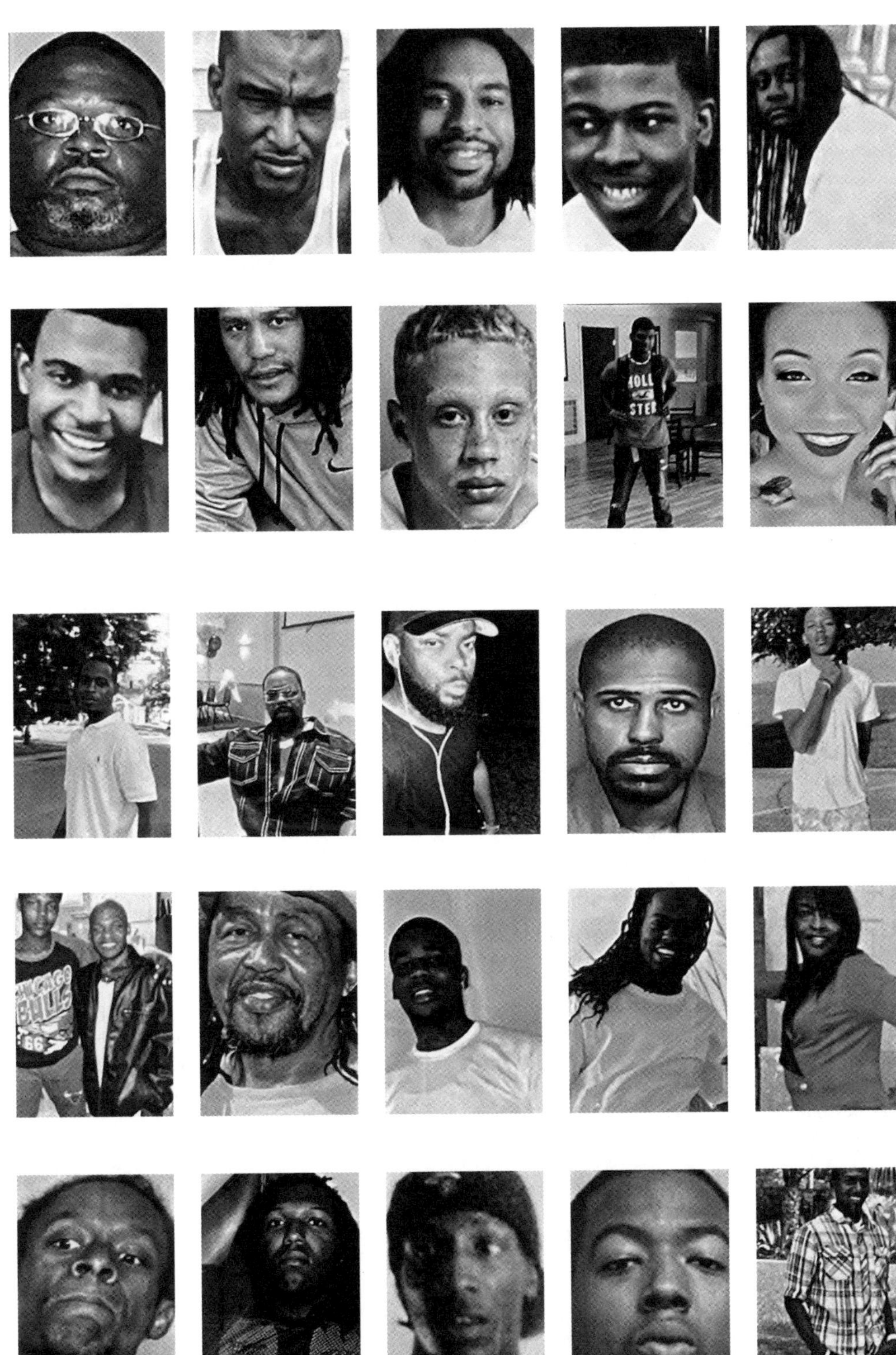
CHICAGO BULLS
66

This book is published in conjunction with the exhibitions

Carrie Mae Weems: Reflections for Now
Barbican, London
22 June–3 September 2023

Carrie Mae Weems: The Evidence of Things Not Seen
Kunstmuseum Basel
4 November 2023–17 March 2024

Exhibition, Barbican
Curators: Florence Ostende, Raúl Muñoz de la Vega
Curatorial Assistant: Amber Li
Exhibition Organiser: Natasha Powell
Assistant Exhibition Organiser: Rita Duarte
Exhibition Designer: Architecture Doing Place
Exhibition Graphic Design: Shaz Madani Studio
Creative Collaboration: Karena Johnson, Vania Gonzalvez, Carmen Okome

Barbican
Artistic Director: Will Gompertz
Head of Visual Arts: Shanay Jhaveri
Senior Manager: Katrina Crookall
Exhibition Manager: Alice Lobb
Production Manager: Maarten van den Bos
Production Technicians: Bruce Stracy, Margaret Liley, Jamie Measure-Hughes
Communications: Ariane Oiticica, Louise Collins, Lily Booth, Georgia Holmes
Marketing: Isobel Parrish, Hannah Moth
Development: Natasha Harris, Alina Tiits, Maria Carroll, Susie Stirling

Exhibition, Kunstmuseum Basel
Curator: Maja Wismer
Assistant Curator: Alice Wilke
Registrar: Monique Meyer
Curator Programs: Daniel Kurjaković
Education and Mediation: Hanna Banholzer, Celina Berchtold
Head of Communication: Karen N. Gerig
Digital Communication: Ana Brankovic, Grace Njoki

Kunstmuseum Basel
Director: Josef Helfenstein
Deputy Director, Head of Art and Research: Anita Haldemann
Head of Art Care: Werner Müller
Head of Finance and Operations: Tim Kretschmer
Head of Marketing and Development: Mirjam Baitsch
Head of Exhibition Management: Matthias Fellmann
Head of Collection Management: Svenja Held

Book
Editors: Raúl Muñoz de la Vega, Florence Ostende, Maja Wismer
Editorial Assistants: Amber Li, Alice Wilke
Project Management: Adam Jackman
Copyediting: Irene Schaudies, Rupert Jenkins, Julie Wolf
Graphic Design: Lacasta Design (Project Management: Paloma Castellanos)
Typeface: Aperçu, GT Alpina
Production: Thomas Lemaître
Reproductions: DruckConcept, Berlin
Printing and Binding: DZS Grafik
Paper: Munken Lynx Rough, 100 g/m²

Published by
Hatje Cantz Verlag GmbH
Mommsenstraße 27
10629 Berlin
www.hatjecantz.com
A Ganske Publishing Group Company

ISBN 978-3-7757-5555-9

Printed in Slovenia

Back cover illustration:
The Glenstone, 2018 © Carrie Mae Weems.
Courtesy of the artist, Jack Shainman Gallery, New York / Galerie Barbara Thumm, Berlin.